Uncertain Democracy

Uncertain Democracy

U.S. Foreign Policy and Georgia's
Rose Revolution

Lincoln A. Mitchell

PENN

University of Pennsylvania Press

Philadelphia

Copyright © 2009 University of Pennsylvania Press

Published by
University of Pennsylvania Press
Philadelphia, Pennsylvania 19104-4112

Printed in the United States of America on acid-free paper
10 9 8 7 6 5 4 3 2 1

Library of Congress Cataloging-in-Publication Data
Mitchell, Lincoln Abraham.
    Uncertain democracy : U.S. foreign policy and Georgia's Rose Revolution / Lincoln Mitchell.
        p. cm.
    Includes bibliographical references and index.
    ISBN 978-0-8122-4127-3 (alk. paper)
    1. Georgia (Republic)—Politics and government—1991– 2. Democracy—Georgia (Republic) 3. Elections—Georgia (Republic) 4. Georgia (Republic)—History—Rose Revolution, 2003. 5. United States—Foreign relations—Georgia (Republic) 6. Georgia (Republic)—Foreign relations—United States. I. Title.
JQ1759.7.A95M58   2008
947.5808'6—dc22   2008031043

Contents

Preface

This book is called *Uncertain Democracy* for two reasons. First, years ago I promised myself that if I ever wrote a book about the Rose Revolution I would avoid a title with expressions or metaphors involving flowers or colors. Second, and probably of greater import, there remains an uncertain quality about Georgia's Rose Revolution. It is still not clear whether democracy will develop in Georgia or to what extent the Rose Revolution was a democratic breakthrough.

Revolution or regime change was not the object of the years of democracy assistance programs funded by the United States in Georgia, nor was the Rose Revolution the product of years or even months of plotting by either Georgians or Americans. As I argue in this book, U.S.-funded democracy assistance programs had far more modest and ambiguous goals. This is not to say that these programs did not have an impact, but that the revolution, when it did come, surprised many. Fair elections, functioning political institutions, and a strong civil society were the stated goals of these programs, but it was thought these would come about gradually within the context of an evolving and democratizing political system in Georgia.

The Rose Revolution had something of an accidental quality for Georgian political activists, politicians, and others who led it. They sought to mobilize citizens to stop the 2003 parliamentary election from being stolen by moving quickly and decisively when an unforeseen opportunity arose after the fraudulent election of November 2003. Demanding President Eduard Shevardnadze's resignation was the most powerful way they could accomplish this, but it was only after a few weeks of demonstrations following the election that the activist leadership began to think that this demand could become a reality and lead to the dramatic events of the Rose Revolution.

Ultimately, the collapse of the Shevardnadze regime was the result of a number of factors, including the strength of Georgian civil society, the strategic actions of the political opposition in November 2003, the impact of U.S. democracy assistance, and the weakness of the regime itself. This volume not only explores these elements, but also examines the events themselves closely, providing background information that is essential for understanding the Rose Revolution. It will also take a close look at the U.S. role and impact on those events.

I hope here to explore the origins and impact of Georgia's Rose Revolution and place it in the framework of the U.S. democracy assistance project and a broader academic context. Although this work has a somewhat academic perspective, my relationship to the Rose Revolution and its leaders is not an entirely academic one.

From fall 2002 through late summer 2004, I lived in Georgia, where I served as Chief of Party for the National Democratic Institute for International Affairs (NDI). NDI is a U.S.-based NGO that works in the area of democracy assistance. The NDI mission in Georgia was funded primarily by the United States Agency for International Development (USAID). According to the mission statement on NDI's Web site, NDI

is a nonprofit organization working to strengthen and expand democracy worldwide. . . . NDI provides practical assistance to civic and political leaders advancing democratic values, practices and institutions. NDI works with democrats in every region of the world to build political and civic organizations, safeguard elections, and to promote citizen participation, openness and accountability in government.

Through my position at NDI, I was not only an observer of the Rose Revolution; I played a role in the events as well. The extent of that role is addressed in some depth in Chapter 6. I also had a chance to work closely with and get to know many of the individuals who played key roles in the events before, during, and after. A number of the observations, descriptions, and comments in this work draw heavily on my personal experience with these people.

Because of my position I had access to information and people during the events covered in this book. While only in a very few occasions do I draw on direct quotes from conversations during this time, I have relied on my notes, observations, and correspondence from 2002 to 2004 to help tell the story of the Rose Revolution as best I can.

This book is not meant to be an account of my role in these events. That book would be neither an interesting nor valuable contribution to our understanding of the Rose Revolution. However, my understanding of these events goes considerably beyond what I could have gotten from doing only academic research. It is my hope that *Uncertain Democracy* combines that access with the benefit of a few years distance from the event to provide a unique analysis of the Rose Revolution. I should add that, although I worked for NDI during a fair amount of the period addressed in this book, the analysis, observations, and opinions are mine alone and do not necessarily reflect those of NDI.

The Rose Revolution remains an ongoing story, the last chapter of which has yet to be written. Demonstrations in November 2007 led to a forceful response, with the government imposing a short-lived state of emergency and calling for snap elections in January 2008, which President Saakashvili, to the surprise of almost nobody, won. The results of parliamentary elections a few months later in May were not encouraging for democracy in Georgia, with the president's party consolidating its strength in Parliament even as a number of domestic and foreign observers raised questions about the quality of those elections.

In August 2008, simmering tensions between Russia and Georgia over the territories of Abkhazia and South Ossetia erupted into war as an ill-thought-out Georgian military advance into South Ossetia met with a strong Russian response that saw Moscow send troops and planes far into Georgian territory. The Georgia-Russia relationship and the status of Abkhazia and South Ossetia are not the primary subjects of this book. They are, however, critically important for Georgia, since the country's democratic future and, indeed, its very sovereignty, remain uncertain given these recent developments.

Chapter 1

Georgia and the Democracy Promotion Project

On November 22, 2003, a group of young Georgian politicians and activists led by former justice minister Mikheil Saakashvili stormed into the first session of the newly—and fraudulently—elected Georgian parliament. Holding aloft a single red rose—the symbol of thousands who had taken to the streets in the days before—Saakashvili marched forward, shouting "Resign!" as President Eduard Shevardnadze stood at the rostrum, addressing the parliament's members. Moments later, a very old and disoriented looking Shevardnadze, known to most people in the West as Soviet president Mikhail Gorbachev's courageous Soviet foreign minister during the waning days of the Cold War, was hustled out the back door of the chamber by his concerned security guards. The next day Saakashvili, former speaker of parliament Zurab Zhvania and sitting speaker of parliament Nino Burjanadze forced Shevardnadze, Georgia's president of ten years, to officially resign.

Shevardnadze's resignation, which took place after almost three weeks of protests and vigils in the center of Tbilisi, Georgia's capital, marked the culmination of what has come to be called Georgia's Rose Revolution. Immediately following the resignation, Burjanadze took over as interim president, as specified by the constitution. Less than two months later, on January 4, 2004, Saakashvili was elected president with an overwhelming 96 percent of the vote in balloting broadly assessed as free and fair.

After Shevardnadze left office, interim president Burjanadze assured the international community that Georgia's new government would place the country on a course oriented toward the West and democracy. Saakashvili, upon taking office, offered the same assurances to the United States and Europe. The United States and Europe, for their part, recognized the Rose Revolution as an important democratic breakthrough and assured Georgia's new leaders that they would provide as much support as needed to help Georgia consolidate its new democracy.

The Rose Revolution can be understood and studied in many ways. It represents more than just the last, best hope for one small, impoverished, semidemocratic country in a remote corner of what once was the Soviet empire. It also can be seen as the beginning of what proved to be a short-lived fourth wave of democratization that quickly spilled over into countries such as Ukraine, Kyrgyzstan, and Lebanon. Others, however, see it as just another case of old wine in new bottles, as the new leaders retreat from their initial democratic promises.

After the Rose Revolution, Georgia was quickly and visibly claimed by the United States and Europe as a success story for democracy assistance. Saakashvili was feted in Washington and other Western capitals. Money poured into Georgia to help the new democracy consolidate its gains. U.S. secretary of state Colin Powell was one of many Western dignitaries who flew to Tbilisi for Saakashvili's inauguration. President George W. Bush and other cabinet members issued statements of support for the new regime and visited Georgia during the first years of Saakashvili's presidency. Not surprisingly, the West's—especially Washington's—previous strong support for Saakashvili's predecessor, Shevardnadze, is rarely mentioned any more.

The story of democracy assistance in Georgia, particularly from the United States, is not, however, the simple success story the post-Rose Revolution American narrative suggests. Looking at democracy assistance and democratization policy toward Georgia both before and after the event makes this clear. The Rose Revolution and the evolution of democracy in Georgia in general also tell us a great deal about U.S. democracy promotion policies. Through a close study of Georgia, it is possible to raise, and answer, central questions about the wisdom of American democracy promotion policies, the efficacy of these policies, and the direction in which they should move in the future.

A number of largely uninformed observers attributed the Rose Revolution primarily to the work of the U.S. government, often through NGOs funded by the United States.[1] This view is held among many in the former Soviet Union, including both supporters and opponents of democratic reforms. Former Russian president Vladimir Putin's remarks shortly after the 2004 Orange Revolution in Ukraine make this view very clear: "It's extremely dangerous to try to resolve political problems outside the framework of the law; first there was the 'rose revolution,' and then they'll [the United States] think up something like 'blue.'"[2] I have encountered similar sentiments frequently in Russia, Kyrgyzstan, and Azerbaijan, where I have been told by politicians and members of parliament that the United States forced Shevardnadze out, created Mikheil

Saakashvili as a political force, and funded the demonstrations. Often those who viewed events in Georgia this way told me they saw little difference between U.S.-supported democracy assistance efforts and the CIA.

Others viewed the events as an indigenous Georgian phenomenon in which the United States played at most a peripheral role. I have heard this view from senior figures in the Georgian government as well as from several Georgian civic activists, many of whom were not deeply involved in the Rose Revolution. Civic activist Giorgi Kandelaki asserted that "many observers have overstated the contributions of civil society and foreign actors to the Rose Revolution. . . . Most of the international actors involved were too willing to compromise and make deals with Shevardnadze despite the demands of the Georgian people." He added: "During the revolution not only were Western actors unhelpful, but at times they were detrimental."[3] While Kandelaki seems to bear a grudge against the West for the role it played in the Rose Revolution, the sentiment he expressed is not uncommon in Georgia.[4] Nor is it without a kernel of truth, as I will show later. For example, one senior official in the Georgian government said, somewhat flippantly, of American support, "What the hell did the U.S. do?"[5] The truth, I argue, lies somewhere in between, which is why examining the actual and perceived impact of democracy promotion work is so important.

Some in the U.S. government sought to encourage perceptions that the United States had played a larger role in the Rose Revolution. Lorne Craner, then an assistant secretary in the Bureau of Democracy, Human Rights, and Labor at the Department of State (he has since become president of the International Republican Institute), and Representative Dana Rohrabacher (R-Calif.), at a July 7, 2004, meeting of the House Subcommittee on International Terrorism, Nonproliferation, and Human Rights, demonstrated the views of some within the U.S. government on this question. Craner remarked that

in the 1990s, the United States supported South Africa's democracy movement, which helped produce a new era of freedom in a country that some believed would descend into chaos. And for the last decade, we've worked with opposition leaders and NGOs in places like Cuba and Burma and Zimbabwe, and also in places like Georgia, where last year, the time and the energy and the heart of our effort, and the effort of so many others, culminated in the peaceful Revolution of Roses.[6]

Rohrabacher added: "Why do they [Georgians] like us now? Because yes, we are taking care of business in Georgia, because we are supporting the democratic elements and the more that our country supports the good guys around the world who want democracy, want their people to live in freedom and to have mutual respect for other people's rights, the more we are going to live in a more peaceful world."

Strong ties between Saakashvili, Zhvania, and important figures throughout the U.S. foreign policy community had certainly existed for years, but the U.S. role was, in fact, relatively ambiguous. Shevardnadze, largely on the strength of his stature in the West, his role in winding down the Cold War, and his warm personal relations with many in Washington, Berlin, Brussels, London, Strasbourg, and other European capitals, had succeeded well into 2003 in maintaining not only Western support, but the perception that he was a reformer. From the time Shevardnadze took over as president of Georgia in 1993 until his resignation in 2003, he was seen almost as much as an engine for democratization in Georgia as the obstacle to change he had become by the end of his term. Accordingly, Georgia received substantial democracy assistance as well as other funds during these years to help reform Shevardnadze's government and move it more toward democracy. Between fiscal years 2001 and 2003, Georgia was given $268.8 million in U.S. support—more than any other former Soviet republic other than Russia and Ukraine, each of which has more than ten times the population of Georgia.[7]

There is ample evidence that by 2003 the United States wanted Shevardnadze to move Georgia in a more democratic direction, with a special focus on the parliamentary elections scheduled for November of that year. Money for various kinds of election support was increased, and high-level visitors—including former secretary of state James Baker, former deputy secretary of state Strobe Talbott, former chairman of the Joint Chiefs of Staff John Shalikashvili, and Senator John McCain—came to Georgia to urge Shevardnadze to conduct fair elections. But there is virtually no concrete evidence that the U.S. sought his overthrow. Moreover, in March 2003 Shevardnadze was one of a small number of world leaders to join the U.S.-led "coalition of the willing" in Iraq. Given how difficult it was for the Bush administration to recruit countries to join the "coalition of the willing," we can be reasonably certain the administration would not have done anything to remove a pro-war government from power.

The U.S. role, the unwillingness of the international community to see Shevardnadze as an obstacle to democracy, and the impact of years of previous democracy assistance form an important battery of questions with regard to Georgia before Saakashvili. The post-Rose Revolution period also raises questions that are central to democracy promotion policy more generally. These concern the depth of U.S. commitment to helping the development of strong, enduring democracy, the ability of democracy promotion tactics to consolidate democratic gains once the breakthrough has occurred, and the viability of democracy in the post-Soviet space.

Why Georgia?

Georgia is an unusual case study of American democracy assistance, but it is a valuable one because it involves many of the key questions at the core of such assistance. Moreover, because the discussion, especially in the popular media, is increasingly dominated by Iraq—a democracy assistance project that is exceptional in many ways—it is important to look beyond Iraq to examine those issues that have bearing on democracy assistance more broadly.

American policy toward Georgia both before and after the Rose Revolution requires special emphasis. Aspects of democracy assistance and other forms of aid from the United States, beginning in the 1990s, played a role. For example, Saakashvili was a former Muskie Fellow at Columbia University, and other civic and political leaders of the Rose Revolution had been trained in the U.S. as well. Saakashvili, Zhvania, and Burjanadze had worked intensively with the party institutes from the U.S. (in the case of Saakashvili and Zhvania, for years preceding 2003). Georgia's vibrant civil society was largely funded by democracy assistance money from not only the U.S., but also the EU, individual European countries, and George Soros's Open Society Institute (OSI).[8] Indeed, the parallel vote tabulation and exit poll that played a key role in persuading the Georgian people that the November 2003 election had been stolen were funded almost entirely by OSI or the U.S. government and supported by American and European expertise.

There is, however, another side to this story. Even as Georgia became a major recipient of democracy assistance, Georgian democracy deteriorated after an initial burst of optimism around Shevardnadze and his party, the Citizens' Union of Georgia (CUG), in the mid-1990s. In spite of years of assistance, by early 2003 many viewed Georgia as a failure of democracy assistance and a virtually failed state. The government had only grown more corrupt and elections more fraudulent. The reformers who surrounded Shevardnadze early in his term, most notably Saakashvili and Zhvania, had left government and were relatively ineffectual in the opposition. The failure of the economy to grow did not help the situation either. The Rose Revolution was, in reality, a surprise to many foreign observers, raising questions about the extent of causality between the millions of dollars of democracy assistance and the democratic breakthrough of late 2003 and how successful these programs actually were.

Later U.S. policy toward Georgia raises a different set of questions and issues about democracy assistance more generally. As discussed above, the United States responded to the Rose Revolution with enthusiasm and support. In the months following those dramatic events, Washington did whatever it could to support the new government. This included increasing assistance for infrastructure and energy and renewing discussions on security cooperation, along with making Georgia one of the countries of the Millennium Challenge Corporation program, which seeks to provide substantial U.S. assistance to countries that have met a series of criteria demonstrating a commitment to reform and democracy.

Yet consolidating the democratic gains of the Rose Revolution has been a difficult task for Georgia. Positive developments in areas like fair elections, fighting corruption, and education reform have been offset by problems regarding separation of the governing party and the state, media freedom, concentration of too much power in the hands of the president, and the crackdown on demonstrators and the state of emergency declared after large street demonstrations in November 2007. The U.S. response to these issues has led to skepticism about how sincere U.S. commitment to true democracy in Georgia really is. This speaks to a very serious issue for democracy promotion, one raised by many of its critics.

Shortly after the Rose Revolution, the United States began to offer unambiguous political support to the new government. It was as if the U.S. government viewed the Rose Revolution not just as a pivotal moment in Georgia's democratic and political development, but as a line that, when crossed, transformed Georgia from a kleptocratic, weak, semidemocratic regime into a consolidated democracy in a period of weeks. Washington reduced democracy assistance to civil society and the media because the government of Georgia was now viewed as the engine of democratization. As will be discussed in Chapter 5, this continued despite evidence that the pace of democratization began to slow dramatically after Saakashvili was elected president in January 2004.

Thus, U.S. policy after the Rose Revolution in Georgia leads one to ask just what kind of democracy the U.S. seeks to help nurture in the politically developing world and how strong the commitment is to strengthening democracy as opposed to simply nurturing and supporting friendly governments. Other less dramatic but equally important questions about democracy assistance after a democratic breakthrough that are relevant not only to Georgia include how to encourage democratic consolidation after a breakthrough and to institutionalize barriers between state and party, particularly in a post-Soviet state.

It remains true that if democracy cannot be consolidated in Georgia, it is not clear where it can be consolidated. As difficult as the challenges are, the outlook in Georgia still looks brighter than in most of the rest of the nondemocratic world. As I argue in this work, the country enjoys numerous advantages that are not shared with most other democratizing countries. First, Georgia is a strongly pro-Western and pro-American country. Both leaders and people see the United States and Europe as the models for political development. Because of this orientation, ideas from the West and American and European support for these ideas are generally viewed as positive. The Rose Revolution was unusual among political transitions in that demonstrators waved American flags—and even a few Israeli flags—while calling for the end of the corrupt Shevardnadze regime. This occurred even though there was a history of U.S. support for Shevardnadze. Within weeks of Shevarnadze's resignation a billboard was erected in downtown Tbilisi displaying the words "Thank You U.S.A." Georgians, like many others around the world, often see democracy as an idea from the outside, specifically from the West, but, in contrast to many other countries, in Georgia there is no negative sentiment attached to that view.

In Georgia, no ideology seriously competes with the Western democratic model. There is little nostalgia for the Soviet Union; no fundamentalist religious model has any support in Georgia; and Asian or corporatist development models have no traction at all. Western democracy is the only political path that has support in virtually any area of Georgian society. Georgia's difficult relationship with Russia, its neighbor to the north, serves to reinforce the country's pro-Western orientation because Europe and the United States are viewed as counterbalances to Russia.

Georgia's pro-Western outlook is buoyed by its leadership. Many of Georgia's new leaders, beginning with President Mikheil Saakashvili, were educated in Western universities and have a strong understanding of how politics works in the West, particularly the United States. Many cabinet members, MPs, and other key leaders of the new government were at least partly trained in the West. Some returned specifically to help build the new Georgia after Saakashvili made an appeal when he became president. Few if any countries in the democratizing world boast a group of leaders who have as much Western education and training as those in Georgia.

Moreover, this leadership has been explicit with domestic and particularly with international audiences that its goal is to make Georgia a modern democratic state. Since the Rose Revolution, Georgia's leadership has maintained that it is committed to building a democratic Georgia even when its actions have suggested otherwise. This is a promise Saakashvili and his team have made to everyone—from farmers in rural Georgia to President Bush. The government cannot easily move away from this commitment and may find its ability to democratize at least a partial component of how its success is measured.

Georgia enjoys other advantages that would seem to predispose it to a smooth democratic transition. The country is relatively ethnically homogeneous. Over 85 percent of the population are ethnic Georgian, with the two biggest minorities being ethnic Azeris and Armenians. While tension certainly exists between these groups and the ethnic Georgian majority, it is not a driving force in Georgia's political life. It continues to be difficult for the government to fully incorporate these groups into the country's cultural, economic, and political life, but there is no violent conflict between groups, as is the case in many democratizing countries.

Georgia is also overwhelmingly Christian, with a small Muslim and a tiny Jewish minority. Georgians see themselves as part of the extended European community—a community that considers democracy absolutely essential. Georgian Christianity is Orthodox, so European and Georgian Christianity do not overlap entirely, but there certainly are Orthodox Christian countries, most notably Greece, that have adapted well to democracy. Huntington (1991) argued that there is a strong link between the spread of Western Christianity and democracy. Western Christianity is not growing very quickly in Georgia, but Christianity, even in its Eastern form, strongly reinforces the country's Western orientation.

Because Georgia lacks valuable minerals, oil, or natural gas, the "resource curse" will not impede democratic development either.[9] Its economy has traditionally been primarily agricultural and remains so today. Economic growth relies on increasing trade, tourism, and foreign investment. For this reason, Georgia's economic future will greatly benefit from strengthening democratic institutions, such as rule of law and an open society.

From this cursory glance it would seem that Georgia is poised to consolidate its democratic gains. However, the challenges are strong. Joblessness and an economy growing too slowly for many Georgians, underdeveloped democratic institutions, and the devastating Soviet legacy demonstrate that even when preconditions for twenty-first-century democratization are as strong as possible, there are still barriers to the American democracy promotion project.

Other countries in the former Soviet Union and other parts of the world enjoy similarly positive positions from which to consolidate their democracy. Ukraine since the Orange Revolution of 2004 is especially relevant. Yet even Ukraine—like Georgia a major recipient of European and American assistance since the democratic breakthrough—finds itself in a more difficult situation than Georgia in terms of consolidating democratization. Ukraine does not enjoy such an unambiguously pro-Western orientation as, Georgia, since its relationship with Russia remains very close even after the Orange Revolution. The divisions between a Russia-leaning east and a more independent-minded western half of the country are much stronger in Ukraine than any comparable division in Georgia. Moreover, the Orange Revolution has stalled more than once because of the continuing strength of Victor Yanukovich's Party of Regions, the candidate who sought to steal the 2004 election from Viktor Yushchenko. Yanukovitch became Ukraine's prime minister in 2006, prompting a difficult period of power sharing with Yushchenko and early elections in 2007.[10]

A Note on Russia

It is not possible to fully understand Georgia, the dominant concerns of the Georgian government and people, and Georgia's behavior in international affairs without looking closely at the relationship between Georgia and Russia. Issues of territorial integrity, particularly in Abkhazia and South Ossetia, energy policy and security, the presence of foreign troops on Georgia soil, the opportunity for export and economic development, indeed, the existence of Georgia as an independent state, are all part of the complex relationship between Georgia and Russia. Russian hostility toward post-Rose Revolution Georgia in particular has represented a major threat and obstacle. Russian efforts to weaken the economy by boycotting Georgian wine and mineral water, intransigence with regard to the disputed territories of Abkhazia and Ossetia, and expulsion of Georgian citizens working in Russia in 2006 are only some of the ways this hostility has made life difficult for Georgia.

Georgia's fate has been closely tied to Russia for several centuries. For over a century, Georgia was the southernmost outpost of the czarist empire, and for more than half a century after that it was part of the far-flung Soviet empire. A central challenge of any government of independent Georgia is to develop a relationship with Russia that guarantees Georgia's independence, resolves frozen conflicts between the two countries, and allows for fruitful cooperation on issues of trade, energy, and the like. This would be an extremely difficult task for any Georgian government.

Georgia's relationship with Russia has been addressed elsewhere.[11] The focus in this volume will be more narrowly on issues of democratization in Georgia. The Georgian-Russian relationship will be discussed where it has bearing upon democratic development in Georgia, but it will not be a central theme in the chapters that follow.

Democracy Assistance and American Foreign Policy

Before turning to a more detailed discussion of Georgia and democracy promotion, it is useful to spend some time on a brief look at the history, theory and practice of promotion of democracy as part of American foreign policy. For decades democracy promotion has been, in one form or another, part of American foreign policy. It was central to President Woodrow Wilson's post-World War I vision of how to organize relationships between states. World War II was at times framed as a battle to protect freedom and democracy. The Cold War era was often similarly framed as a conflict between the democratic West and authoritarian communism, but during this period anti-communism in practice trumped democracy promotion among policymakers and scholars. This meant there was little U.S.-backed effort to support democratization in authoritarian noncommunist regimes. However, late in the Cold War democracy promotion began to reemerge, initially in the guise of Jimmy Carter's emphasis on human rights during his presidency in the late 1970s.

As democracy promotion has been given a more central role in foreign policy, the foundations underlying it have evolved and changed. Not surprisingly, the policy has also come under substantial criticism. For President Woodrow Wilson at the end of World War I, democracy promotion rested on the notion of making the world a safer place for the United States. This was a forerunner of what has come to be known as the peace rationale for democracy promotion. The rhetoric of making the world safe for democracy that characterized World War II and the Cold War was an extension of Wilson's ideas and proposed democracy as an alternative to, and bulwark against, first fascism and then communism.

During the Cold War, democracy promotion was generally seen only in the context of anti-communism, but the rationale for the limited democracy promotion that took place during this period was that freedom and democracy were an appealing alternative to communism. Unfortunately, the notion that these were also appealing alternatives to right-wing authoritarians regimes seemed to be lost on too many Cold War era policymakers in the United States.

It was America's first born-again Christian president, Jimmy Carter, who introduced an explicitly moral dimension to democracy promotion by stressing the import of human rights in foreign policy.[12] Carter's notion that the internal workings and human rights record of a country should influence American policy toward that country was initially scoffed at by many who felt that during the Cold War the only consideration was how a government aligned itself between the two superpowers.[13] However, as we will see later, it was the neoconservatives during the presidency of George W. Bush who, ironically, revived this morally driven view in their strong support of democracy promotion—even in some countries which were U.S. allies but not democratic.

Carter's introduction of human rights into American foreign policy gave way to the presidency of Ronald Reagan and the prosecution of the Cold War with renewed vigor. Reagan incorporated democracy promotion into his Cold War strategy through "Project Democracy," which included exchange programs and other cultural activities aimed at exposing people from communist countries to American-style democracy.[14] These programs were, not surprisingly, focused on the ideological struggle of the Cold War and sought to contrast Reagan's America with, for example, late and post-Brezhnev Soviet Union. The battleground of the Cold War at that time was primarily Central America, where the leftist Sandinista revolution had just occurred in Nicaragua, so much of Reagan's democracy promotion, like his Cold War strategy in general, was focused on that region.

Reagan's democracy promotion strategy was not, however, limited to these types of programs. In 1983, the administration, with support from Congress, funded and initiated the National Endowment for Democracy (NED), an organization that funds democracy assistance advocates in the U.S. and abroad as well as providing funding for its core grantees, including NDI and the International Republican Institute (IRI). NDI and IRI are U.S.-based implementing organizations with similar democracy assistance mandates. They are loosely affiliated with the Democratic and Republican parties respectively.

Thus, much of the infrastructure for the modern era of democracy promotion was created in the 1980s and initially perceived as part of an effort to win the Cold War. The perception of the NED as an instrument of the Cold War changed somewhat after the NED supported democratization efforts in the Philippines in 1986 and the presidential plebiscite in Chile in 1988. Interestingly, not only did this infrastructure continue after the Cold War ended, but the post-Cold War period saw these organizations' biggest impact.

The collapse of authoritarian regimes in the late 1980s and early 1990s—especially in Eastern Europe and the Soviet Union—also consolidated the idea that democracy was a human right rather than the system of government or ideology of a handful of countries.[15] The Vienna Declaration on Human Rights, adopted by the UN General Assembly in 1993, declared democracy a universal right, adding that "The international community should support the strengthening and promoting of democracy, development and respect for human rights and fundamental freedoms in the world."[16] The evolution of democracy from a political ideology and system of government to one of the poles in the bipolar world of the Cold War and then to a political right, the consensus form of government, and ultimately a human right, is a key development for international politics and democracy promotion.[17]

With the end of the Cold War, democracy promotion began to take on a qualitatively different role in U.S. foreign policy, and to a lesser extent in many European countries as well. For the United States, it was no longer an abstract principle with a vague impact on policy, nor did it continue to be seen as an often inconvenient consideration when broader strategic questions were examined. Instead, it began to become increasingly central to foreign policy with programs and budgets to match this centrality. These budgets remain a relatively small fraction of overall foreign policy monies, but budgets are bigger than ever.[18] Moreover, measuring democracy promotion's import simply by looking at how much money goes to democracy promoting organizations misses a great deal because democracy promotion can also take other forms, such as the public statements of diplomats and policymakers and the components of larger aid packages. Furthermore, democracy promotion programs are not usually expensive because they rarely include the direct delivery of goods or services.

In the initial period following the end of the Cold War, roughly 1989 to 2001, democracy promotion began to focus on the post-Communist countries of Eastern Europe and the former Soviet Union. Once the dust had settled on the rapid transformation of the former Soviet empire, Europe and the United States began to commit resources to building democratic institutions throughout the region. Although the collapse of the former Yugoslavia, along with genocide and wars there throughout the 1990s dominated the news, there are also many, quieter success stories as countries like Hungary, Poland, the Czech Republic, and the Baltic states made rapid strides toward democracy before joining the European Union in the early twenty-first century.

Democracy promotion and democratization in the 1990s were not limited to the post-Communist world. The third wave of democratization that had begun in Southern Europe in the 1970s broke onto the shores of Asia, South America, and Africa as well.[19] Taiwan and South Korea continued to consolidate their democratic gains from previous years; dramatic breakthroughs occurred in Chile, South Africa, and elsewhere; and less dramatic steps toward democratization took place in other countries in other parts of Africa, Asia, and South America.

Although democracy made substantial gains globally throughout most of the 1990s, a number of formerly authoritarian countries seemed to slide backward as the decade came to a close. Other countries had proved to be very difficult environments for building democratic institutions as some parts of the world, notably China, North Korea, and the Middle East, had shown themselves to be largely unaffected by the third wave of democratization. Thus, as the new century began there was still a great deal of democratization to be done, but the initial excitement had worn off. Instead, a structure of donors, NGOs, governmental organizations, consultants, and private businesses had emerged to implement the complex American democracy promotion policies, which had begun to assume a more a more central position in American foreign policy.

Democracy promotion became a central component of American foreign policy during the administration of President Bill Clinton. In the 1995 National Security Strategy of Engagement and Enlargement, the Clinton administration identified democracy promotion as one of its three central security goals. The document also asserted that

All of America's strategic interests—from promoting prosperity at home to checking global threats abroad before they threaten our territory—are served by enlarging the community of democratic and free market nations. Thus, working with new democratic states to help preserve them as democracies committed to free markets and respect for human rights, is a key part of our national security strategy. One of the most gratifying and encouraging. (22)

Nonetheless, it was America's second born-again Christian president, George W. Bush, who was strongest in stressing the moral dimension of democracy promotion. In the years following the terrorist attack on September 11, 2001, democracy promotion assumed an even more central role in foreign policy as Bush aggressively, and with stunning lack of success, sought to democratize the Middle East, one of the world's least democratic regions. Bush made democracy promotion a centerpiece of his foreign policy and linked it closely to American wars in Afghanistan and Iraq.

Bush spoke explicitly about the moral dimension of democracy. He often referred to democracy, or "freedom," as a right that had been given to all humanity by God. This moral dimension informed more than just Bush's words as his presidency was marked by an aggressive democracy promotion strategy that included military interventions in Iraq and Afghanistan, substantially increasing resources for democracy promotion programs around the world, linking fair elections to attempts to resolve decades-old problems such as the Israel-Palestine situation, claiming strong links between democracy abroad and security—primarily from terrorism—at home, and supporting, and in some cases encouraging, democratic breakthroughs in countries like Ukraine and Lebanon in addition to Georgia. Bush's support for democracy promotion was so strong that many on both sides of the country's increasingly partisan divide began to view democracy promotion as a Republican policy, ignoring its deep, bipartisan roots.

While Bush's rhetoric regarding democracy promotion differed in quantity and emphasis from his predecessors, democracy assistance programs under the Bush administration did not look very different than they had under Clinton. Election support, assistance to legislatures, local governments and other government institutions, support for nascent civil society organizations and NGOs, as well as the occasional program seeking to expand political participation on the part of women or young people remained the primary ways the United States sought to strengthen democracy around the world. The exception was, of course, Iraq, which has dominated almost all discussions of Bush foreign policy, including democracy assistance, and will be discussed in more depth later. Yet if Iraq is taken out of the equation, and Bush's rhetoric is discounted, there is strong continuity between democracy assistance during the presidencies of Bill Clinton and George W. Bush.

As democracy promotion has taken on an increasing role in U.S. foreign policy, it has matured as an "industry" as well. Before the mid-1980s, it would have been impossible to discuss a democratization "industry." To the extent that democracy promotion, as distinct from anti-communism, was part of American foreign policy, it was an element informing decisions on military and financial assistance, sanctions, clandestine operations, trade policy, and other traditional foreign policy approaches. It also was part of American propaganda efforts abroad through organizations like the United States Information Agency (USIA). However, very few organizations or individuals saw their work strictly in terms of building and promoting democracy overseas.

Although this situation began to change in the mid-1980s, it was largely beginning in the 1990s that a democracy promotion industry began to emerge and mature. While this industry is in many respects less developed than many other industries, it is a significant sector of the foreign policy community. The democracy promotion industry today can be said to include governmental organizations, such as parts of the U.S. Agency for International Development (USAID) and the Middle East Partnership Initiative (MEPI); nongovernmental organizations like the NED, NDI, IRI, Freedom House, American Bar Association (ABA) and International Foundation for Electoral Systems (IFES), all of which rely heavily on the U.S. government for funding; numerous private contracting companies such as Chemonics, Associates in Rural Development (ARD), Management Systems International (MSI), Development Associates International (DAI), Development Associates (DA), and hundreds of small businesses, consultants, and scholars.

In recent years this business has become more professionalized with fewer firms and organizations using volunteers and one-time consultants for projects, relying instead on a growing network of trained and experienced professionals. As democracy assistance has matured it has begun to take on the characteristics of many other industries that rely on the government for a substantial amount of their funding. While it is still far too soon to speak of a democracy industrial complex, some of these issues are worth exploring.[20]

Unlike twenty or even ten years ago, there are now dozens of American businesses and thousands of American individuals who have a financial stake in the perceived needs not just for democracy promotion, but for the U.S. approach to democracy promotion, aspects of which rely substantially on expensive training and resident American experts, consultants, and staff and offices in the United States. It is not my intention to propose that the democracy promotion business is characterized by financial self-interest or corruption, but merely to suggest that the financial motives, particularly among the for-profit contractors, for maintaining and expanding democracy promotion exist, are becoming stronger, and play some role in discussions of democracy assistance and its implementation.

As the policy implementing apparatus entrenches itself more in the government, private, and NGO sectors, it has become more difficult to evaluate the needs of democracy promotion. "Will this country benefit from direct democracy promotion assistance?" is rarely asked about a particular country. Instead, the question "what kind of democracy promotion will benefit this country?" or even "what kind of political party/civil society program will benefit this country?" are increasingly among the first questions asked. In some respects this is a positive development: the need to promote democracy no longer must to be explained or defended in a particular country. However, it also reflects an implicit assumption that the best way to support democratization in every country is through an essentially similar battery of democracy promotion programs.

The Democracy Assistance Debate

As George W. Bush's first term in office came to an end in 2004, a debate had begun to reemerge in foreign policy circles about the wisdom and efficacy of democracy promotion. Although this debate had been around for years, new life was breathed into it during the Bush administration. To some extent, this debate began to get traction because of the use of democratization by the administration as a way to justify the unpopular war in Iraq, but the debate was much more complex than that, with many critiques and defenses along numerous different dimensions. Moreover, it did not lend itself easily to partisan or ideological leanings.

Proponents of democracy promotion based their support on several occasionally overlapping notions. Some shared the moral outlook of President Bush, believing that democracy was, essentially, a God-given right that Americans should help the rest of the world to achieve. Others took a more ideological and less moral view, simply arguing that democracy was the best and most fair system of government and that all people should have the right to self-governance. Arguments based on stability, security, and economic development were made as well.[21]

In general, views on democracy promotion can be grouped along two dimensions: the moral-ideological dimension and the U.S. interest dimension. There are several positions on the moral-ideological dimension. First, there are proponents who for ideological, moral, or religious reasons believe that democracy is the right thing for all people and that the United States should do its part in helping people by promoting democracy whenever it can. This has been the position of the Bush administration, but it is shared by others as well. For years, the notion that people should have a right to choose their own government was a core value of the American non-communist left. This seems to be changing now.

Within this moral-ideological dimension two arguments can be found to oppose democracy promotion. These two arguments overlap to some degree but are presented differently. The first, often associated with the right, is that not all people are ready for democracy. With regard to some countries, the argument is that a longstanding attachment to another form of government, overarching religious views, or lack of political modernity leaves the people simply unprepared for democracy. While few academics make this precise point, it is a frequently encountered sentiment in opinion pieces, blogs, and comments by politicians. This belief is often presented with a tone of exasperation as if the speaker or writer were stating the obvious. A comment by Senator Chuck Hagel (R-Neb.) sums this view up very succinctly "You cannot in my opinion just impose a democratic form of government on a country with no history and no culture and no tradition of democracy."[22]

The second argument, generally associated with the left, is that democracy promotion on the part of the United States is not genuine. Rather, it is thinly veiled self-interest and a twenty-first-century form of imperialism. This critique is particularly prominent when applied to countries like Iraq, where democracy promotion has been accompanied by military intervention, but it is also used to describe countries where U.S.-supported elections have led to a new government, more friendly to the United States, taking power.[23]

The second dimension of the democracy promotion debate is centered around the idea that expanding democracy worldwide is somehow good for the United States. The best-known explanation for why democratization is good for the United States is the theory of the democratic peace. This theory holds that no two democratic countries have ever gone to war with each other, therefore increasing the number of democratic countries would reduce the possibilities for war in different parts of the globe.[24] After September 11, 2001, the democratic peace position was expanded so that building democracy was considered an important defense against terrorism. A NED strategy document from January 2002 summed this view up well, asserting that the "global defense of democracy is the appropriate and most effective response to the threat posed by Islamic extremists . . . the universal aspiration for democracy is the banner under which the battle for the defense of our national interest can most effectively be waged."[25] This view was not grounded in much empirical data, but it dovetailed well with the Bush administration's democracy promotion agenda.

Democratization was also viewed by many as in the U.S. interest because democracies were seen as the most stable form of government.[26] Stability is in the interest of the United States because instability and failed states can produce terrorists or other threats to national security. Once the stability of the Cold War ended, the United States worked quickly to replace that system with another stable system in much of the world.

Economic reasons have also been used to explain why democratization is in the interest of the United States. Democratic countries are viewed as good trading partners. Because markets in these countries are governed by their legal systems, Americans doing business are on stronger footing in democratic countries. Moreover, democratic countries are usually less corrupt, so businesses do not need to pay bribes or risk being at the caprice of corruptible, undemocratic leaders. This was the position of the Clinton administration in the 1990s.[27]

While most critics agree that democratic countries generally do not go to war with each other, there have been several critiques of using the democratic peace theory to support a policy of democracy promotion. Some have argued that while democratic countries do not go to war with each other, they are no less likely to go to war with nondemocratic countries. Therefore democracy in some countries does not preclude those countries going to war. The exception to this might be a whole region, for example, Eastern Europe after the Cold War, that democratizes more or less together. Indeed, the likelihood of war in Eastern Europe is now quite small, unless Belarus becomes more belligerent with its neighbors.[28] Others have argued that while democratic countries do not go to war with each other, the process of democratization, particularly with an emphasis on elections, can lead to instability and violent conflicts, including wars with neighbors, disputes over territories. and civil wars.[29] Some have posited that it is not democracy but affluence that keeps countries from going to war with each other, and that as less affluent countries become democratic they will remain likely to get involved in wars over resources or other economic issues.[30]

Democracy promotion, perhaps in a less public and militarily oriented fashion, is likely to remain part of U.S. foreign policy. For this reason, it is useful to move beyond discussions of whether or not democracy promotion is the right policy for the United States and to ask whether we are doing it in the most effective way possible.[31] Policy makers, some of whom may question the wisdom of democracy assistance generally, rarely question whether our democracy promotion programs are actually the best way to promote democracy. However, democracy promotion programs themselves have come under scrutiny by a number of scholars

Carothers (2002) has pointed out that the battery of U.S.-funded democracy promotion projects look similar across very different countries with quite different challenges and histories. It may be that, for example, civic education about anti-corruption, campaign training for political parties, watchdog NGOs, and workshops for lawyers and judges really are necessary in every democratizing country, but it is also possible that different countries have different needs. Political development professionals now speak of a "standard political party program" or "the typical democracy and governance program" in a particular country.

Carothers and other scholars of democracy promotion have further asserted that practitioners lack sufficient knowledge of non-American forms of democracy; that many in the field lack sufficient language skills and cultural familiarity to do their jobs; and that democracy assistance programs are viewed in the host countries as founts of grant money and little else. The first part of this criticism seems less true now than it did five or ten years ago as American NGOs and contractors increasingly use people from many different countries in their efforts to find the best match for the challenges of a particular democratizing country.

The USAID reliance on a training approach to democratization reflects the abilities of democracy assistance organizations more than the needs of democratizing countries. Stressing training suggests that democracy is just a technical concern that must be understood better so it can be implemented. While there is a technical side to most aspects of democracy, this reliance on training and technical issues often forces implementers of democracy promotion policies to focus less on the political aspect of democratization, which is often more critical.

What Kinds of Democracies?

A key question for the democracy assistance community and the government agencies and officials who are making policy is what kind of democracy. This is particularly relevant in the case of Georgia. The question of when a country can be considered a democracy is central to understanding and evaluating democracy assistance. Freedom House offers a graded scale along two dimensions, the civic and the political, that are updated and evaluated annually. The Freedom House measurements are used by many to categorize regimes for the purposes of further study.[32] Others, such as Huntington (1991), argue that changing governments through free and fair elections is the lynchpin of democracy. Dahl (1989) described eight institutional guarantees that must exist in a democracy. Linz and Stepan (1996) argue that a country has consolidated democracy when democracy is viewed as the "only game in town." In practice, the U.S. government makes decision about democracy assistance based on when countries have reached certain, often subjectively measured thresholds in areas such as election fairness, civic freedoms and strength of democratic institutions.

Democracy, even in advanced democratic countries like the United States or much of Europe, is also not yet complete and is constantly evolving and developing. Questions of the rights of immigrants, the role of money in politics, or whether gay people should be allowed the legal rights and protections of marriage are seen as central to defining Western democracies. Advanced democracies are characterized by intense debates over expanding rights and freedoms and balancing liberties and claims between competing groups that result in policies that expand suffrage, grant civil rights to previously excluded groups of people, or offer new protections to citizens. The democracy that is built in the developing world should be equally vibrant with institutions that are able to allow citizens to resolve these types of issues.

Building mature democracies able to engage in these serious issues is extremely difficult, but must be the goal of democracy assistance. We should not be satisfied with weak democracies that do not offer citizens the full range of choices and freedoms we enjoy in more advanced democratic systems. Much of the literature on democratization has sought to create taxonomies to describe the various kinds of semidemocratic or democratizing systems.[33] Looking more closely at these systems is important, but we must recognize that democracy assistance must seek to do more.

Ordinary citizens in democratizing countries, particularly in the post-Communist world, where the promise of democracy and its associated benefits has been so strong, often become disenchanted with democracy, making it much tougher to build strong democracies. This disenchantment is often exacerbated because citizens have been told that the semidemocratic post-Soviet, corrupt system they have is actually democracy. U.S. democracy assistance programs must be careful about contributing to this problem by defining countries as democratic before they have established a resilient democracy. In this way, the U.S. imprimatur that democracy is in place for states that have not yet achieved democracy may well undermine the future of democracy in those places. The extreme example of this is Iraq, which has sometimes been described by President Bush as a democracy, but other examples include numerous semidemocratic states such as Egypt and, indeed, Georgia.

A related challenge, which is particularly acute in the post-Soviet world, is that people have unrealistically high expectations for democracy. Many citizens of these countries expect democracy to alleviate poverty, create jobs, return stability to the country, and rebuild the infrastructure relatively quickly. When these unrealistic goals are not met, confidence in the new system wanes and democratic consolidation becomes very difficult.

Civic education programs in democratizing countries often are quite successful in communicating key aspects of democracy, such as voting procedures, roles of local government or citizen's rights to citizens. However, it is often equally important to explain to citizens of new democracies what democracy is not. Democracy is not a guarantee of a job, freedom from crime or terrorism, or a quick way for the country to grow rich. By managing these expectations, democratizing countries can give their new democratic institutions a better chance of becoming stronger.

It is in the context of these challenges regarding democracy assistance that we will begin to look at democratization in Georgia before, during, and since the Rose Revolution, as well as the role of democracy assistance in this development. There has been backlash, both in the United States and internationally, against democracy assistance. The international backlash has occurred largely because authoritarian leaders do not want any color revolutions in their own countries. At the same time, in the United States democracy promotion has been misused to explain the problems in Iraq. By learning from cases like Georgia, this critical policy can be retooled and become effective again.

Chapter 2
Illusions of Democracy

The First Years of Independence

During the last two decades of the Soviet Union, Georgia was one of the most affluent of the country's fifteen republics. An economy buoyed by the sale of wine, tea, fruit, and mineral water as well as its position as one of the major tourist destinations of the Soviet Union meant that Georgians enjoyed a higher standard of living than most of their compatriots in other parts of the USSR. In these years, Georgia was also viewed as an important cultural center where artists, film makers, and others worked and had an impact on the entire USSR. Distance from Moscow and the relatively competent leadership of Communist Party first secretary Eduard Shevardnadze from 1973 to 1985 also contributed to quality of life in Georgia.

The impact of the Soviet Union on the development of Georgian nationalism in the twentieth century is important for understanding the struggles that country now confronts.[1] The 1921 Soviet takeover destroyed the nascent, independent Georgian state, but it did not destroy Georgian nationalism; it froze it. As in other areas of the Soviet Union such as Ukraine, nationalist uprisings in Georgia persisted well into the 1920s, primarily in the difficult to access mountainous regions. These uprisings were brutally repressed. However, when the Soviet Union began to collapse, Georgian nationalism began to thaw. For Georgian nationalists, there is a strong continuity between the 1920s and the 1980s and 1990s. The activism of the late 1980s and early 1990s opposed the authoritarian Soviet regime, but independence and self-determination, not democracy, were the movement's primary goals.

The end of the Soviet period instigated dramatic change throughout the fifteen newly independent countries that had once formed the Soviet Union, but Georgia was something of an extreme case. Georgia had been one of the wealthiest of the constituent republics of the Soviet

Union, but its economic decline was greater and more rapid than that in almost any of the others, and by 1995 it was one of the poorest of the newly independent states.

Ironically, the newly independent Georgia might have seemed to an outside observer in 1991 like a likely prospect for a smooth evolution toward stability and democracy. As a small republic with a relatively homogeneous population by Soviet standards; a border with Turkey, a NATO member, potentially important ally, and trading partner; an educated population; and an established market niche, Georgia seemed to have many positives. Sadly, by the mid-1990s, all this had been squandered; the country had devolved into an impoverished, wartorn, almost lawless country in a period of only a few years.

The modern Georgian state was born in March 1991 when the Georgian people overwhelmingly approved a ballot referendum calling for independence. A few months later, they went to the polls again to elect the government for the new state. The winning party in that election, Round Table, was led by Zviad Gamsakhurdia, a dynamic, popular Georgian nationalist who was viewed as one of the leaders of the renascent Georgian nationalist movement. Gamsakhurdia was not, however, either a democrat or prepared for the task of governing.

Georgia's first years of independence under the leadership of Gamsakhurdia were not easy ones. Rather than initiate a new democratic era, Gamsakhurdia sought to create a new one-party system. The Round Table, which had come together during the late Soviet years as a rallying point for Georgian independence activists, proved unable to govern. Although elected by a substantial majority in an election that was essentially free and fair, Gamsakhurdia was in many ways an undemocratic leader. He did not tolerate opposition, often calling political opponents traitors and other epithets. Effective institutions such as courts, legislative bodies, and bureaucracies did not evolve during these years. Gamsakhurdia's behavior became increasingly erratic and divisive. He did, however, manage to maintain a reasonable degree of popularity among the Georgian people who had elected him to office.[2]

Under the ineffective leadership of the Round Table in the early 1990s, Georgia rapidly slipped into civil strife, territorial instability, and economic collapse. Indeed, Gamsakhurdia's inability to govern effectively led to a descent into nearly anarchic conditions. The government failed to deliver services, maintain infrastructure, or implement the law. The economy rapidly collapsed as infrastructure fell into disrepair or was destroyed or stolen. Difficult relations with Russia, Georgia's largest trading partner, rapidly dismantled the tourist market as well as the external market for products such as wine, mineral water, and other foodstuffs.

Political strife of various hues exacerbated the economic collapse. First, two regions of Georgia, South Ossetia in 1991 and Abkhazia in 1992 (inhabited by Georgians as well as Ossetians and Abkhazians), declared independence, precipitating civil conflicts that ended in 1993 when Georgia lost control over both regions. The Abkhaz and Ossetian opponents of Georgia were supported by Russia, but their actions can also be partly attributed to Gamsakhurdia's heated nationalist rhetoric. Efforts to bring them back into Georgia through some kind of federalist arrangement are still being undertaken and remain central to the ongoing tension between Russia and Georgia. An estimated 250,000 Georgians living in those regions fled to other parts of Georgia, creating a problem of resettling internally displaced persons (IDPs) that has still not been resolved.

A third region, Ajara, also declared de facto independence from Tbilisi during this time. The regime of strongman Aslan Abashidze, who would later play a key role in the Rose Revolution, remained semi-autonomous until May 2004, when Abashidze, in the face of aggressive efforts from the new government, fled to Russia and Tbilisi regained control of Ajara.

Even with Ajara, Abkhazia, and South Ossetia excluded, Georgia was still far from stable. Civil strife between supporters of Gamsakhurdia and opponents of various stripes were rampant. Armed gangs controlled parts of western Georgia, particularly in the Samegrelo region. In 1991–92, civil war appeared imminent as armed conflict took place on the streets of Tbilisi, the parliament building was shelled, and armed gangs intimidated residents of the capital, bringing work and commercial activity to a virtual standstill. Georgia, in short, was on the verge of collapse.

A motley collection of Gamsakhurdia opponents, including gangsters, intellectuals, former Communist party leaders, businesspeople, and even a few democrats, sought to replace the democratically elected president with someone who might be able to hold the country together, bring it sorely needed international recognition and support, and perhaps even behave a little bit more rationally and democratically. The man they turned to was the former first secretary of Georgia, who had moved on to international renown as the foreign minister of the USSR. Thus Eduard Shevarnadze returned to his native Georgia from Moscow to serve as its second post-independence leader.

In the West, the return of Shevardnadze was viewed, and to a great extent continues to be viewed, as unambiguously positive for Georgia. The experienced and mature Shevardnadze, so the narrative goes, a man of international renown, respected all over the world for his tenure as Soviet foreign minister, was being asked to return to his native Georgia and try to pick up the pieces left by the failed presidency of the erratic, undemocratic, slightly nutty Zviad Gamsakhurdia. Shevardnadze shared this view, often referring to his return to Georgia as one of the proudest moments in his career.[3]

The truth is more complicated. Gamsakhurdia, for all his many failings, was a democratically elected president. Shevardnadze was not elected to replace Gamsakhurdia; he was appointed by a collection of elites, some with strong ties to organized crime. While clearly a more competent, experienced, and perhaps even decent leader, Shevardnadze had no democratic foundation for his return to Georgia in 1992, when he was appointed acting chair of the Georgian State Council, effectively becoming the country's leader. His assumption of this position may not have been a coup in the classic sense, but it certainly veered in that direction. Failure to understand this fact and how it influenced the feelings of ordinary Georgians toward their first secretary turned State Council chair (and in 1995, following constitutional changes, president) was central to many of the problems the West encountered in its democracy assistance policies during Shevardnadze's tenure as president.

Shevardnadze's Return to Georgia

When Shevardnadze became Georgia's leader in 1992, he immediately faced the daunting tasks of bringing stability and the rule of law, establishing diplomatic ties with the West, rebuilding Georgia's economy, keeping what was left of the state from disintegrating further, and beginning democratic reforms. The future of the Georgian state rested on resolving at least some of these problems.

The first few years of Shevardnadze's presidency produced markedly mixed results. The unrest in Abkhazia and South Ossetia had begun during Gamsakhurdia's tenure, but in Abkhazia the actual shooting began under Shevardnadze. The conflicts wound down with Georgia losing both regions, roughly 20 percent of its territory. Additionally, the moribund economy recovered only partly and very slowly, so unemployment and poverty remained enormous problems for the state and its new president. The country's infrastructure, which had collapsed with the Soviet Union, also recovered only slightly; power outages and disruption of gas and water supplies continued to plague most of Georgia through the mid-1990s.

There were, however, positive signs as well during the early years of the Shevardnadze administration. First, Shevardnadze brought enormous personal prestige to the presidency, and Georgia benefited directly and indirectly from that prestige. Internationally, Georgia was the only former Soviet state other than Russia with a president who was well known and respected globally. The names of leaders of other post-Soviet countries, such as Azerbaijan and Tajikistan, were completely unknown in the West, but Shevardnadze did not have this problem. Through his formidable network of relationships and personal ties at the highest levels of dozens of foreign governments, Shevardnadze was able to accelerate Georgia's diplomatic recognition. With Shevardnadze leading Georgia out of the chaos of the Gamsakhurdia period, foreign countries began to establish diplomatic ties, setting up embassies, forging bilateral agreements, and providing much needed foreign aid.

On taking office, Shevardnadze began to bring a measure of stability back to Georgia. The civil conflicts that had reached as far as the capital toward the end of Gamsakhurdia's time in office decreased. Working with both business leaders and criminal elements, Shevardnadze was able to rein in the most dangerous and unlawful elements in Georgia, including Jaba Ioseliani's Mkhedrioni, a paramilitary ultranationalist group based in western Georgia that was heavily involved in criminal activities. The country's infrastructure was not rebuilt during this period, but it did improve so that more Georgians had slightly more access to gas, water, and electricity.

Shevardnadze positioned himself as the guarantor of Georgian stability, especially when interacting with foreigners. This role was largely accepted by the international community as diplomats and foreign policy makers were relieved to see a friendly and competent face at the helm of one former Soviet republic. However, Shevardnadze continued to be perceived differently by foreigners and Georgians, a theme that would continue throughout his presidency. Many Georgians saw Shevardnadze as an improvement over his predecessor and were grateful that some stability had returned to their lives, but they did not accept the Western narrative, which Shevardnadze promoted, in which the Soviet foreign minister had come back to his native land to save the teetering independent state. They remained frustrated with his failure to expand the economy, rebuild basic infrastructure, bring real democracy, or curb the corruption that continued to plague Georgia throughout the 1990s.

The modicum of stability that returned to Georgia in fact made it possible for corruption to become more formalized and to infiltrate every aspect of life. The police were little more than an organized crime ring, shaking down motorists for bribes, planting drugs on innocent people and demanding money for the charges to be dropped, and buying and selling positions in the police force. The education system gave way as poorly paid professors and dishonest university officials sold grades and college degrees to students of the newly rich corrupt business class. Ties between government and business were strengthened as government officials grew rich accepting bribes from business interests or stealing tax revenue and foreign assistance money. By 2000 it was virtually impossible to find an area of Georgian life untainted by corruption.

This view of the situation is borne out by Transparency International's Corruption Perceptions Index. This watchdog group's annual survey ranks "more than 150 countries by their perceived levels of corruption, as determined by expert assessments and opinion surveys."[4] It does not rank every country for every year, but the data for Georgia, when available for the last years of Shevardnadze's administration, are startling. In 1999 Georgia ranked 84th of 99 countries; it ranked 85th of 102 countries in 2002 and a remarkable 124th of 133 countries in 2003 (countries are ranked from least corrupt to most corrupt).

Democracy in the Early Shevardnadze Years

Democratic development in Georgia during the first years of Shevardnadze's presidency was mixed. The extreme illiberal democracy and chaos of Gamsakhurdia's time gave way to a regime with elements of what Carothers (2002) has called "feckless pluralism." A weak state placed virtually no restrictions on assembly or speech. Georgians quickly made up for decades of not being allowed to enjoy these freedoms by forming civic organizations and political parties, creating newspapers and television stations, and engaging in other forms of civic activism. Think tanks and advocacy groups emerged that were critical of the government and pushed for reforms of the political system. Newspapers and talk shows were filled with pundits, politicians, and others commenting, often very critically, on political developments.

Georgia during these years was generally viewed as the most democratic of the non-Baltic former Soviet countries, with the greatest freedom of media, assembly, and civic life. Although this description was somewhat akin to likening it to the tallest building in Topeka, there was clearly democratic space in Shevardnadze's Georgia. There was a vibrant civil society and free media, and the government generally left people alone to live their lives. During this time the parliament emerged as an important and visible institution. By the late 1990s, the Georgian assembly was a place where different political voices were heard, issues were debated, and different views on subjects were aired. In this regard, Georgia was quite different from most of the other countries in the region.

Table 1 shows the Freedom House scores for the countries of the former Soviet Union from 1991 to 2003.[5] The total scores are the combined total for the civil liberties and political rights indices used by Freedom House to determine the extent to which a country is free. Scores are given on a scale of 1 through 7; lower scores indicate countries that are

TABLE 1. Freedom House Scores for Post-Soviet Republics

Year covered	1991	1992	1993	1994	1995	1996	1997	1998	1999	2000	2001	2002	2003
Armenia	10	7	7	7	8	9	9	8	8	8	8	8	8
Azerbaijan	10	10	12	12	12	11	10	10	10	11	11	11	11
Belarus	8	7	9	8	10	12	12	12	12	12	12	12	12
Estonia	5	6	5	5	4	3	3	3	3	3	3	3	3
Kazakhstan	9	10	10	11	11	11	11	11	11	11	11	11	11
Kyrgyzstan	9	6	8	7	8	8	8	10	10	11	11	11	11
Latvia	5	6	6	5	4	4	3	3	3	3	3	3	3
Lithuania	5	5	4	4	3	3	3	3	3	3	3	3	3
Moldova	9	10	10	8	8	7	7	6	6	6	6	7	7
Russia	6	7	7	7	7	7	7	8	9	10	10	10	10
Tajikistan	6	12	14	14	14	14	12	12	12	12	12	11	11
Turkmenistan	11	13	14	14	14	14	14	14	14	14	14	14	14
Ukraine	6	6	8	7	7	7	7	7	7	8	8	8	8
Uzbekistan	11	12	14	14	14	13	13	13	13	13	13	13	13
Georgia	11	9	11	10	9	8	7	7	7	8	8	8	8
Mean	7.33	7.80	8.53	8.20	8.27	8.20	7.93	8.00	8.07	8.33	8.33	8.33	8.33
Mean without Baltic states	8.83	9.08	10.33	9.92	10.17	10.08	9.75	9.83	9.92	10.33	10.33	10.33	10.33

Source: "Freedom in the World Country Ratings 1972–2006," at http://www.freedomhouse.org/template.cfm?page=15

freer. Aggregate scores range from 2 to 14, with 2 representing a very free and democratic country and 14 an extremely repressive regime. In addition to the individual country scores, the table shows the mean score for all 15 countries and for the 12 non-Baltic countries.

The years in Table 1 span the beginning of Georgian independence to the last years of Shevardnadze's presidency. The data show that during the early years of independence, under Gamsakhurdia, Georgia was less free than most former Soviet republics, even when the Baltic states are excluded. This changed in the mid-1990s with the election of Shevardnadze to a full term as president and the liberalization of Georgia. Beginning in 1996, Georgia's scores were lower than the mean for the region (significantly lower when the Baltic states are excluded). The only countries with comparable scores for this period are Armenia (slightly higher), Ukraine (virtually identical), and Moldova (slightly lower).

Although Georgia was significantly freer than many of the countries of the former Soviet Union, it was not a democracy. Elections were not free; the rule of law was not strong; democratic institution such as functioning bureaucracies did not exist; and corruption was ubiquitous. Moreover, the state, while stronger than during Gamsakhurdia's presidency, was still extremely weak. In many parts of the country, legislation and regulations were of only peripheral import as local governors appointed by the president, powerful and corrupt businesspeople, or gangsters capriciously exercised the real power. In other areas there was no real authority at all.

The exception was the southwestern province of Ajara, where Aslan Abashidze had consolidated a dictatorship through which he strictly controlled the region and its population of roughly 120,000 and enjoyed semi-autonomy from Tbilisi. In Ajara there were almost no civic organizations, fundamental freedoms, or political opposition. Abashidze's regime was involved deeply in organized crime, allegedly including smuggling drugs, stolen goods, and weapons. He personally enriched himself tremendously through this activity.

The regime was characterized not only by widespread ties to organized crime and a lack of freedom unlike anywhere else in Georgia but also by a cult of personality around the very eccentric Aslan Abashidze. Abashidze cultivated a kind, grandfatherly image for himself. He was known throughout Ajara as *babu*, Georgian for grandfather. His tranquil face shone out from billboards and posters throughout the region in which he was frequently pictured with his own grandchildren or groups of Ajaran children. Visitors to his palace in Batumi, the capital, were often treated to a monologue that lasted several hours, during which Abashidze would explain his family's history over the last several centuries, the artistic and cultural achievements of Ajara, and the superiority of his regime to that in the rest of Georgia. Abashidze wore only black, gray, or white clothing and lived and worked in a palace with high ceilings and almost no decorations on the white interior walls other than numerous flat-screen television sets.

Thus, by the late 1990s, Georgia had evolved into a semidemocratic hybrid in which the governing regime was neither strong nor authoritarian, but processes were fundamentally unfair and government decisions were not made in a way that could be called democratic. The parliamentary elections of 1995 and 1999, as well as the presidential election of 2000 in which Shevardnadze was reelected, were viewed as flawed by foreign and domestic observers. The government during this period was also working more closely with corrupt business interests. But the strong civic life, relatively functional legislature, and the president's ambiguous attitude toward democratic reform made Georgia an intriguing country with regard to democratic potential.

One of Shevardnadze's first acts as president was to create a political party, the Citizens Union of Georgia. The CUG quickly grew to dominate Georgian politics, with the president, most of the legislature, the bureaucracy, and other government leaders members or supporters of the party. There were several opposition parties such as the People's Party, Traditionalist Party, Labor Party, and Industrialists, but none of them played a central role in the government. The exception was the Revival Party, the dominant party in Ajara.

Shevardnadze sought to bring a broad swath of Georgia's political and social leadership into the CUG as a way to help bring the country together after the chaos of the Gamsakhurdia years. While this effort was partially successful, the result was that by the late 1990s Georgians were living under their third one-party rule in a ten-year period. It was not to be their last. The CUG rule was relatively benign, but it severely stunted democratic growth in Georgia and made it difficult for groups to compete through democratic structures such as elections. As in all one-party systems, struggles for power within the party and disputes over party policy were much more important than elections and parliamentary processes, the way such issues are usually resolved in democratic countries. Thus, while the parliament was a place of vibrant debate, most of this occurred entirely among members of the governing CUG.

The CUG was far from unified; its leadership included reformers, corrupt business people, former communist elites, and others. The reform wing was led by Zurab Zhvania, a charming and brilliant Shevardnadze protégé who had been brought into the CUG from the Georgian Green party. Zhvania possessed an understanding of, and commitment to, democracy not often seen in post-Soviet political leaders. Fluent in

English, well connected in foreign policy circles throughout Europe and the United States, and possessing a brilliant political mind and a deep understanding of how government works and how to get things done in a country like Georgia, Zhvania seemed like precisely the kind of leader Georgia would need after Shevardnadze. Zhvania was an extraordinary raconteur with a good sense of humor who could make anybody feel comfortable in his presence. He had the valuable political gift of making whomever he was speaking with feel they were the most important person in his world. During these years, Shevardnadze supported Zhvania, promoting him to Western leaders as the best hope for Georgia's future and using him to indirectly demonstrate his own commitment to democracy and reform.

Zhvania was not the only reformer in the CUG. Throughout the 1990s he drew into his circle other reformers, often but not always young, generally English speaking, and partly trained in the West. They included people like Gia Baramidze, Zurab Noghaideli, and Misha Machavariani. By the late 1990s, the team Zhvania had assembled looked like the next generation of CUG leaders, who would be able to lead the reform efforts in Georgia. They were seen as in the ascendancy within the CUG and as enjoying the favor of President Shevardnadze, who usually drew attention to these reformers in his discussions with foreigners.

These young reform-oriented politicians did not form the majority in the CUG, which was dominated by corrupt and inefficient elements. The question why these reform oriented leaders stayed in the CUG as long as they did is critical. There are several likely reasons. First, none of the other parties in the 1990s were a good fit for them either. Abashidze's Revival Party was dominated by corrupt and criminal forces, and most of the other parties were either also corrupt or irrelevant. Second, Shevardnadze regularly indicated to the reformers themselves and outside the party that the reformers were the next generation of party leadership and all they needed to do was to wait a few more years. Last, many of these reformers probably felt that in a de facto one-party system, they could only make a real difference from within the party.

The most visible, talented, and important reformer Zhvania would bring into his circle was a young Georgian lawyer, Mikheil Saakashvili, who upon completing his LLM through a Muskie fellowship at Columbia University had gone to work at the "white shoe" Manhattan law firm of Patterson, Belknap, Webb, and Tyler. Zhvania lured Saakashvili away from a promising and lucrative legal career to return to Georgia and serve first as an MP and then as justice minister. Saakashvili quickly developed into an enormously talented and energetic politician.

In addition to his studies in the United States, Saakashvili had studied in Ukraine during the Soviet period. He was fluent in English, Ukrainian, French, Dutch, and Russian. Although he had been born into an elite Tbilisi family, Saakashvili possessed an extraordinary ability to communicate with ordinary Georgians. He was also quite young when he returned to Georgia. Born in December 1967, he had not yet reached his thirtieth birthday when Zhvania urged him to return to help rebuild his country.

The Last Years of Shevardnadze's Georgia

After the 2000 election, when Shevardnadze was reelected handily in an election viewed as deeply flawed—poorly prepared voter lists, voters casting ballots more than once and other forms of fraud—the seventy-two-year-old president seemed in a strong position. He had avoided any serious opposition in his reelection campaign and kept his party, which still dominated the legislature and Georgian politics generally, unified throughout the campaign. He remained broadly respected internationally for his role in ending the Cold War and bringing Georgia back from the precipice of disaster. This term was to be his last, before he planned to retire as a respected elder statesman of both international and Georgian politics.

Shevardnadze played an enormous role in late twentieth-century Georgia. By the time he left office in November 2003, he had been leader of Georgia, as Soviet republic or independent country, for 22 of the previous 30 years. For an additional 6 of those years, when Shevardnadze was Soviet foreign minister, Georgia was governed by Jumbar Patiashvili, a Shevardnadze loyalist. Shevardnadze was more than just the long-time leader of Georgia: he was a man of extraordinary political talent who began life as a poor youth in the mountains of the rural region of Guria and rose to be one of the most powerful men in the world. Moreover, he did so in the competitive, often nasty world of Soviet politics.

After he returned to Georgia in 1992 he again became the sun around which Georgian politics revolved. Politicians positioned themselves not according to any ideology but by their degree of support or opposition to Shevardnadze. His behind the scenes machinations could set opposition parties squabbling with each other for weeks. By the end of his tenure as president, both opposition and government blocs in parliament were filled with people he had appointed, recruited, or supported. When he needed to remind Georgians about his status, he would drop the name of a U.S. president or secretary of state or other world leader with whom he enjoyed a personal relationship. Those who stayed close to him could access these resources; those who had never been close to him would have a hard time getting a phone call returned in Washington, London, Berlin, Strasbourg, or Brussels.

Shevardnadze's personal prestige and relationships in the West prevented many observers and policy makers from becoming aware of the depth of Georgia's problems. These people had a difficult time recognizing that the man who had worked so closely with the United States as Soviet foreign minister could be part of a regime that was profoundly corrupt and dishonest and that, for example, stole elections. They wanted to believe Shevardnadze was fighting for reform and were reluctant to blame him personally for the corruption, election fraud, economic stagnancy, and other problems Georgia was experiencing. Shevardnadze, who seemed genuinely torn between the reform and corrupt wings of his party, encouraged this perception by showcasing Zhvania, Saakashvili, and the other reformers in the party, charming foreigners with recollections of the Cold War, and allowing a substantial amount of freedom in Georgia.

Many Western leaders, in addition to not fully understanding the undemocratic aspects of Shevardnadze's regime, also critically misunderstood the view of Shevardnadze held by many Georgian people. Ordinary Georgians believed Shevardnadze was deeply and personally responsible for the economic and political problems in Georgia. Even those Westerners, particularly during the last years of his presidency, who were critical of Shevardnadze were baffled as to how the man who did such a good job as Soviet foreign minister could be so unsuccessful as president. Georgians asked themselves the precise opposite question: How could the man who was a bad first secretary of the Communist Party in Georgia and an even worse president have done such a good job as foreign minister of the Soviet Union?

The years 2000–2003 did not go well for the newly reelected president. He continued to be unable to deliver any kind of meaningful economic development for Georgia as unemployment remained high, foreign investment did not grow, and tourism and trade with neighboring countries did not return either. Nor was Shevardnadze able to make progress toward bringing South Ossetia and Abkhazia back under Georgian control or returning internally displaced people, who by the late 1990s numbered roughly 250,000, to their homes in these regions. Shevardnadze also failed to make any serious effort to reduce corruption, so that problem continued to grow, damaging the economy, destroying the education system, frightening off foreign investment, and generally making life in Georgia very difficult for its shrinking population. Throughout these years thousands of Georgians left for Russia, the United States, Germany, Israel—virtually anywhere where they would have an opportunity to make a living and send money home.

The 2000 election would prove to be a turning point. Shevardnadze's major opponent was Jumbar Patiashvili, who had once served as first secretary during Shevardnadze's tenure as Soviet foreign minister. Patiashvili was not well liked in Georgia, largely due to his support for the Soviet Union during the independence movement in the late 1980s and his role in the violent suppression of the April 9, 1989, demonstration in Tbilisi.

Shevardnadze was almost certain to beat Patiashvili, but his supporters and parties committed numerous cases of electoral fraud anyway. The report from the Office of Democratic Institutions and Human Rights (ODIHR) of the Organization for Security and Cooperation in Europe (OSCE) described "problems . . . in the following areas: interference by State authorities in the election process; deficient election legislation; not fully representative election administration; and unreliable voter registers." The report also noted that "The authorities did not behave impartially and gave strong support for the election campaign of the incumbent. Also, there was no clear dividing line between State affairs and the incumbent's campaign."[6] Human Rights Watch addressed the Georgian elections in its country report for Georgia for that year, stating that the elections were "marred by irregularities" but also adding that "nontraditional religious minorities were harassed, attacked, and subjected to baseless charges during the run up to the election."[7] In short, it was a typical post-Soviet, undemocratic election, even if the outcome was more or less what the voters wanted.

The 2000 presidential election was not the only fraudulent election in the late Shevardnadze years. The 1999 parliamentary election was also marred, but unlike the presidential election, the fraud, intimidation, bribery, and violence had a substantial impact on the outcome of the election and the makeup of the new parliament. In many respects, the flawed 1999 election laid the groundwork for the parliamentary election of 2003, so it is important to take a closer look at that election, its outcome and the politics surrounding it.

Interestingly, the ODIHR report on the 1999 election painted a much more positive picture than was perceived by most Georgians. The basic conclusion of ODIHR was that

the conduct of this election represented a step towards Georgia's compliance with OSCE commitments, although the election process failed to fully meet all commitments. In the areas where elections were held, voters were mostly able to express their will and, despite some irregularities, were generally able to vote without interference in an atmosphere largely free from intimidation. However, some instances of intimidation and violence observed during the pre-election period and on Election Day, raise concern.[8]

The 1999 parliamentary election, like that of 2003, sought to elect 235 people to the Georgian national legislature through a mixed electoral system that consisted of party list and majoritarian components.[9] The party list component was a single, nationwide list where 150 seats would be divided, based on proportion of the vote received, among parties that won 7 percent or more of the votes. The remaining 85 MPs were elected in districts that were coterminous with rayons.[10] Only 75 of these were actually elected since ten seats were reserved for Abkhazia, which was not at the time under Georgian control. Because these majoritarian seats were based on rayons, the population of these districts varied dramatically, from fewer than 15,000 to more than 100,000. Surprisingly, this discrepancy never seemed to be an issue for Georgian reformers. The political reality was that the party list part of the election was of most concern, as most conceded that the majority of the district-based seats would be won by local corrupt business people loyal to the government. Unlike the 2000 presidential elections, where no politician was able to compete with Shevardnadze on a national level, the 1999 parliamentary elections were very competitive since Shevardnadze's policies of allowing freedom of speech and assembly led to the creation of a number of strong opposition parties seeking to win seats from the governing CUG.

The CUG ran an aggressive campaign, combining modern campaign techniques such as polling, mail, and television advertisements with fraud and intimidation. The architect of this campaign was the CUG's most prominent reformer, Zurab Zhvania, who by then was also speaker of the parliament.

Zhvania's role in the election partially undermined his reformist credentials and weakened his position with the Georgian people. One key decisions for which Zhvania's critics held him responsible was raising the threshold for parties seeking representation in parliament from 5 to 7 percent. Importantly, most followers of Georgia in the West, still wanting to believe the best about Shevardnadze, never really understood the extent of fraud in that election, or of Zhvania's critical role in committing that fraud. This was reflected in the generally positive assessment of the election by ODIHR.

The CUG efforts to ensure a resounding victory led to multiple voting, particularly in the heavily ethnic Azeri region of Kvemo Kartli and the heavily Armenian region of Samskhe-Javakheti; it saw faulty voter lists throughout Georgia and widespread bribery and intimidation. However, this was not enough to guarantee the result the CUG wanted, so after Election Day the counting process was falsified as well. Most at stake was which parties would cross the 7 percent threshold and send members to parliament. Because this threshold was relatively high, and there were 150 seats to be divided among parties that crossed it, any party that received 7 percent of the vote was guaranteed at least ten seats in the new parliament, enough to form an official faction.[11] In addition to keeping some parties out of parliament, the CUG sought to raise its proportion of the vote so as to have the largest number of MPs possible.

Going into the election two parties, the CUG and Revival, were all but guaranteed to pass the 7 percent threshold. But it was not at all clear which, if any, other parties would pass the threshold. Revival was in a strong position because, as the ruling party in Ajara, it had the ability to steal as many votes as needed to get into parliament. Not surprisingly, a number of individuals and political parties sought to make a deal with one of these parties to run as a coalition or for their leaders be given a place on either the CUG or Revival list.

The result of the election was that two parties, the CUG and Revival, passed the threshold easily. The early results showed that two more parties, the moderate or pseudo-opposition Industrialists and the radical, anti-Shevardnadze Labor Party were close. Ultimately, the Industrialists made it into parliament with 7.08 percent of the vote, while Labor narrowly missed with 6.69 percent of the vote. The widely held, probably accurate, belief in Georgia was that the Industrialists were allowed into parliament because they came up with more money to bribe the election committee during the counting period.

The ODIHR report, while not explicitly supporting the Labor Party claim that it was deliberately kept out of parliament, makes it clear that there were many problems with the counting procedure at the central level.

The procedures followed were not sufficiently transparent. The figures released by the CEC (Central Election Commission) were based on the summation of precinct results arriving by fax from various DECs (District Election Commissions) in a random manner. . . . The tabulation was conducted in the CEC premises, which was not accessible to party representatives. Even some CEC members, particularly those from the opposition, were denied access to these premises. . . . The tabulation was conducted by a limited number of CEC technical staff with standard statistical software, which did not include special safeguards against technical errors. In case such errors occurred and they needed to be corrected, no trace was left for the wrong record after the corrections were inserted.[12]

The Labor Party and its leader, Shalva Natalashvili, were furious over these results and brought about several unsuccessful court cases seeking entrance into parliament. Natalashvili's public anger at the CUG and Shevaradnadze did not subside over the following years. He held a special disdain for Zurab Zhvania, whom he seemed to view as a false democrat who had personally led the drive to keep Labor out of parliament.

The new parliament, like the old, was to be dominated by a diverse CUG block consisting of reformers, corrupt business and political interests, and former communists. Neither of the two opposition parties figured to pose a serious threat. Revival, if left to do what it wanted in Ajara, was not going to make trouble for the CUG. The Industrialists, led by beer magnate Gogi Topadze, were not strongly opposed to the CUG and would cooperate in exchange for support for their business interests. Thus, the major challenge for the CUG, and party leader in parliament Zurab Zhvania, was to hold the party together. This would prove to be difficult as the tensions within the party continued to grow. The roots of the party system of 2003, which would eventually lead to the Rose Revolution and the overthrow of Shevardnadze's regime, lay in the CUG's inability to remain a single cohesive party in the face of growing internal tension.

Structural issues contributed to the breakdown of the CUG in parliament after the 1999 election. The difference between a legislature organized by party and one organized by faction is subtle but, it turned out, extremely important. Once the parliament is elected, rather than forming large blocs for each party, any group of at least ten MPs can form a faction. A faction in this sense does not refer to an informal group of likeminded members within a party. In the Georgian parliament, factions are recognized formally. Each faction is given an office and representation on the committee that sets the agenda, media attention, and other perks. Thus, there is an incentive for the parliament to be disunified, which of course contributes to an imbalance between the executive and legislative branches of government. This structure is not at all uncommon in the former Soviet Union and contributes to weak legislatures across the region.

Mikheil Saakashvili was the first reform politician to formally break with Shevardnadze. Saakashvili's return to Georgia and tenure as justice minister and then MP had not been easy. While he won accolades from the Georgian media, civil society, and many international observers for his uncompromising efforts to fight corruption, these efforts were significantly less appreciated from colleagues in the government, many of whom were deeply involved in the corruption. Saakashvili became increasingly frustrated before resigning in September 2001. After resigning, he ran for parliament as a majoritarian from Vake rayon in Tbilisi in late 2001 with support from the CUG. Vake is the most visible and elite rayon in Georgia, so the office of MP from Vake takes on a special significance. Saakashvili handily won the election. Saakashvili's break with Shevardnadze was not entirely complete at that time, as Shevardnadze campaigned in support of Saakashvili during his race for parliament.

In 2000, while serving in parliament as a CUG majoritarian MP, Saakashvili became increasingly exasperated with Shevardnadze's failure to support a reform agenda. Finally, in October 2001, he publicly broke with Shevardnadze and announced the formation of his own party, the National Movement-United Front (NM). He was able to persuade more than ten of his fellow MPs, all originally elected as CUG members, to join him in forming an NM faction in parliament. Thus, although the NM had not been in existence during the 1999 elections, it was formally recognized as a faction in parliament with all the requisite perks.

Saakashvili's departure from the CUG was seen as a blow to Shevardnadze, but because Saakashvili had always been an outsider in the CUG, never attaining major party leadership positions, it was not devastating for Shevardnadze, who was still able to maintain his reputation as a reformer by pointing to another young reform leader, Zurab Zhvania, who was still speaker of parliament and held a leadership position in the CUG.

Zhvania's break from Shevardnadze in fall 2001 was more devastating for Shevardnadze and not easy for Zhvania, who agonized for weeks before publicly separating himself from the man he considered his mentor and who often spoke about Zhvania like a son. Zhvania not only resigned as speaker of parliament and formed his own party, the United Democrats (UD), but he brought 22 MPs with him to make the UD faction the biggest in parliament. Zhvania was replaced as speaker by Nino Burjanadze, who would wait until the summer 2003 before breaking with Shevardnadze and joining the opposition.

Before the formation of the NM and the UD, led by Saakashvili and Zhvania respectively, another faction had broken off from the CUG. The New Rights, led by insurance magnate David Gamkrelidze—who, like Zhvania and Saakashvili, was under forty, spoke English, and was brought into politics by Shevardnadze—also claimed to be a reform oriented opposition party. Unlike the UD or the NM, the New Rights was not widely viewed as an opposition party. Instead, many saw them as a party of businesspeople supported, or even created, by Shevardnadze as an attempt to shift attention and support away from the growing opposition and demand for reform within the CUG.[13]

The New Rights took much of its style and approach from Gamkrelidze, who had been a doctor before making his fortune in insurance. Gamkrelidze was conservative in both politics and personality, and had a strong affinity for the U.S. Republican Party. He was put off by Saakashvili's impatience and more radical edge, preferring to make more cautious and calculated decisions. Politics did not come easily to him, and he never seemed to be fully comfortable with the machinations and maneuverings essential for a good leader of a political party.

The line between CUG and the opposition parties was becoming murky in Georgia by 2001 and 2002, as many Georgians initially found it difficult to believe Shevardnadze's top protégés were now leading many of the major opposition parties. Nonetheless, as the spring 2002 local elections approached, the new party system was more firmly in place. Of the three parties in parliament, the two pro-government parties were Revival and the CUG. While the CUG had begun to fracture and weaken, Revival was still unified in support of Abashidze's authoritarian regime in Ajara, but its coalition partners from the 1999 election, most notably the Traditionalist Party, had broken off and informally become part of the opposition. The Industrialist Party remained unified, continuing to be a weak opposition voice but a frequent supporter of the CUG.

The opposition parties were divided between those who had never been part of the CUG, notably the Labor Party, a left-leaning party whose platform called for government spending on programs to help Georgia's poorest voters. Labor frequently touted its credentials as never having been part of the CUG. The second group was the the breakaway factions/parties that had once been part of the CUG. These included the NM, UD, and New Rights. There were numerous smaller parties that had no representation in the 1999 parliament and were desperately trying to remain relevant. The most prominent of these were the National Democratic Party (NDP) and the People's Party, both of which had been active in the movement for Georgian independence in the late 1980s, but by the beginning of the new millennium were no longer very relevant in Georgia.[14]

A few other aspects of the political party system were important as well. First, other than a social-democratic position taken on economic and social issues by the Labor Party, ideology was not very relevant in partisan differences. Most parties claimed to be center-right and to support market reforms, but rarely fleshed that position out or even demonstrated a clear awareness of what the term "center right" meant.

Instead, the issue that defined this party system was a party's position relative to Shevardnadze. Moreover, as time passed and the president grew less popular, each party, other than the CUG, claimed to be the most genuine and strongest in its opposition. By 2003, the phrase "we are the only real opposition party in Georgia" was the boast of virtually every non-CUG party. Revival and the Industrialists based this claim on the fact that they had won seats in parliament independently of the CUG; Labor on having run on an aggressive anti-CUG platform in 1999 and been prevented from taking its rightful seats due to CUG election fraud. The NM and UD based their claim on having visibly broken with CUG leadership and by using their seats in parliament to form an anti-government group in that body. When parties were not asserting their reasons for being the only true opposition, they were often attacking the opposition credentials of the other parties.

There was not a lot at stake in the local elections of 2002 because most power in Georgia was centralized, but the balloting was viewed by many as a test for several of the newly formed parties and a preview of the 2003 parliamentary elections. These local elections were held in towns, cities, and rayons around the country, including a party list election for the Tbilisi city council. The voting was not altogether free and fair, but because there was so little at stake it was more so than either of the recent national elections. The three big winners were the New Rights, who won more seats nationwide than any other party, although this was in substantial part due to vote buying and bribery; the Labor Party, whose strong anti-Shevardnadze message resonated throughout Georgia; and the National Movement, which won seats throughout the country and, running under the slogan "Tbilisi without Shevardnadze" won a plurality of seats on the Tbilisi city council. The National Movement and Labor were able to form a majority on the city council, making Saakashvili the speaker of that body, a very visible position in Georgia. Because Tbilisi's mayor was not directly elected but appointed by the president, Saakashvili was the highest ranking elected official in Tbilisi.[15] He used this position for great political and symbolic gain. Zhvania's United Democrats got a late start in these elections as the details of the split between Zhvania and the CUG took some time to resolve, but Zhvania's party did respectably, winning a handful of seats throughout the country and in Tbilisi. Thus, the political environment had begun to take on more clarity as the parliamentary elections of 2003 approached.

Defining the Shevardnadze Regime

Categorizing Shevardnadze's Georgia as a particular type of regime is a complex task. Examining Shevardnadze's rule in this way, however, is important because this process helps clarify the Rose Revolution. For example, to determine the extent to which the Rose Revolution was a democratic breakthrough, or in fact a revolution, depends substantially on how the regime that preceded it is understood. The relevance of the Rose Revolution as a model to other countries struggling for expanded democracy also depends on how comparable the Shevardnadze regime is to other nondemocratic regimes.

The combination of a substantial amount of freedom, a weak state, restricted political competition, extensive corruption, powerful non-state actors, fraudulent elections, a strong presidency but a visible legis-lature—all of which characterized Shevardnadze's Georgia—was unusual. While it is clear that Georgia during this period was neither democratic nor authoritarian, it is not clear whether it was in transition or was some kind of consolidated semidemocratic regime. If one views it as being in transition, it is equally unclear whether it was a period of transition to democracy or part of a lengthy transition, which began in the late 1980s, away from the Soviet system.

When Shevardnadze's regime finally came to an end in November 2003, it was obvious that a key turning point in modern Georgian history had been reached, but it was less obvious precisely what that turning point represented. Shevardnadze, like many other post-Soviet leaders, was an old communist-era politician who had been in power in Georgia or the broader Soviet Union for at least a generation. He was not a reformer or democrat, nor did he represent a decisive break with the past.

Although nobody would say so at the time, we can now see that to a considerable extent Shevardnadze's regime was a restoration of at least some of the old Soviet system after the brief Gamsakurdia interregnum. Gamsakhurdia was a strongly anti-Soviet figure who wanted to restore independent Georgia and sever political, cultural, and economic ties with Russia. He represented a radical break with the Soviet period that reshuffled economic and political power. Shevardnadze's ascension to power after several years of Gamsakurdia's failed leadership, while far from a return to the Soviet system, put a number of Soviet-era figures back in power and was a much less radical break.

It was not until the Rose Revolution, which brought to power a generation of leaders who had not been politically relevant during the Soviet period, that the transition was really complete. Only then did the last generation of Soviet communists truly relinquish power. Equally significant, the end of the Shevardnadze period indicated an even further reorientation away from Moscow. In this framework, his regime could be described as a semidemocratic caretaker regime governing during a period of extended post-Soviet transition, but that description is too specific, even sui generis, and is of limited analytical value.

How then can Shevardnadze's semidemocratic regime best be characterized? Carothers describes semidemocratic regimes as falling mainly into two groups: feckless pluralism and dominant power politics. This is a useful taxonomy, but not one that can be easily applied to Shevardnadze's Georgia. Countries experiencing dominant power politics are described as having "limited but still real political space, some political contestation by opposition groups, and at least most of the basic institutional forms of democracy."[16] This description fits Georgia under Shevardnadze very well. But Carothers continues by describing this system as one where "opposition parties that do exist are hard put to gain much public credibility" and there is a "deep-seated intolerance for anything more than limited opposition." Georgia during this period had vibrant opposition parties and more than limited opposition, so this type does not quite fit Shevardnadze's Georgia.

Carothers's description of feckless pluralism also seems to sketch the outlines of Shevardnadze's Georgia. These states have "significant amounts of political freedom [and] regular elections," an apt description of Shevardnadze's Georgia. But they are also characterized by "alternation of power between genuinely different political groupings," which does not apply.

Andreas Schedler describes electoral authoritarian regimes as "play-[ing] the game of multi-party elections by holding regular elections for the chief executive and national legislative assembly . . . subject to state manipulation, so severe widespread and systematic that they do not qualify as democratic."[17] This description fits Georgia, but Schedler's further remark that electoral authoritarian regimes "preach democracy but practice dictatorship" is a bit strong; Georgia was clearly not a dictatorship under Shevardnadze.

Marina Ottaway introduces the notion of semi-authoritarian regimes as "combin[ing] rhetorical acceptance of liberal democracy, the existence of some formal democratic institutions and respect for a limited sphere of civil and political liberties with essentially illiberal or even authoritarian traits."[18] Of critical import is that semi-authoritarian regimes are not "imperfect democracies struggling towards improvement and consolidation" (3), nor are they in a period of transition. They are regimes that have the appearance of democracies and democratic institutions primarily as a means of deflecting criticism and appearing more palatable to the West.

This description seems to apply reasonably well to Shevardnadze's Georgia, particularly during the later years of his presidency. It was clear by the turn of the twenty-first century that Georgia under Shevardnadze and what remained of the CUG was not moving toward democracy, but was a nondemocratic country with a fair amount of political and civic freedom and "essentially illiberal traits." Ottaway's description of semi-authoritarianism is, however, quite broad. The term applies to many countries, including what she describes as "decaying democracy," "institutionalized semi-authoritarian" regimes, and "decaying semi-democratic regimes." While it is difficult to fit Georgia into any of these groups, describing Shevardnadze's regime simply as semi-authoritarian does not reveal with enough precision the characteristics of the regime.

Levitsky and Way describe competitive authoritarian regimes as ones in which "formal democratic institutions are widely viewed as the principal means of obtaining and exercising political authority. Incumbents violate those rule so often and to such and extent, however, that the regime fails to meet conventional minimum standards for democracy."[19] This description also seems to fit Shevardnadze's Georgia reasonably well. Interestingly, while Levitsky and Way give a number of examples from the former Soviet Union, they do not identify Georgia as a competitive authoritarian regime, perhaps because of hesitancy to view a country with such a high degree of political and civic freedom as a modified authoritarian regime.

Shevardnadze's regime is thus not easy to classify. It had some of the characteristics of a number of different semidemocratic systems, but did not quite fit any of them. It was marked by an unusual combination of one-party dominance, strong civil and even parliamentary institutions, freedom of speech and assembly, fraudulent elections, and high degrees of corruption and lawlessness. Ultimately, the regime also proved weak and undisciplined. This combination raised challenges for democrats and members of the opposition because of the incongruity between tolerance for freedoms and dominance of the one-party system and pervasiveness of electoral fraud and theft.

Perhaps the most important characteristic of the Georgian state under Shevardnadze was its weakness, which limited the government's options in a range of areas. The government lacked the capacity to rebuild the infrastructure, stimulate the economy, fight corruption, or even hold the country together. These failings contributed to the extreme unpopularity of Shevardnadze and his government by the early years of the new century.

This weakness also played a role in the high degree of civic and political engagement Georgians enjoyed during the Shevardnadze years. Shevardnadze may or may not have truly believed that his regime that stole elections, failed to deliver services, and looted millions of dollars from the people was somehow more democratic if it did not repress free speech and allowed for political opposition. However, what he actually believed was largely moot because by 2001 the regime clearly lacked the strength to repress freedoms.

Chapter 3
The Accidental Revolution

As the parliamentary elections of 2003 approached, Shevardnadze's regime was rife with corruption, unable to deliver basic services or economic growth of any kind and relying increasingly on Shevardnadze's reputation, continuing mastery of politics and ability to keep the Georgian opposition disunified. The local elections had shown how unpopular Shevardnadze had become in the two years since his reelection: the biggest winner in that election, Saakashvili's NM, had campaigned under the unambiguous slogan "Tbilisi Without Shevardnadze."

Preparations for the Election

As soon as the 2002 local elections ended, parties began to prepare for the November 2003 parliamentary elections, which were broadly viewed as the main event for which the local elections had simply been the warm-up. Long before the elections, it became clear that the balloting would push Georgia in a new political direction. At the beginning of 2003, the CUG was in shambles and could no longer present itself as having a reform wing at all. Moreover, in the years since the last presidential election, there had been no decline in corruption or improvement in the Georgian economy. The CUG clearly had little hope of winning these elections fairly. Instead, it would have to rely on even more fraud, intimidation, and bribery than it had in 1999.[1]

Politically, Shevardnadze found himself in an interesting position. On several occasions, he publicly stated that he did not intend to seek reelection when his term expired in 2005, so this was to be the last election in which he would be a major actor. Shevardnadze was likely to become a lame duck president after the election, particularly if his party did not do well. One result of this was that the parliamentary election was something of an informal primary to see which opposition party would offer the strongest presidential candidate in 2005. The leader of the party that won the most seats in the new parliament would be in a good position to run for president in 2005.

Because he was not personally on the ballot, Shevardnadze might have been able to avoid playing an active role in the campaign and simply agreed to work with whatever parliament the people elected. For a man increasingly focused on his legacy, this would have been a wise decision. Unfortunately, Shevardnadze, a consummate politician, was unable to avoid the temptation of becoming involved in one last election. This proved to be a politically fatal mistake.

As with many elections in semidemocratic countries, the 2003 parliamentary elections were framed by two key questions: who would win and how fair the elections would be. Accordingly, the opposition parties confronted a dual challenge, winning the elections and working to ensure their fairness. The distinction between these two goals is critical and often lost on political parties. Winning votes through effective communication, mobilization, and organization is not sufficient if the election will be stolen anyway. Similarly, fighting for fair elections, while always a worthy goal, is of limited value to a political party that does not campaign and secure votes. Most of the major Georgian opposition parties understood this and pursued both paths throughout 2003.

There were a number of important issues on the political agenda in Georgia that directly tied into election fairness, including a new election law that had the potential to make election fraud more difficult; the make-up of the Central Election Committee (CEC), the body responsible for administering the election and making final decisions about outcomes and vote totals; whether voter marking would be used; the process for assembling and checking voter lists, the size and character of the international election observation mission; the possibility of meaningful pressure for fair elections from the United States and Europe; the size and quality of the domestic election monitoring effort; and the specific problem of Ajara, where the Revival Party had the ability to inflate its numbers and claim more than its share of seats in the national legislature.

By mid-2003, only a few of these questions had been resolved. The OSCE/ODIHR was preparing an international observer mission consisting of an experienced full-time staff of about 12 people, along with 20 long-term observers (LTOs) who would be dispatched to various regions of Georgia to closely observe election preparations beginning in early September, two months before the election; another 400 short-term observers (STOs) were to observe election day and the few days before the election. Julian Peel Yates, leader of the mission, was a dedicated, engaged, and experienced Englishman. Reformers in Georgia viewed the direction of the ODIHR mission as positive.

The establishment of a strong ODIHR observation mission was certainly a sign that the West was going to push somewhat seriously for the elections to be conducted freely and fairly. However, overall the message from the West was mixed, with indications that the West was not going to pressure the Shevardnadze government as hard as it might. A late summer trip by former U.S. Secretary of State James Baker, acting as a personal envoy of President Bush, also reinforced these mixed messages as Baker pushed for fair elections, but refrained from criticizing Shevardnadze directly in this regard. Moreover, the United States seemed willing to trust the government on a variety of preelection issues, such as preparation of voter lists, that suggested largely unwarranted confidence in the Georgian government's intentions to conduct fair elections.

For most Georgian politicians, civil society leaders, and ordinary citizens, the domestic monitoring effort was just as critical as the ODIHR mission. The leading nonpartisan domestic group to monitor this election was the somewhat grandiosely named International Society for Fair Elections and Democracy (ISFED). ISFED had observed elections in Georgia for years and enjoyed a reputation as the group whose views on election fairness and evaluation of a particular election were the most accurate and impartial and who did not get involved in partisan politics. ISFED's efforts would be supported by a number of other civic organizations in Georgia, most notably the Georgian Young Lawyers Association (GYLA). Both ISFED and GYLA were funded by the USAID. GYLA received its funding, approximately $230,000, through a subgrant from IRIS, a U.S.-based NGO, while ISFED was funded by a subgrant of roughy $250,000 from NDI.[2]

ISFED hired a new executive director, Zurab Tchiarabishvili, for the parliamentary elections. A civic activist with the pro-democracy Liberty Institute and a freelance journalist, he brought to the position a network of strong political and civic relations, good organizational skills, media savvy, fluency in English, and no small amount of self-confidence. ISFED sought not only to observe the elections but to implement a parallel vote tabulation (PVT) as well. A PVT is a technique to determine the extent to which the official vote count matches the actual votes counted and thus demonstrate whether fraud has occurred in this phase of the election. If fraud has not occurred during the counting phase, the PVT results will be similar to those released by the government and can help build confidence in those results. As will become clear, a PVT does not capture fraud such as bribery, multiple voting, or police intimidation.

Implementing a PVT consists of essentially gathering a large, statistically significant sample of voting in various voting places around the country and comparing that sample to the numbers given by the election authorities after the count. Election observers are dispatched to the sample poll sites where they spend the entire day, counting the number of actual votes cast, and staying for the ballot counting in the polling place. When the ballots are counted, the numbers for each party are called into a central headquarters and entered into a database. The PVT requires a great deal of preparation, including training observers, ensuring that they are able to stay in the polling place all day, good data entry and analysis, and overcoming myriad logistical and communication challenges that are exacerbated by the poor infrastructure in a country like Georgia. The PVT was an enormous challenge for ISFED. The group was aided by technical and financial support from NDI in this endeavor.

In early summer a new election law was passed that called for more transparency in the voting and reporting process. This was viewed as only a minor step toward better elections, as most people recognized changing the law was not going to be sufficient in Georgia, where rule of law was very weak. The new election law also remained ambiguous about how the CEC would be appointed. This issue, which will be addressed more fully later, was a major point of contention between the parties even after it was resolved in late summer of 2003.

The new election law also called for marking the fingers of voters with indelible ink in order to combat multiple voting. This decision was controversial as rumors and superstitions about the nature of the ink circulated, raising the possibility that some voters would not vote because of fear of the ink's effects. These fears were assuaged through a voter education campaign that included flyers and television advertisements explaining what the ink was. A letter from the leader of the Georgian Orthodox Church, stating that the ink was in no way part of a satanic plot, was made public and posted at every voting place in the country.[3]

Most of the other issues remained unresolved or, more precisely, were resolved to the detriment of fair elections. Although the ODIHR LTOs were diligent in observing the months preceding the election in Ajara, it was increasingly clear that the Tbilisi government was not going to do anything to prevent the Ajaran authorities from stealing as many votes as they wanted. More disturbingly, the Ajaran authorities were forcibly preventing any campaign activities by parties other than Revival.

The voter list issue remained unresolved as well, and as the election approached it became clear that accurate voter lists would not be assembled in time for the election. The import of good voter lists is evident. Without accurate and comprehensive voter lists, not everybody will be able to vote and some people will be able to vote more than once.

Manipulating voter lists is a good way to disenfranchise supporters of the opposition.

The handling of the voter list issue by the Georgian government and the international community revealed a great deal about the intentions and views of both. Creating good voter lists requires a great deal of time, so the government would have needed to start no later than February or March. The failure to do this was seen by many as further evidence that the government was not going to work to make the elections more free and fair. Additional months of inaction furthered this perception. Few people among the diplomatic corps or in foreign capitals interpreted this delay this way. Instead, they indulged the excuses of the Georgian government.

Ultimately, the United States contributed several million dollars to help the Georgian government set up a sophisticated computerized system for entering and upgrading voter lists. However, this system still relied on government data. The list it produced was an improvement on existing lists, but still far from comprehensive or accurate. The voter list issue was a top priority in the spring and early summer of 2003, but for many in the opposition the question of who would sit on the CEC soon overshadowed concern about voter lists.

Georgia's extremely weak tradition of rule of law meant that many viewed the substance of the new election law as far less important than the question of who would be responsible for implementing and interpreting it, and ultimately counting the votes after the election. Who would sit on Georgia's CEC was also of critical concern to the opposition parties, which feared a CEC dominated by Shevardnadze supporters or a coalition of Shevardnadze and Abashidze supporters. In the end, this is precisely what they got.

There are various models for national election committees in democratizing countries. Some opt for professional election committees of technocrats, others for election committees led by prominent and respected representatives of civil society. The third common model is to constitute the election committee from political parties. The first two models can lead to nonpartisan election committees, but this was not possible in Georgia, where there were few competent technocrats and the NGO leaders were not viewed as nonpartisan. Most of the political parties could agree that the CEC should be drawn from the political parties. The question was from which parties.

Resolving this question was one of former Secretary of State Baker's primary accomplishments in Tbilisi in July 2005. The agreement he brokered, known in Georgia by the somewhat clumsy name "Baker's version," called for a thirteen-person CEC with two presidential appointments, two CUG appointments, eight opposition party appointments, and a CEC chair to be chosen by the president from three candidates submitted by the OSCE. Baker left Tbilisi thinking an agreement had been reached, but the parties had not yet finalized how the eight opposition seats would be allocated.

This is where the government legitimately outsmarted the opposition. Once Baker was safely out of the country, the CUG, Revival, and Industrialist representatives in parliament voted that the parties that had passed the 7 percent threshold in the 1999 parliamentary election—Revival, CUG, and Industrialists—would get two seats each, while the four parties that had passed the threshold in the 2002 local elections in Tbilisi—NM, UD, Labor, and New Rights—would get one seat each. All other parties would receive no seats. This meant that the twelve-member CEC would have four solidly pro-government votes—those of the two presidential and two CUG appointees. It would also have four likely government votes from the Industrialists and Revival and four solid opposition votes from NM, UD, Labor, and New Rights. In practice this meant that the government had a working 8-4 majority and could do more or less what it wanted on the CEC. The government's strength was increased when the OSCE included Nana Devdariani, a supporter of the president, as one of the three nominees for chair of the CEC. This list was presented to the president, so that he could choose one of the candidate's to be the CEC chair. Devdariani's inclusion was another mixed signal from the international community regarding its real commitment to pressuring the government to conduct the elections freely and fairly. Not surprisingly, Shevardnadze chose Devdariani.

The Political Context

The political environment through early and mid-2003 was also in flux. As we have seen, Georgian political parties were not divided along clear ideological or demographic lines, but by their relationship with, and position towards, Shevardnadze. This was further complicated because most of the opposition parties were led by politicians who were protégés of Shevardnadze, and exacerbated even more by personal ambitions and tensions between opposition party leaders, most notably Gamkrelidze, Natalashvili, Saakashvili, and Zhvania.

Natalashvili, about fifteen years older than the other three, refused to view them as opposition leaders at all. Rather, he somewhat dismissively characterized them as the "new CUG."[4] To fully understand the Rose Revolution, it is absolutely essential to note the almost completely forgotten reality that, at the time, this characterization resonated with many voters as well. For most of 2002 and 2003, Natalashvili and his Labor Party were either the first or second most popular party in Georgia. Labor's claim to have never been part of the CUG and or to have supported Shevardnadze was a very appealing claim for most voters. It also was, for the most part, the truth. Natalashvili's assertions that the other leaders' breaks with Shevardnadze were essentially too little, too late also rang true with voters, particularly with regard to Gamkrelidze and Zhvania. Many saw the former as more or less another corrupt businessman who had benefited under the Shevardnadze regime and the latter as Shevardnadze's top political operative who had been responsible for fraudulent elections in 1999 and 2000.

Natalashvili was an important political leader in Georgia in the years leading up to the Rose Revolution. A series of tactical blunders beginning in November 2003 made him a substantially less important figure today, but his role before then is often overlooked. Even in 2001–2003, when he was either the first or second most popular politician in Georgia, he was usually underestimated or ignored by many Western observers, particularly outside Tbilisi.

Natalashvili's Labor Party was the closest thing Georgia had to a party calling for a return to communism. Although more social democratic rather than communist in orientation, the Labor Party called for free health care, education, and more jobs for ordinary people, which for many harkened back to the late Soviet days. Due to this stance, Natalashvili was often ridiculed by Georgian and foreign elites as a "populist." Few knew the meaning of this epithet with which they dismissed Natalashvili, or were aware of the appeal of a populist message in a poor country with a small, visible, corrupt wealthy class.

In addition to being a "populist" in a country where every other party referred to itself as "center-right," largely to win approval from the West, Natalashvili faced other obstacles when it came to the international community. He did not speak English, so he could never match the relationships and influence in the West enjoyed by Zhvania and Saakashvili. Few Georgians who spoke English or traveled frequently in the West were supporters of Labor or Natalashvili, so his strength was always downplayed by these people. Nonetheless, Labor did well in the 2002 local elections, probably broke the threshold in the 1999 elections for parliament, and by mid-2003 was poised to come in first or second in the parliamentary elections of that year.

There was another side of Natalashvili as well. He was transparently dishonest. He peppered his conversations with falsehoods that were often patently ridiculous but occasionally quite serious. Rumors of corruption surrounded his party and its top leaders. He also brought in a number of former Communist Party leaders, some of them broadly disliked by most Georgians. In a country where parties were often dominated by their leaders, Labor was extreme even by Georgian standards.

There was little to the party other than its leader, who made all the decisions and public appearances, and thousands of his supporters.

Gamkrelidze, Zhvania, and Saakashvili in turn did not show any good will toward Natalashvili. Their voices joined those ridiculing him as a "populist" and suggesting that he had ties to Shevardnadze through corrupt business interests. Indeed, only Saakashvili actually competed with Natalashvili for the votes of the mostly poor and rural Georgians who supported the populist message of the Labor Party.

Natalashvili's disdain for and suspicion of what he referred to as the "new CUG," as well as his preference for a more left leaning economic policy made it clear that he represented a distinct segment of the Georgian electorate, but the distinctions among the remaining three major opposition parties were much more vague. Nonetheless, throughout the preelection period competition between the NM, UD, and New Rights was intense. Thus, the three parties failed to unify and form what would have been a very powerful block, capable of working together to win votes and combat election fraud.

The differences between these three parties were so intense largely because they were so personal, particularly between Saakashvili and Zhvania.[5] The two were roughly the same age, equally well connected and respected in the United States and Europe, and equally ambitious. Both saw themselves as the best hope for Georgia's future. Moreover, much of their support came from the same segment of Georgian society, educated young democrats who wanted to make Georgia into a European style democracy. The key difference was that Zhvania's support was largely limited to this demographic, while Saakashvili was able to build well beyond this to appeal to the Georgian electorate more broadly. In addition to occasionally differing on political questions, Zhvania and Saakashvili bickered, usually playfully, about things like who spoke better English or who knew more members of the U.S. Congress.

Saakashvili and particularly Zhvania surrounded themselves and built their parties with smart and competent people. Below the most senior leadership, there was often cooperation between the NM and the UD, and at times the New Rights as well, but as the elections approached it was clear that the rivalries between the leaders were too strong; the opposition vote was going to be split between these three parties as well as Labor; and, more damagingly, the parties would be competing with each other for votes and likely end up in a position to make deals with the CUG and those who were planning to steal the election.

While the opposition leaders were squabbling with each other and seeking to undermine each other's reform credentials, the CUG was trying to reinvent itself and build a coalition for the election. In the spring, the CUG leadership formed a coalition called For a New Georgia (FNG) that would allow it to contest the election without having to use the CUG name, which had little appeal among voters. FNG was not a real coalition: it was the CUG and a number of very small parties whose leaders were given spots on the FNG list. The list of small parties grew to include the Socialists, Greens, Christian Democrats, and National Democratic Party, which sounded impressive, but these parties only had a few thousand supporters among them. Nonetheless, it was hard not to get the impression that the government was considerably better organized than the opposition.

Of the three parties that had broken away from the CUG, the NM was the strongest. Saakahvili, unlike Gamkrelidze or Zhvania, had an ability to appeal to voters who were poor and rural. These people constituted a majority of the electorate, and often favored the NM or Labor because of Labor's populist message and Saakashvili's populist style. The New Rights through their network of local elected officials, deep pockets, and complex relationship with Shevardnandze seemed likely to do well enough in the elections to secure seats in the new parliament. The same could not be said of the UD, which was hobbled by Zhvania's lack of popularity outside his base and an image as a party of the Tbilisi elite.

The picture became more complicated with the rise of Nino Burjanadze as a political force by late spring of 2003. This was one of the major unexpected developments of 2003. Burjanadze had been elected in a close vote to replace Zurab Zhvania as speaker of parliament after Zhvania resigned the position in 2002. Burjanadze was thought of as something of a political lightweight who would not be able to measure up to Zhvania's energy, creativity, vision, and political skill as leader of the legislature. This assessment proved not to be completely inaccurate, but overlooked Burjanadze's broader appeal among ordinary voters.

Burjanadze, like Gamkrelidze and Zhvania, had been elected to parliament on the CUG list and, like all three of the young opposition leaders, had been brought into politics by Shevardnadze. However, her break from Shevardnadze came much later. As late as spring 2003 it was not clear whether she would align herself with the opposition or position herself as leader of the new reform wing of Shevardnadze's CUG. Her recognition of the fruitlessness of the latter direction, as well as what seemed like a genuine desire to help bring democracy to Georgia, pushed her toward becoming part of the opposition.

Burjanadze's even temperament, warm personal style, and democratic instincts not only increased her popularity among voters in her own country, but won supporters overseas as well. On a spring trip to the United States, she impressed Washington as a strong, competent leader with a bright future. This trip helped strengthen her position as a new more moderate democratic hope for Georgia and a contrast to Natalashvili and Saakashvili, who were both viewed as too hot-headed and confrontational for U.S. tastes.

While it was becoming increasingly clear that Burjanadze would align herself with the opposition, it was not clear what form this decision would take. She explored the idea of starting her own party and conducted negotiations regarding creating a coalition with one or more of the opposition parties. Labor was the only major opposition party with whom she did not conduct these negotiations. Natalashvili had no interest in working with her, and Burjanadze viewed Natalashvili as a populist and something of a demagogue.

The UD, NM, and New Rights pursued Burjanadze as if she were a star ballplayer choosing with which team she was going to sign. She delayed her decision until August, before deciding to join Zhvania's United Democrats. The United Democrats and Zurab Zhvania were a good fit for Burjanadze. Their rhetoric and tone, like hers, was democratic and moderate.

Zhvania seemed to understand the need to accommodate Burjanadze and use her to the political advantage of his party. He gave her the number one position on the party's list, put her face on campaign posters and advertisements, and even registered the party as the Burjanadze Democrats (BD) for the election. Burjanadze was also the public face of the campaign, campaigning throughout Georgia, holding rallies, and attending meetings with groups of voters. Zhvania reduced his public appearances dramatically once Burjanadze joined his party. However, as she was to learn the hard way, the party remained very much Zhvania's in spite of its new name and top candidate.

Shortly after this coalition was formed, another minor opposition party, the Traditionalists, led by another former parliamentary speaker, Akaki Asatiani, also joined. This helped make the BD look like a real coalition. Furthermore, the presence of one sitting and two former leaders of parliament made it seem like the party most prepared to lead parliament. It is hard to overstate how much Burjanadze helped the BD. Before she joined the party, it was not at all certain the UD would pass the 7 percent threshold to make it into parliament. The polls following the creation of the BD showed the party soaring to a virtual tie for first place with Labor and the NM. With one impressive political deal, Zurab Zhvania had transformed his party from teetering on the edge of the threshold to frontrunner.[6]

The fact that political analysis like this could be made in summer 2003 speaks to the complexity of Shevardnadze's semidemocratic regime. Throughout that summer, the Georgian media published public opinion polls that appeared accurate and scientific; at the same time, candidates were able to campaign and speak to voters in most parts of the country. Nonetheless, political analysis always was done in the context of the assumption, which everybody knew was false, that the elections were going to be fair. Thus, analysis of the horserace was paired with questions about how far the government would go to steal the election and what deals might be made with which parties to reduce tension and arrive at a parliament with which the government and the people could both live.

The Campaign

The merger between the UD and Nino Burjanadze was the final major political event before the campaign began in earnest in early September. By fall 2003 seven parties had a legitimate chance at breaking the 7 percent threshold and getting into parliament. Although the FNG was extremely unpopular, it was recognized that the governing party was going to do whatever was necessary to get into parliament. The question was whether it would be content to steal its way to 10 to 15 percent or try to get more. Revival, because of its ability to get as many votes as it wanted in Ajara, was also viewed as certain to pass the threshold. Five remaining parties—Industry, Labor, BD, NM, and New Rights—also had a chance. Several smaller parties were preparing to contest the election but enjoyed virtually no support from the electorate.

Political parties were not the only major participants in the campaign, however. Civic organizations continued to play an essential role in politics during this period. ISFED conscientiously monitored the preparations for the elections. Through press conferences, public statements, public events, and briefing the international and diplomatic community, it drew a great deal of attention to various kinds of election fraud that occurred in the preelection period. These included ongoing problems with voter lists, FNG abuse of government resources and facilities, attempts to bribe and coerce election commission members and voters at the local level, and other hijinks. Organizations such as the GYLA and the George Soros-funded Liberty Institute also drew attention to the shortcomings and undemocratic behavior of the government during these critical months. Again, the freedom enjoyed in Shevardnadze's Georgia and the regime's tolerance of civic activism contributed to the strengths of these organizations.

Summer and fall 2003 saw the emergence of a new kind of civic organization in Georgia. Kmara, Georgian for "enough," was a hybrid: social movement and virtual NGO. Consciously modeled on the Serb NGO Otpor (the Serbian word for "resistance"), which had played a crucial role in the defeat of Yugoslav president Slobodan Milosevic in 2000, Kmara was a movement of young people, mostly students, who were fed up with the corruption, dishonesty, and failures of the Shevardnadze regime. Kmara was nonpartisan but understood to be supportive of Saakashvili and his NM. Its members were trained and advised by the Liberty Institute and funded by OSI. By mid-2003 both these prominent Georgian NGOs were also viewed as more or less aligned with Saakashvili. However, Kmara's behavior and tactics were genuinely nonpartisan. Rather than promote any one politician or political party, they focused on criticizing the regime and creating a sense that there was a large anti-Shevardnadze movement brewing.

Faced with the challenge of creating a large-scale social movement, strong enough to be of concern to the government and to convince voters that change was inevitable and they should support the opposition, Kmara's solution was a tactic that was a devastatingly brilliant and simple piece of political theater. Members spray-painted the word "Kmara" on walls, buildings, streets, bridges, and everywhere else they could in virtually every corner of Georgia. This effort was supplemented by a handful of more mass-based events such as demonstrations and an aggressive media campaign that successfully drew attention to Kmara and its efforts.

The spray-painting campaign was brilliant for several reasons. First, it enabled Kmara's relatively small number of members to make a visible impression on the Georgian people. Second, it successfully branded the opposition as well as the government. The word *kmara* was increasingly recognized, signaling anger at the current government and demand for change. Third, because spray-painting one word in a public place is a simple and inexpensive means of political participation, anybody could do it and thus feel part of Kmara. Traveling around Georgia in the late summer and fall, one saw *kmara* painted in a number of remote places. It is unlikely that the leaders of Kmara knew each of the people painting the word on walls or buildings.

Kmara, perhaps not entirely consciously, contributed to a new prototype for a twenty-first-century social movement. Drawing on some outside funding in the form of OSI grants, good media skills (including using the Internet to communicate with supporters inside and outside Georgia), and a decentralized branding campaign, Kmara was able to raise its profile and communicate its message throughout Georgia. In American campaign terms it raised the government's negatives, or softened them up, so that the opposition parties could concentrate on campaigning and communicating their own messages to voters.

From early September to early November, the campaign was in full swing. The FNG, aware of its high negatives and lack of popular leaders now that the party had split, ran a two-tiered campaign. First, its media campaign included posters with drawings that looked as if they had been made by children, along with pictures of children, relatively bland future-oriented slogans, and absence of pictures of Shevardnadze or other government or party leaders. The second and more important tier remained the efforts to lay the groundwork for a fraudulent election through increased pressure on local government and elected officials, efforts to bribe or intimidate voters, and the like, euphemistically known as "using administrative resources."

Revival's campaign, which was entirely within Ajara, also put effort into ensuring that the election fraud would come off as planned, buttressed by a positive campaign oriented around the cult of Aslan Abashidze's personality. Revival and the Ajaran authorities continued to stop other parties from any kind of campaigning in Ajara, often resorting to force to break up rallies.

The real campaigning took place primarily among the opposition parties. To a large extent this campaign was about dividing up, and fighting over, the substantial proportion of the voters who did not want to vote for FNG and lived outside Ajara. Voters in Ajara, of course, were simply going to be counted, in some cases more than once, as Revival Party voters. The campaign was occurring in a gray area because of the likelihood of widespread election fraud, but since nobody knew how much fraud there would be or how accurately the votes would be counted, the opposition parties had to pursue a two-tiered strategy of their own, winning the elections and ensuring their fairness.

All four opposition parties campaigned aggressively. Posters covered the streets of Tbilisi and most other major cities. Parties purchased a great deal of television time to advertise their party. The media, particularly the television station Rustavi Two and the newspaper *24 Hours*, covered the election extensively and reasonably well. However, the four parties did not campaign equally well. After an early start, the New Rights campaign stalled a bit under the guidance of American consultant Michael Murphy. Murphy, an experienced and respected Republican Party consultant, had been hired because of his Republican Party ties and reputation. The New Rights saw themselves as a right-wing party ideologically similar to the U.S. Republican Party, so they reached out to Murphy. The New Rights hoped Murphy would provide not only campaign guidance but also access to senior figures in the American government. However, Murphy produced material that did not strike the right chords with the Georgian electorate and never called in any important favors in Washington for his Georgian client. His work was high quality, but it had the feel of generic American political campaigns with feel good spots introducing Gamkrelidze and the party. The New Rights Party finally began to regain some of its lost momentum when it replaced Murphy with a Georgian media advisor in the last two weeks of the campaign.

Labor's campaign seemed considerably less sophisticated, with fewer financial resources than the other opposition parties. Nonetheless, Labor's older, poorer and more rural electorate responded to the low budget posters, often printed on newsprint, with a picture of Natalashvili striding confidently into the future. Throughout the summer and early fall, Labor generally led or was a close second in the polls.

The BD and NM campaigns were the most intriguing during September and October. After making substantial gains in the polls and becoming one of the front-runners when Burjanadze first decided to join Zhvania's party, the BD, somewhat bafflingly, failed to expand or even keep that support. Burjanadze, who remained popular, campaigned throughout the country. As the only woman in the race, and a relatively new face in national politics, she was well positioned to be the image of change, something the Georgian people desperately wanted. But the BD campaign was surprisingly lackluster, with a message and campaign materials that did not stand out as different in the crowded media context during the election.

The NM campaign got off to a late start, and was the last major party to put up posters and go on the air with television commercials. However, once it got started, it ran a brilliant campaign. For months preceding the election, Saakashvili and other NM leaders traveled to every corner of the country to make campaign appearances and speak to voters. Saakashvili met with pensioners in cities like Tbilisi and Kutaisi, impoverished grape farmers in Kakheti, old women in remote mountain villages, unemployed youths throughout Georgia, and virtually every other group in the country. He brought a great deal of energy to this project, delivering his message of the need for change and hope to the entire country.

This required tremendous effort and time, as many villages in Georgia are difficult to reach due to the poor conditions of the roads. On one occasion, Saakashvili was forcibly prevented from campaigning in the Azeri region of Kvemo Kartli by the region's pro-Shevardnadze governor Levan Mamaladze. Mamaladze's troops actually fired at Saakashvili after he insisted on his right to campaign wherever he wanted to. This was particularly noteworthy because the NM was the only party that sought to campaign in Kvemo Kartli, rather than write the entire region off to massive government-backed election fraud. His attempt to campaign there was publicized throughout Georgia and further increased support for his party.

The energetic campaigning by Saakashvili and other NM leaders was buttressed by an outstanding media campaign. Campaign posters of Saakashvili looking strong and confident, wearing an open-collared shirt and a leather jacket, appeared throughout the country, projecting an image of fearless and honest leadership. The commercials were excellent as well, no different in quality from what one would expect in a competitive race for U.S. senator or governor. The strong NM finish paid immediate dividends; by mid-October, polls showed voters moving from the BD and other parties to the NM in substantial numbers.[7]

As the election approached, fears that all these campaign efforts would not accomplish anything grew as it was becoming increasingly clear that fraud would be widespread on Election Day and during the counting period. The government's two-thirds CEC majority was deciding every case in favor of the government. The voter list as finally released was far from comprehensive. Rumors of increased intimidation and bribery were spreading as well. Because of this environment, the political leadership of the opposition, particularly from the NM and UD parties, became increasingly aware of the need for a postelection strategy to protect their hard-won votes and ensure that the votes would be counted fairly.

The postelection strategy on which the two parties decided was remarkable both on its own merit and because the parties were able to agree on it even while actively competing with each other for votes. The first component of this strategy was to conduct an exit poll that, in the likely case of widespread fraud, would demonstrate to the Georgian people that the election had been stolen. Georgian polling firms were viewed as partisan and not trustworthy, so a prominent American firm, the New York-based Global Strategy Group (GSG), was brought in to design, supervise, and analyze the results. Importantly, GSG was not recruited or hired by any U.S. government representative, but through OSI, which also paid the GSG fee. OSI had been working closely with the NM and BD on the postelection strategy and had been deeply involved in trying to make the elections fair. The hope was that the exit poll would complement the PVT and make it clear to everyone that the results were fraudulent, or in an even better scenario, the exit poll and PVT would lead to enough pressure on the government that the CEC would have to count the votes fairly.

The second component of the postelection strategy was mobilization of people. As soon as the results of the exit poll, which would be available before the PVT, or official results, were announced, people would gather at their rayon election office to demand fair vote counting. Mobilizing hundreds of people in most of Georgia's 75 rayons was a substantial organizational challenge. Ultimately, this part of the strategy was not executed precisely as planned.

The Election

After months of campaigning and even more months of political positioning and deal making, November 2, Election Day, finally arrived.
Unfortunately, Election Day was more or less what everybody expected.
Voter lists proved flawed as thousands of voters, primarily supporters of
the opposition, were not on lists. Polls opened late in Tbilisi and parts
of Kutaisi, Georgia's second largest city and one of the places the BD
expected to do very well. Violence, multiple voting, and voter intimidation were widespread, particularly in Kvemo Kartli, where the FNG
needed to get a lot of votes. In this region gun toting thugs stormed into
polling places, threatening voters and disrupting the voting process. In
some cases ballot boxes were stolen or upended, making an accurate
vote count nearly impossible. In short, in most of Georgia, the election
was looking like a standard order post-Soviet stolen election.

During the day, however, the quality of the election varied substantially across Georgia. In Ajara and most of Kvemo Kartli, intimidation,
violence, and multiple voting were widespread, in the former region for
the benefit of the Revival party, in the latter for FNG. In other areas like
Kutaisi, where polls eventually opened several hours late and were kept
open late to make up for the lost time, the elections were merely bad in
a relatively typical post-Soviet way, characterized by a lower level of fraud
and intimidation then in Ajara or Kvemo Kartli. There was a a fair
amount of incompetence on the part of election officials, but some sem-
blance of voter preferences was reflected through the voting process. A
third category, which included most of Tbilisi and a few isolated areas
around Georgia, ended up with elections that were acceptable by post-
Soviet standards. Again, incompetence, bad voter lists, and low level
harassment prevented them from being good, but in these places the
voting reflected voter preferences reasonably well.

In Ajara, however, the election was much worse. Georgians and foreigners had anticipated that elections would be worse in Ajara than in
the rest of the country. Abashidze was known for running up Saddam
Hussein-like majorities and inflating the vote total so his party would
have a greater share of the overall national party list vote. Ajara was a
notoriously difficult place not only for opposition parties to campaign,
but for domestic election monitors to observe elections. For this reason,
ISFED had sought and received extra funding to bring in election monitors from Russia and Ukraine to count the voters and observe the count
in the PVT polling places.[8] ISFED reasoned, accurately, that Abashidze
would have some scruples about intimidating foreign election monitors,
particularly from Russia and Ukraine, two countries with which Ajara
maintained friendly relations.

The election in Ajara was even worse than most people expected. Widespread multiple voting; security forces, government officials, and others in the polling place to intimidate voters; extremely fraudulent counting; and huge pro-Revivial and pro-Abashidze media and visibility surprised nobody. But this was not the extent of Abashidze and Revival's efforts to steal the election in Ajara. Two specific incidents went above and beyond this. First, a Georgian election observer, Georgi Mshvenieradze from GYLA, was arrested inside a polling place. The charges were assaulting a representative of the government. I went to the voting place minutes after this happened and visited Mshvenieradze at the police station later that day. From what I was able to determine from other witnesses and my discussion with Mshvenieradze, he was arrested and charged with beating members of the Ajaran security forces. The charges were a clear and outrageous lie; in reality, Mshvenieradze was the one who had been roughed up, but Mshvenieradze, a frightened, and courageous youth of twenty-one, spent weeks in jail before being released through the intervention of the U.S. embassy, which negotiated directly with Abashidze. This arrest, early in the day, sent a very clear message to the other Georgian election monitors, who either left Ajara immediately or spent the rest of the day in fear.

The second incident was a somewhat bizarre and reasonably creative attempt to strike fear into voters, observers, and others in Batumi, Ajara's capital and largest city. At around noon, one of Abashidze's former bodyguards, who allegedly had connections to organized crime, was gunned down while sitting at the wheel of his late model Mercedes waiting for a light to change.[9] Everybody in Batumi understood that Abashidze was behind it. The shooting occurred directly in front of Batumi's largest polling place, which further intimidated and frightened voters.

When most of the polls closed at 8 p.m., it was not at all clear who had won the elections or what the government parties in Tbilisi or Batumi would do. Counting and announcing numbers was a critical stage in the election, but it did not begin right away. Instead, the first information released was the exit poll. Rustavi Two, Georgia's most popular television station, began broadcasting the results of the exit poll about three hours after the polls closed. Erosi Kitsmarishvili, owner of Rustavi Two, had helped fund the exit polls and understood their value both politically and as a news story.

The exit polls made an immediate impact because they were the first news of the election results made available. They showed the National Movement winning with 26 percent of the vote, followed by FNG at 19 percent, Labor at 18 percent, BD at 10 percent, Revival at 9 percent, and New Rights at 7 percent. These numbers were revealing. First, it was a resounding victory for the opposition. The three most outspoken opposition parties—Labor, NM, and BD—combined for more than 50 percent of the vote. Second, the numbers showed a clear defeat for FNG. More than 80 percent of the Georgian electorate, according to the exit poll, opted, in the face of threats, coercion, and bribery, to vote against the party that had been ruling Georgia for a decade. Rarely has a governing party been handed such an unambiguous verdict from an electorate.

The exit poll results also showed that among the opposition parties, NM and Labor, who were first and second, were the winners. The BD had done much more poorly than expected. Because the opposition viewed this election as, to a great extent, a contest among themselves to show which party was poised to elect its leader as president in 2005 (when Shevardnadze was planning to retire), the exit poll caused great problems for the BD.

The early release of the exit poll results was a major tactical step forward for the cause of fair elections. An apparently nonpartisan coalition of media and NGOs, supported by an American polling firm with a strong reputation, had reported numbers that were widely accepted. As soon as these numbers became public, it became considerably more difficult for the government to commit fraud in the counting phase of the election. Unfortunately, as will be discussed later, this did not stop it from trying.

The day after the election, the government's task of committing more fraud was made even more difficult because the PVT numbers were announced. While many in the West are less familiar with PVTs than with exit polls, among Georgians it was probably viewed as more important than the exit poll. ISFED, the group that carried out the PVT, had a strong reputation, a director who was increasingly well known and respected, and had spent months explaining the PVT to the media, political parties, government, and international community. Having a PVT and an exit poll, however, was a risky strategy because if the two tools revealed different outcomes it would bring into question the validity of both.

At noon on November 3, the day after the election, Zurab Tchiabarashvili, ISFED executive director, stood in front of a press conference overflowing with media, diplomats, Georgian politicians, civic activists, and election observers and dramatically projected the PVT results onto a screen in the ballroom of the Tbilisi Marriott. The PVT had the NM winning with 27 percent, followed by FNG at 19 percent, Labor at 17 percent, BD at 10 percent, Revival and NR at 8 percent, and Industrialists at 5 percent. While not identical to the exit poll numbers, they were close enough to reinforce the three major findings from the exit polls.

TABLE 2. November 2, 2003 Election, Reported Results (%)

	Official results	PVT	Exit poll
FNG	21	19	19
Revival	19	8	9
NM	18	27	26
Labor	12	17	18
BD	8	10	10
NR	7	8	7
Industry	6	7	5

Going to the Streets

At this moment, when the PVT and the exit polls showed that the government had been soundly defeated, the opposition was deeply divided, in a way that was easily exploitable by the government. The NM believed it had won a decisive victory and that party leader Mikheil Saakashvili was well positioned to become Georgia's next president in spring 2005.[10] The BD was smarting from the PVT and exit polls, which both indicated that it was a distant third among opposition parties and fourth or fifth overall. Labor and New Rights seemed to be comfortable with the numbers, which showed Labor a clear second and New Rights slightly above the threshold needed to get into parliament.

The CEC began to release its numbers late in the day on Monday, November 3. It was immediately clear that the CEC was not daunted by PVT or exit poll evidence. The first numbers released showed FNG finishing first, followed by the NM and Labor close together in second and third place, followed by the Industrialists and NR at about 9 percent and BD hovering around the 7 percent threshold. Significantly, Revival was doing very poorly, with the CEC claiming that ballots from Ajara had not yet been received. The late arriving Ajaran ballots were to play an important role in the coming weeks.

Table 2 shows the final official results, PVT data, and exit poll findings. These official results were not released until almost two weeks after the election, when Ajaran authorities finally sent their results to Tbilisi.

Labor and the New Rights seemed willing to accept the fraudulent CEC data as long as their positions in the polls did not change too much. The Industrialists were by this time making little effort even to present themselves as an opposition party. This left the BD and NM the only parties in a position to express opposition to the increasingly fraudulent vote counting. By Monday evening they were discussing plans to mobilize people to demonstrate against the ongoing election fraud. Both understood that now was their last chance to show unity and work together. However, the two parties had different complaints with regard to the counting, and this difference could have been exploited by the CEC and the ruling party.

The NM wanted to be recognized as the winner of the election, not just the opposition party with the most votes, but party with the most votes overall. With this recognition would come the largest delegation of MPs and a chance to be a powerful force in parliament. The NM position was simple. The exit poll and the PVT both showed it had won the election, a victory for which it had worked very hard and for which Saakashvili and others had campaigned tirelessly. The NM wanted the CEC to recognize this.

The BD position was significantly more complicated. On one hand was concern about ending up below 7 percent when all the votes were tallied. This was a distinct possibility because with the PVT and exit polls both showing BD hovering only slightly above the threshold, the CEC could place it below the threshold relatively easily. But winning seats in parliament would not solve the BD's larger problem: it would still be the smallest party in parliament. Perhaps more significantly, based on the preliminary CEC returns, the parliamentary delegations of both Labor and the NM were likely to be two to three times larger. The BD position within the opposition would not be strong, and Burjanadze's presidential ambitions for 2005 would be weakened. A few days after these results were released, the BD announced it would not enter the parliament at all because it did not want to recognize the fraudulent elections. This struck some as a display of principle, but others as an attempt by Zhvania to undermine a parliament where Saakashvili and Natalashvili would be the dominant opposition figures. In any case, this proposal was abandoned after a few days.

Perhaps not surprisingly, the government was in a good position to exploit the positions of the two parties and diffuse the demonstrations before they began. It could have agreed to add a few points to the BD total and take a few away from the NM. This would have satisfied the BD, which in exchange would have agreed not to take part in the demonstrations. The NM could not demonstrate alone because Zhvania and Burjanadze were viewed as the more "rational" members of the opposition. Had the BD leaders stopped criticizing the election, Saakashvili would have been isolated and viewed as an extremist.

The government also could have made a deal with the NM, agreeing to give it first place and keep the BD out of parliament. This would have reduced total parliamentary opposition, but Saakashvili would still have been viewed as the leader of the opposition. Had this deal occurred, he would have stopped his party from participating in the demonstrations. Without NM support, the BD would not have had enough support from the people for credible street demonstrations.

Not a moment too soon, the parties decided to work together and refused to agree to either deal.[11] Another option, supported by the BD, was to call for new elections. This, however, was relatively quickly seen as a partisan rather than fair election-oriented solution.

The demonstrations began the Wednesday after the election. Very quickly the central demand of the demonstrators became the resignation of Shevardnadze. Although this demand was at first viewed by the organizers as unrealistic, it was broadly understood to be the best message for mobilizing people. Georgians wanted fair elections, but ridding themselves of the president to whom they attributed the rampant corruption, poverty, and unemployment in their country was a much more powerful motivator.

The demonstrations were organized by two parties: the NM and BD. A few minor parties, such as the Traditionalists and the People's Party, immediately joined. Other opposition parties such as the New Rights and Labor made what turned out to be a fatal mistake by opposing the demonstrations. By refusing to support calls for Shevardnadze's resignation, these two parties lost their credibility as opposition forces. Although the leadership of the demonstrations came from two major parties, by late November the demonstrators were supporters of many other parties as well, most notably Labor, whose members were demonstrating on the streets of Tbilisi while their leaders made statements against the demonstrations.

Burjanadze, Zhvania, and Saakashvili quickly emerged as the principal leadership of the demonstrations. Saakashvili soon became the primary leader; he was the most popular and most able to motivate the crowds with his energetic and fiery speeches. Nonetheless, Zhvania's political sophistication, constant negotiating with the government, and planning ability were instrumental to the success of these demonstrations.

The demonstrations began on November 5 and continued until Shevardnadze resigned on November 23. These two weeks have become the founding myth of the Rose Revolution. Like all such myths, it includes a fair amount of exaggeration and hyperbole.

The popular understanding of the Rose Revolution is that it looked something like Ukraine's Orange Revolution, with hundreds of thousands of people coming to the streets in support of a unified opposition. This is, to a great extent, the narrative the Georgian government has encouraged. Saakashvili, for example, wrote in a 2004 opinion piece in the *International Herald Tribune* that "hundreds of thousands of Georgian citizens . . . took to the streets," and referred to "three weeks of massive demonstrations."[12]

The Tbilisi demonstrations in November 2003 were in fact significantly smaller than this. They are perhaps better understood as a vigil.

For the first ten days or so, the size of the demonstrations varied from a few hundred to about fifteen thousand, but there was almost always some protest activity in front of the parliament, as the vote counting continued in the nearby CEC headquarters.

During the first few days, the demonstrators were primarily young people and supporters of either BD or NM, and mostly residents of Tbilisi. But information spread quickly and easily, and toward the end citizens throughout Georgia became actively involved.

While the demonstrations in front of parliament were a variation of the postelection plans made by the UD and BD in October, the opposition did not have a clear idea of what would happen after they brought people to the streets. Many feared the demonstrations would dissipate after a few days as momentum would be hard to maintain.[13] Few believed Shevardnadze would actually resign. The international community, particularly U.S. ambassador Richard Miles, European Commission ambassador Torben Holtze, and other European diplomats, began to negotiate with both sides, urging them to accept the results of the PVT. This would have satisfied the NM, but not the BD. However, the government decision to refuse the PVT results and continue to count the ballots in its own creative way, made it clear that the conflict would not be negotiated away.[14]

The rivalry between the BD and the NM was also a central dynamic for at least the first ten days or so of the demonstrations. Publicly, the NM, BD, and more important, their leaders, seemed unified. They worked hard to demonstrate this by never attacking each other in public, coordinating and planning together, and frequently being photographed and filmed together. Behind the scenes, however, the rivalry continued. Zhvania's calls for new elections, a partisan solution to the problem, were met by Saakashvili's reminders that he had beaten the BD by a margin of almost 3–1. Saakashvili and Zhvania, through his surrogate Burjanadze, vied for leadership of the opposition and the demonstrations. Conversations I had with leaders of the two parties at this time revealed that under the surface the disunity was still quite intense. I was frequently told by people from the BD that the NM did not have solid enough opposition credentials because it did not want new elections, while the NM told me that the BD had no support from the people.

A central turning point occurred on Friday, November 14, when the largest demonstration to date took place. Roughly 25,000 people came to the parliament that afternoon and evening to hear speeches and demand a fair vote count, and most important, Shevarnadze's resignation. That evening was also the day Saakashvili's primary leadership in the uprising became clear. He led the crowd brilliantly, asking them to march from the parliament to the CEC building and back to the chancellery, a total of about one mile through the heart of Tbilisi. The crowd responded to his leadership and his insistence that demonstrators conduct themselves peacefully.

The size of the demonstration that day was precipitated by the Ajaran election commission's decision to release vote returns from Ajara. They had waited until the counting was largely complete before turning in the vote count from. As expected, the Ajara results were completely fraudulent. But the degree of fraudulence surprised many. The Ajaran authorities turned in so many votes from Ajara that Revival leaped to first place in the count. Revival had managed to steal more votes in relatively tiny Ajara than FNG was able to steal in all of Georgia.

The only thing that democrats in Georgia opposed more than a fraudulent FNG victory was a fraudulent Revival victory. A Shevardnadze regime propped up by support from Ajara promised to be much less tolerant and democratic than the regime had been for its first decade. It was clear to the opposition leaders that the FNG and Shevardnadze had turned to Revival for electoral and political assistance. FNG and Revival cooperation created a new sense of urgency for the opposition because it seemed that a government dominated by these two parties would move away from holding elections to succeed Shevardnadze in 2005.

Shevardnadze's Resignation

The last week of Shevardnadze's presidency, and of a political career that had spanned five decades, began quietly for the man once recognized in the West as one of the major architects of the peaceful resolution of the Cold War. The large demonstration from Friday the 14th had ended peacefully as the demonstrators went home awaiting further instruction from the now clear leader of the opposition, Mikheil Saakashvili. The vigil of a few thousand people in front of parliament remained, but it was not at all clear what would happen next.

The CEC was due to announce the final results of the election sometime early in the week; and the new parliament was scheduled to be seated on Saturday November 22. Meanwhile, opposition activity had begun to spread beyond the capital as sporadic protests and civil disobedience were increasing in the regions of Georgia, particularly Western Georgia. A trip by Shevardnadze to the eastern region of Kakheti, once a base of support, was cut dramatically short as protesters surrounded the airport making it impossible for his plane to land. Instead, Shevardnadze returned to Tbilisi.

Having nowhere else to turn, Shevardnadze flew to Ajara, where Aslan Abashidze received and vowed to support him. A day or two later, Abashidze's help arrived in the form of busloads of demonstrators brought to Tbilisi from Ajara to demonstrate in support of Shevardnadze and demand the seating of the parliament as announced by the CEC. As the Ajaran demonstrators began to occupy the space in front of parliament, it became clear that calling for help from Ajara had been a mistake by Shevardnadze.

The Ajarans were viewed by the residents of Tbilisi, more or less accurately, as outsiders and thugs, sent by a dictator to force acceptance of a stolen election. Their presence in the capital not only reinvigorated the opposition and energized the support of thousands of ordinary Georgians but raised the stakes for them as well. Saakashvili, Zhvania, and Burjanadze understood that if Shevardnadze was turning to Abashidze at a time like this, then the next government would be heavily influenced by Abashidze and his Revival Party. The official CEC data had the Revival Party dropping into second place behind the FNG, but it would still have an enormous amount of formal power in the parliament as well as whatever informal power came out of a Shevardnadze-Abashidze alliance at this key moment. In other words, Abashidze's influence on Shevardnadze would bring any chances of continuing reform, and presidential elections in 2005, to a halt.

Time, however, was running out for the opposition. When the new parliament was seated it would elect a pro-government leader, most likely former state minister Vazha Lortkipanidze,[15] bringing the opposition's momentum to a halt. When the Ajarans came to Tbilisi, Saakashvili went to western Georgia to bring more opposition supporters for a possible showdown with the Revival Party. The government sought to block the major roads into Tbilisi on Wednesday and Thursday when the buses of opposition supporters began to flood into the capital. But the thousands of supporters of Saakashvili and his agenda were not to be deterred by a few roadblocks and quickly swept the blockades aside.

Many feared that when the demonstrators arrived, the presence of the Ajarans would mean an end to the nonviolent tone that had thus far characterized the demonstrations. However, although the Ajarans remained in the capital until Saakashvili and his supporters stormed into parliament on November 22, creating a very tense situation, they finally left late that day, avoiding any confrontation with the demonstrators.

The showdown between the opposition and Shevardnadze could no longer be avoided, but it was not clear precisely how it would take shape. The culmination of weeks of demonstrations occurred on the afternoon of Saturday, November 22, when a frail and elderly looking Eduard Shevardnadze was removed from the podium and taken out of Georgia's parliamentary chamber by his own bodyguards, still clutching the text of his speech welcoming the new parliament.

When Saakashvili and his supporters burst into the parliament, disrupting Shevardnadze's speech and causing him to flee the room, it was a dramatic and somewhat oedipal moment that was broadcast around the world. The symbolism of Saakashvili assuming Shevardnadze's position at the podium and drinking what remained of Shevardnadze's tea was primal, and unmistakable.

Behind the dramatic imagery was a savvy political calculus. Until the new parliament was seated, Nino Burjanadze was still speaker and next in line for the presidency. If Shevardnadze resigned while Burjanadze was still speaker, the opposition would control the presidency and ensure a much smoother and clearer transition. However, once the new parliament was seated its first move would be to elect a new speaker, if not Lortkipanidze than someone more pro-government. Shevardnadze's resignation at that point would accomplish very little. Ironically, had Shevardnadze not insisted on making a very long-winded Communist style speech welcoming the new parliament, it would have moved to the business of electing a new speaker, causing major problems for the opposition, long before Saakashvili and his supporters entered

Immediately after fleeing from parliament, Shevardnadze sought to hold onto his power by declaring a state of emergency. Rather than causing fear among the population or reducing the number of demonstrators, this decision contributed to increasing the numbers of protestors in the streets, now in the tens, if not hundreds, of thousands, as opposition leaders called for more support to maintain the momentum. By late in the day on November 22 opposition supporters had seized the buildings of the parliament and the State Chancellery and burned Shevardnadze's chair in front of the Chancellery.

Early on the morning of November 23, while Shevardnadze was still technically president, Defense Minister Davit Tevzadze declared that he would not use force against his fellow Georgians. Tevzadze's decision was most likely based on his awareness that the political winds were shifting, along with a genuine reluctance to see innocent Georgians killed by their own military. Shevardnadze's frequent claims that he refused to use force during these days is rendered somewhat less impressive by the reality that by the morning of his last day as president, it was clear that he no longer had the ability to use force. He did not call out the security forces because, after not being paid their full salaries for months, they were no longer loyal to the president and would probably not have followed orders to shoot fellow Georgians.

Events moved very quickly after that. On the afternoon of November 23, less than 24 hours after the incident in parliament, Zhvania and Saakashvili met privately with Shevardnadze at his official residence as thousands continued to demonstrate outside. The two opposition leaders spent less than twenty minutes with the man who had not too long ago referred to them as his sons before Shevardnadze emerged from his office and announced to the waiting reporters and the crowd of protestors that he was "going home."

Chapter 4
How Democratic Was the Rose Revolution?

When Shevarnadze resigned, it was not Mikheil Saakashvili, the most prominent leader of the Rose Revolution, who assumed the leadership of Georgia. Instead, in accordance with the constitutional procedure for replacing a president after death or resignation, parliamentary speaker Nino Burjanadze, who had also played a key visible role in the demonstrations, became president of Georgia late in the day of November 23.

Immediately after Shevardnadze's resignation, Burjanadze spoke to the international media. A young, confident, strong-looking woman, Burjanadze, speaking calmly and convincingly in English, pledged her country's commitment to democracy and the West. She was unlike any post-Soviet leader the world had seen before. Her earnest and mature demeanor was perfect for demonstrating that Georgia's new leadership was serious, willing, and able to work with the United States and Europe. Shevardnadze, for all his failures as president, was still viewed by much of the outside world as the guarantor of stability in Georgia. Burjanadze began to persuade observers that Georgia's new leadership could guarantee stability as well.

At least partly due to the image projected by Burjanadze as well as Zhvania and Saakashvili, her partners in leading the Rose Revolution, the events in Georgia were immediately greeted by Europe and the United States as a tremendous victory for democracy and for Georgia. In the first days and weeks following. Shevardnadze's resignation, the new leaders received congratulations and pledges of support from the West. In the next few weeks, the West agreed to provide more support for the snap presidential election, which had been scheduled for January 4, 2004, as well as the rescheduled parliamentary election, winter heat programs to ensure that Georgia was able to pay its heating bill (primarily to Russia), and millions of dollars worth of new government programs.

Shevardnadze had been supported by many policy makers in the West until just days before his resignation, but these leaders were far less generous after he resigned. Leaders in these countries, particularly the U.S., seemed to slip into some kind of political amnesia, conveniently forgetting how strongly they had supported Shevardnadze in previous years. Shevardnadze fell into something of a political purgatory. Aware of his place in history and what was left of his reputation in the West, the new Georgian leadership was too smart to prosecute or bring injury to their former president. Instead, Shevardnadze spent his days in his dacha writing his memoirs, all but forgotten by the rest of the world.[1]

For many, however, a closer look at the events of that November raised questions about the peaceful and democratic nature of the Rose Revolution. How could a transition be considered democratic when it rested on a president being forced to resign by a relatively small number of demonstrators? What kind of democracy begins by storming the parliament building and forcing the president out of the room? Shevardnadze, after all, had not even been on the 2003 ballot.

Clearly, in a narrow procedural sense, the events that brought down Shevardnadze's government were not democratic, but they rested very heavily on democratic institutions and foundations. Saakashvili's party, after all, had won an election. An effort was made by the government to deny this victory, to keep the BD out of parliament illegally, and to increase the representation of the FNG and Revival in parliament through illegal and undemocratic means. Moreover, the extremely peaceful nature of the demonstrations, and the immediate call for new presidential and parliamentary elections by the new government, demonstrated a strong commitment to grounding the Rose Revolution in democratic processes.[2] The nonviolent nature of the Rose Revolution also speaks to its democratic foundations. Its leaders did not want to seize power in a coup; they wanted democratic processes to be followed. They also demonstrated a commitment to the rule of law by following the constitutional prescription for what was supposed to happen in the event of a presidential resignation.

The defining moment of the Rose Revolution, however, was the storming of the parliament. Bursting into parliament and shouting down the president of the country are not peaceful acts. Nonetheless, there was no physical violence associated with them. Weapons were not brandished; pro-government members of parliament were neither beaten nor threatened. Shevardnadze did not flee parliament due to an actual physical threat, but was hustled out by his bodyguards, who were acting with perhaps too much caution. Moreover, a number of those who burst into parliament, including Saakashvili, were in fact newly elected members of that body.

The day after the Shevardnadze's resignation, Saakashvili first floated the term "velvet revolution" to describe the just completed events in Georgia, but that phrase was already taken by the Czechs, so within a few days the new government and the international media had decided on the term "Rose Revolution." Naming the Rose Revolution was the beginning of creating the official narrative. A critical component of this narrative was to suggesting that the demonstrations were five to ten times larger than they actually were. This exaggeration not only diverted people from the real story of the Rose Revolution but sought to suggest that the leaders of the demonstrators enjoyed more popular support than one might have assumed at the time, based on the actual number of demonstrators.

However, this exaggeration was unnecessary. The events in the days leading up to Shevardnadze's resignation made it clear that the thousands of demonstrators on the streets of Tbilisi, while not huge in number, represented the tip of an iceberg that included most of Georgia. This is why Shevardnadze found himself with nowhere to turn in the waning days of his presidency, when ordinary citizens from around the country were forbidding the president's plane to land, taking down roadblocks, rejecting orders from bus company owners not to drive their buses full of demonstrators, and generally assisting and supporting the opposition in whatever ways they could.

The January 2004 presidential election made the legitimacy of Saakashvili's government clear to the entire world. Overstating the size of the demonstrations, however, creates a narrative in which the opposition seems more heroic and brave, moving perceptions away from the reality that the regime the Rose Revolution toppled was, in fact, a very weak one.

The Transitional Government

In the days following Shevardnadze's resignation, the first task for the new leadership, after ensuring the rest of the country, and the rest of the world, that Georgia was in mature and democratic hands, was to schedule presidential elections as well as to reschedule the parliamentary elections that had originally occurred on November 2. The constitution called for immediate presidential elections to replace a president who was unable to finish his term, so the election was called for January 4, roughly six weeks after Shevardnadze's resignation. The constitution was less clear with regard to parliamentary elections, so it was agreed to postpone those until spring.

The critical question regarding the presidential election was who would be the candidate of the Rose Revolution. This candidate would be ensured victory, but the temporary unity between the three leaders was already beginning to fray, so the question had become somewhat divisive. Saakashvili continued to argue for his candidacy based on his party's victory in the parliamentary election and his status as the de facto leader of the Rose Revolution. Burjanadze and Zhvania raised concerns that because Saakashvili was anathema to Abashidze, a Saakashvili presidency might precipitate more violence and resistance from Abashidze. These concerns were the bases of their argument that Burjanadze should have been the candidate for president. When this gambit failed, Zhvania and Burjanadze proposed that Saakashvili become president—but with the presidency reduced to a figurehead comparable, for example, to the presidency of Israel. This was only the beginning of another round of political and institutional maneuverings which would characterize the next weeks.

As we all know, Saakashvili won this battle and became candidate for president in early December. Importantly, Saakashvili's candidacy was presented to the public as something on which all three leaders agreed. This gave the impression of preserving the unity of the Rose Revolution leadership. During the weeks between the announcement and the election, Saakashvili was treated as the president-elect, a view that was strengthened when no other serious candidates emerged to run against him in the election which had been scheduled for January 4.

As the presidential election approached, with Saakashvili's victory already understood to be a fait accompli, the new government sought to make sure that elections would be different with Shevardnadze gone. It demonstrated its commitment to democracy by conducting a free, fair, and transparent election.

The January 4 election was much different from other elections in Georgia up until that time. The ODIHR report on this election begins by noting that

The 4 January 2004 extraordinary presidential election in Georgia demonstrated notable progress over previous elections, and in several respects brought the country closer to meeting OSCE commitments and other international standards for democratic elections. In contrast to the 2 November 2003 parliamentary elections that were characterized by systematic and widespread fraud, the authorities generally displayed the collective political will to conduct a more genuine democratic election process.[3]

Although broadly recognized as free and fair, this election was more a confirmation of Saakashvili as Georgia's new leader, rather than an election where voters were given a choice. Running virtually unopposed, Saakashvili won slightly more than 96 percent of the vote. This enormous majority raised suspicions about the fairness of the election, but the problem with the balloting was not lack of fairness but lack of competition. Saakashvili's popularity had scared away all other politicians, so only a few fringe candidates bothered to challenge him. On Election Day, the feeling of unanimity was strengthened when Shevardnadze himself spoke to the media for the first time since his resignation. The former president told the media that he had already voted—and that he had cast his vote for the man who had deposed him.

What Made the Rose Revolution Possible?

In the previous chapter, I described the events leading up to and during November 2003. The organization, political savvy, and hard work not just of the three major leaders of the Rose Revolution but of many others in the opposition played a key role in these events. Additionally, the clumsy miscalculations of Shevardnadze and his government as well as their puzzling underestimation of the opposition also were important. The election provided a catalyst for the opposition and brought all of this to a head

Other factors contributed to these events as well. The freedom Georgians enjoyed during Shevardnadze's presidency ultimately led to a strong and diverse civil society able to educate, organize, and mobilize people throughout the country. Groups like Kmara were able to focus Georgians' anger on Shevardnadze and raise people's belief that, as the slogan indicated, enough was finally enough. ISFED was able to operate relatively freely before, during, and after the election to make the case to the Georgian people that the elections had been stolen. Other civic organizations like the Liberty Institute and GYLA were able to maintain a steady drumbeat of criticism of the government through public statements, reports, and media appearances. Political parties, while occasionally harassed, were allowed to communicate with voters and campaign in most parts of the country.

Georgia's media also played a key role in the Rose Revolution. The presence of free, critical, and well respected media made it possible for the leaders of the opposition to communicate effectively with supporters throughout Georgia, and, correspondingly, for ordinary citizens to follow the events in Tbilisi. State-controlled Ajaran television ran very negative coverage of the demonstrators and their leaders, but this had no traction outside Ajara, and little even inside. Georgian state television station could not compete with the popular independent networks, such as Rustavi Two.

Ironically, Shevardnadze's commitment to freedom, whether because he believed in it or because he thought it would help keep foreign criticism at bay, ultimately led to his downfall. Unfortunately, many leaders of other post-Soviet countries learned from Shevardnadze's experience that allowing too much freedom can be a devastating mistake for an authoritarian or semidemocratic regime.

Another important contributing factor to the Rose Revolution was that by November 2003 Shevardnadze's government was extremely weak. A decade of corruption in a country without any significant natural wealth had left the country and the government poor. Although a number of government officials had skimmed substantial personal fortunes from years of corruption, the amount of money stolen was, in absolute numbers, far less than in many countries, simply because there was less to steal. The result was that after the officials had taken their share of the budget, the government did not have enough money left to do anything like maintain an infrastructure, perform simple governance tasks, exercise sovereignty over substantial parts of the country, or pay the security services.

Shevardnadze's weakness was exacerbated because he had no reservoir of personal support from any region or ethnic group to whom he could turn. No group in society was willing to come to the defense of the president. His failure to keep the state functioning in virtually any way meant that even the security forces were not loyal, because they had not been paid or treated well during the last years of his administration. Thus, Shevardnadze's post-Rose Revolution claim that he kept the situation peaceful because he did not call out the security forces against the demonstrators was somewhat misleading. The only people he could mobilize were the Ajarans, who at the key moment decided they were not interested in supporting Shevardnadze because their loyalty was to Abashidze.

These partial explanations of why the Rose Revolution occurred in Georgia in 2003 help us understand its origins, but it is also important to look at it in a more analytical and rigorous fashion. The roots of the Rose Revolution are clearly complex. Major contributing factors include the weakness of the Georgian state, the strength of civic life in Shevardnadze's Georgia, the political skills of the opposition (notably Zurab Zhvania, Nino Burjanadze, Mikheil Saakashvili, and several other key actors), and Georgia's unique political and social characteristics.

These explanations only go so far, because it is also essential to examine how these conditions came about. Democratic breakthroughs similar to the Rose Revolution have occurred in other parts of the post-Communist word in the years preceding and immediately following 2003.[4] Moreover, countries in other regions of the world—for example, the Philippines—experienced similar breakthroughs in the 1980s. Looking at Georgia in this context can help us understand the origins of the Rose Revolution.

While there have been electorally based democratic breakthroughs in the former communist block, Georgia was the first of its kind in the former Soviet Union itself. However, most countries of the former Soviet Union held regular elections beginning in the early or mid-1990s. Many were comparable to those in Shevardnadze's Georgia in that they were not conducted fairly, with fraud, bribery, and ballot box stuffing rampant, but none led to significant democratic breakthroughs.

What made it possible for this kind of breakthrough to occur in Georgia, but until that time, no other countries in the region, and why 2003, as opposed to earlier Georgian elections, was the election that led to this breakthrough, are critical to better understanding the Rose Revolution. It occurred only weeks after larger demonstrations in neighboring Azerbaijan were put down by with violence, and only a few years after two different national elections in Georgia were stolen. Both these cases were treated as business as usual, but in November 2003 something was different.

One approach to answering the question has been to show the ways that Georgia is different from the former Soviet Union. This might be called Georgian exceptionalism. These works, such as those by Nodia, Wheatley, Karumidze and Wertsch, and Kandalaki, tend to focus on the details of what happened and the unique political environment in Georgia as a means to explain why the Rose Revolution occurred in Georgia. Showing how it could not have happened anywhere else does not really explain why it occurred in Georgia. Clearly, there are some aspects of politics that are unique to Georgia and must be understood to fully understand political developments there. Many of these issues have been addressed in this work. However, relying too heavily on this approach makes it difficult to bring any analytical or comparative rigor to efforts to understand the Rose Revolution or to place it in the context of democratization or democracy promotion more broadly.

This type of exceptionalism is a not uncommon problem in case studies, but it seems to be more extreme in the case of Georgia. It might be called the wine and *khachapuri* fallacy.[5] People who have spent time in the former Soviet Union frequently comment, with a fair degree of accuracy, that upon arriving in Georgia, the food and wine taste better, the weather is nicer. less Russian is spoken, people are friendlier, and there is less general Soviet feeling than in other countries in the region. This carries over to the political arena, where even in the Shevardnadze years Georgia felt freer than many other countries in the region. Georgian politicians have long been more conversant in English, possessed a stronger understanding of how politics in the West works, and had stronger ties to politically powerful Westerners than comparable figures in other parts of the region. In short, Georgia stands out from the rest of the former Soviet Union in so many ways that it is easy to overlook Soviet and post-Soviet influence and the extent to which Georgia is similar to other post-Soviet states.

Georgia's unique history, culture, and cuisine notwithstanding, it is still a post-Soviet country sharing many of the challenges of the rest of the region. The Soviet legacy contributes to the lack of trust between citizens, leading to a collective action problem that makes solving basic problems difficult. It also contributes to the general sense of suspicion with which many Georgians approach government and the difficult relationship between Georgia and Russia. The legacy of Soviet economic policy is clear throughout the economically devastated country, as it is throughout the former Soviet Union. Industrial production has ground to a halt; joblessness is epidemic, and the infrastructure has been destroyed. Thus, while political, historical, and social context specific to Georgia were contributing factors to the Rose Revolution, they do not sufficiently explain why it occurred in Georgia in 2003, nor do they reduce the value of more comparative approaches.

Other common explanations for the Rose Revolution taking place in Georgia cite the maturity and strength of civil society during the Shevardnadze years.[6] Many key elements of civil society were supported financially by Western money and were able to draw on Western expertise and technical support. However, this explanation does not fully account for why civil society was so strong and free during this period. The most frequent answer to this question is that Shevardnadze was less repressive than many other former Communist leaders and allowed more freedom in Georgia. But why did he take this approach? While some vague commitment to democracy is possible, there is no real evidence that Shevardnadze took this position out of altruism or tolerance. It is at least worthwhile to explore other possible reasons for Georgia's strong civil society during these years.

Shevardnadze was never able to consolidate power in Georgia in the same way as others such as Nazerbayev in Kazakhstan, Aliev in Azerbaijan, or, to pick an extreme case, Turkmenbashi in Turkmenistan. Although, during his tenure as president Shevardnadze sought to present himself to the West as the guarantor of Georgian stability, the reality was quite different. In addition to losing control of South Ossetia and Abkhazia, Shevardnadze's government in Tbilisi exercised very little sovereignty over Ajara or even the northwestern province of Samagrelo, which borders on Abkhazia and had been Zviad Gamsakurdia's political base. For most of the Shevardnadze years, Samagrelo was under the de facto control of bandits and powerful local clans. This was, perhaps to a lesser extent, true of the northern province of Svaneti as well.

The weakness of the Georgian economy and state was a dominant issue in political life during these years. The precipitous economic decline following the collapse of the Soviet Union weakened the Georgian state to the point where it could no longer function. Shevardnadze had no resources with which to build a strong state. Georgia had no natural resources, little international trade once the artificial Soviet economy wound down, no remaining industry, and a decreasing population. Georgians during these years survived largely on agriculture (Georgia is a fertile country with a long agricultural history), along with remittances from family working outside the country and whatever foreign aid trickled down from the corrupt government. In many respects, the evolution of Georgia's civil society is as much attributable to these circumstances as to Shevardnadze's benevolence or commitment to freedom.

Not all weak states develop vibrant civic organizations and civil life, so again this explanation only helps somewhat. There were strong strategic considerations for Shevardnadze's commitment to allowing political, media, and associational freedom. Support from the West was of particular import. His reputation in the international community was his most valuable and only unique political asset. Through cleverly using this reputation, Shevardnadze was able to bring a disproportionately large amount of foreign assistance to Georgia. Cracking down on civic freedoms would have likely been a step too far and might have finally alienated his government's Western supporters. This was a chance Shevardnadze could not take.

Another way to look at the question is to ask why democracy assistance from the United States and the West was more effective in Georgia than elsewhere in the region. While Georgia did receive more democracy assistance money per capita in the years leading up to the Rose Revolution than most other post-Soviet countries, it was a difference in degree, not in kind.[7] Therefore, attributing the Rose Revolution too strongly to U.S. democracy assistance policy raises as least as many questions as it answers. Georgia's neighbors in the South Caucasus, Armenia, and Azerbaijan received support for civil society, local government, and strengthening of their legislatures and political parties, but those programs had far less impact.

In Georgia, however, what Carothers (1999) called the "basic package of democracy programs" including "election assistance around each national election . . . a parliamentary strengthening program . . . judicial reform work . . . attempts to strengthen local government; money and training for various NGOs"[8] contributed substantially to the evolution of a strong democratic alternative and ultimately to the Rose Revolution itself. Civil society organizations were supported by American money and expertise in U.S. efforts to hold the corrupt regime accountable, push for fair elections, and mobilize citizens to demand their rights, while political parties had developed the skills to contest the election by presenting a vision and persuading voters they had a better alternative. Years of support to the Georgian parliament had helped that institution become a focal point for political action, helping keep politics legal and nonviolent.

Georgia during these years was fertile ground for U.S. democracy assistance. The pro-Western orientation and dependence on foreign assistance, as well as absence of any internal source of wealth or political strength, made the regime dependent on foreign aid. It would have been very difficult for Shevardnadze to reject democracy assistance, which amounted to a small fraction of overall U.S. support to Georgia, while accepting the rest of the assistance package. To have done so would also have further undermined the perception in the West, which he worked so hard to cultivate, that he was a reformer who wanted to bring democracy to Georgia.

The dependence of Shevardnadze's regime on Western support was exacerbated by the regime's relationship with Russia, the other natural place Shevardnadze might have looked for support. As we have seen, Georgian feeling toward Russia, as made clear by the tension between the two countries since the Rose Revolution, is much closer to the feelings in the Baltic states than in those in Central Asia. For a leader of independent Georgia to be too close with Russia would have severely damaged support for that government among much of the Georgian public.

There was an additional issue that made it difficult for Shevardnadze to turn to Russia for support. Like many other leaders of newly independent states, Shevardnadze had been a prominent leader during the Communist years as well, but he would not have been able to easily use this connection to build a strong relationship with Russia had he wanted to move in that direction. Shevardnadze's tenure as foreign minister at the end of the Cold War clearly cemented his reputation in the West, but it had the opposite effect in Russia. Particularly among mid- to high-ranking communist apparatchiks who had made their way into positions of power in post-1991 Russia, he was largely viewed as the man who helped destroy the Soviet Union. Shevardnadze was not even Russian; he was the Georgian who gave away the Russian empire.

Shevardnadze was never well liked or fully trusted by Russia while he was in power and was pushed toward the United States more than other leaders in the regions, most of whom shared his roots in the leadership of the Communist Party. Georgian opposition forces were able to take advantage of this situation to build both a civil and political opposition and exploit the opportunity that arose when Shevardnadze tried to steal one too many elections in 2003.

Chapter 5
Governance by Adrenaline

Mikheil Saakashvili's election raised hopes both in Georgia and internationally that a new political era would begin in Georgia, one in which democracy, transparency, and the rule of law would replace the old regime of corruption, stolen elections, and kleptocracy. Saakashvili himself encouraged these expectations through his speeches and comments about the new direction in which Georgia was moving.[1]

Georgians were exhausted and angry that the first twelve years of post-Soviet independence had brought little besides declining economic conditions, chaos, crumbling infrastructure, and a dishonest and uncaring government. For many of them the Rose Revolution and Saakashvili's election represented nothing less than a rebirth of independent Georgia. The Soviet period was finally completely over now that the country was no longer governed by a former Communist Party first secretary. Saakashili, thirty-six years old at the time of his election and with no political roots in the Soviet period, clearly represented a new generation, and new outlook and direction, in Georgian politics.

Internationally, the events in Georgia were greeted with great hopes as well. It was hoped that the Rose Revolution in Georgia would reinvigorate the third wave of democratization that seemed to have ebbed in the former communist world. It was also hoped that Georgia would rapidly consolidate its democracy and demonstrate that democracy promotion was a worthwhile policy goal in the twenty-first century.

The New Constitution

It was clear that advocates and opponents of democracy and democracy assistance would be watching the new Georgia very closely. For these reasons, the constitutional changes that occurred within 20 days of Saakashvili becoming president were particularly surprising and troubling.

While the substance of the constitutional changes, discussed below, should have raised concerns about the new government's commitment to meaningful democratic reform, the process in which they were passed was perhaps more disturbing. The new constitution was rushed through parliament in a one-week period immediately after Saakashvili took office. There was no opportunity for public input or review. The new government asserted, somewhat implausibly, that most of the changes had been discussed by the parliament in 2000 and therefore did not require further deliberation.

Members of the old pre-Rose Revolution parliament who were still in place at this time were reportedly coerced to support the amendments, in some cases even threatened with investigations or persecutions; the amendments themselves changed several times during this period, making it difficult for any real debate in the media or civil society to occur. All this occurred without a critical word of any kind from the United States or Europe. The Venice Commission was asked by Saakashvili to offer an opinion on the proposed changes, but the changes went through so quickly that by the time the commission issued its report, the proposed changes had already passed.[2]

The constitutional changes of February 2004 were far from minor and resulted in the reshaping of Georgia's government and in a great deal of power being concentrated in the president. According to the new constitution, the president appoints the prime minister and the cabinet, can disband parliament if it rejects his budget three times, and exercises control over an executive branch of government that dominates the weaker legislative branch. The president also retained the right to nominate judges, university provosts, some big city mayors, and other officials. Under the new constitution, Saakashvili enjoys more formal power than Shevardnadze ever did.

The new constitution also created a powerful prime minister who would be appointed by the president. The prime minister, in consultation with the president, would then appoint and run the government. This arrangement not only concentrated power in the hands of the president, but substantially reoriented the relationship between the legislative and executive branches. The creation of the office of prime minister and the other constitutional changes meant that parliament would be less powerful.

The weakening of the parliament was no accident because the constitutional changes were the next, and last major, step in the ongoing struggle for power between Saakashvili, Zhvania, and Burjanadze. One goal of the changes was to make sure that each of the three major leaders of the Rose Revolution received an important position in the new government. The office of prime minister was created for Zurab Zhvania, whose administrative skills, international connections, and experience made him the perfect candidate for the position, while his lack of popularity among voters meant that his path to power needed to be through appointed office. Zhvania's involvement in the new government was essential for its success. However, changing the constitution to fit one person is rarely a wise idea.

The new constitution cut the political legs out from under Nino Burjanadze, who had graciously agreed to return to her position as speaker of parliament after Saakashvili replaced her as president. By weakening the branch of government that was the base of Burjanadze's power, Saakashvili also weakened the only other Georgian politician who shared his revolutionary credentials and approached his popularity with voters. Saakashvili's desire to reduce Burjanadze's power was understandable, although his tactics were far from exemplary. In addition to viewing Burjanadze as a potential threat, Saakashvili had never regarded her as genuinely part of the opposition because she had supported the CUG government for far longer than Saakashvili and had waited until mid-2003 before definitively casting her lot with the opposition.[3]

More difficult to understand was Zhvania's participation and support of the new constitution. Zhvania's brilliant political skills had been central to the success of the Rose Revolution. It was he who kept dialogue going with the Shevardnadze government and the security forces during the three critical weeks in November. This dialogue was instrumental in maintaining the peaceful nature of the Rose Revolution. The basic components of the post-election strategy including foreign exit polls and demonstrations had also been his ideas.

Zhvania's relevance in Georgian politics after the November 2 election, however, was due largely to Nino Burjanadze. Although the showing of the Burjanadze Democrats at the polls was disappointing, had Burjanadze not been leading the party's election efforts, the old United Democrats would almost certainly not have gotten the votes to have even been close to reaching the 7 percent threshold and Zhvania's political career would have all but finished.

These circumstances made Zhvania's decision to support Saakashvili against Burjanadze all the more puzzling. As a smart and sophisticated politician, Zhvania must have know that by doing this he was violating one of the most basic rules of politics: "Dance with the one that brung ya." Burjanadze was the one who had "brung" Zhvania, and Zhvania sacrificed her as part of his deal with Saakashvili. In addition to treating Burjanadze poorly, Zhvania ended up putting himself in a very difficult position

The incentive for Zhvania to join with Saakashvili to weaken parliament and therefore Burjanadze, was, of course, the position of prime minister.[4] This post created for Zhvania was a perfect match for his skill set. Zhvania was, however, not just prime minister: he was prime minister in a government led by President Saakashvili. Zhvania's longtime personal rival was now his boss. Saakashvili's leadership style, already clear before he became president, of making quick decisions without consulting anybody, making big promises, and general governance by adrenaline were certain to make the prime minister's position a difficult one. Zhvania knew all this, but he still sided with Saakashvili at this moment. Perhaps Saakashvili's popularity at that time made Zhvania think it was impossible to oppose Saakashvili as he pushed through constitutional changes to weaken democratic institutions and concentrate power in the president. Perhaps, Zhvania felt that his participation in government was the only potential check against Saakashvili. Perhaps he simply could not abide being left out of the government after the essential role he had played in the Rose Revolution.

Zhvania's tenure as prime minister was short and difficult. Responding to Saakashvili's ever changing policies and government personnel and knowing that he served at the pleasure of his longtime rival was never easy. Zhvania's time in this position was tragically cut short when he died under mysterious circumstances in Tbilisi in February 2005.

Zhvania's Death and Its Impact

Early on the morning of February 3, 2005, Zurab Zhvania was found dead in the apartment of a friend, Raul Usupov, in Tbilisi. Zhvania had gone to visit Usupov around midnight on February 2. After not getting any responses to attempts to call him on the phone or knock on the door, Zhvania's security people broke in to the apartment at around 3:30 A.M. and found both Zhvania and Usupov dead. According to reports, Zhvania was in an armchair in the living room and Usupov was in the kitchen. The cause of death was quickly stated to be carbon monoxide poisoning from a faulty heater.

There was little evidence of efforts to throw open windows or turn off the heater, which is what most people do if they are awake and begin to suspect the presence of poison gas. Most people who die of carbon monoxide poisoning die in bed in their sleep, not while sitting in the living room or standing in the kitchen. On the other hand, because of the old and poorly made heating systems on which many in Georgia depend in the winter in the absence of central heating, death by carbon monoxide poisoning is not that rare in Georgia (the $30 carbon monoxide detector a colleague brought over from the United States may have saved the lives of me and my family one cold night in the winter of 2002–3). Like most Georgians, Usupov did not have one of these detectors. Usupov's heating unit, however, had only recently been installed.

The government investigation of Zhvania's death, conducted jointly with the FBI, ruled that the death was an accident. The report was issued only days after Zhvania's death and before forensic examination had even begun. Zhvania's family, including his widow and his brother, challenged the finding and urged further investigation.

There is still a substantial amount of uncertainty surrounding Zhvania's death. Many believe the Russians were somehow behind it, as they might have viewed getting rid of Zhvania as a way to accelerate instability in Georgia. A significantly smaller number of people, generally radical opponents of the government, have suggested that Saakashvili had a hand in the incident, although no evidence has ever been produced to suggest that this is true.[5]

The precise circumstances and causes of Zhvania's death may never be known, but its effect on Georgian politics is clear. Zhvania was a unique, and not uncontroversial, figure in Georgia. As discussed earlier, he was seen quite differently by his fellow Georgians and foreigners, particularly Americans and Europeans. The former viewed him with a fair amount of suspicion and distrust, while the latter group generally saw him as Georgia's leading democrat and an unequivocally positive force for his country. The truth, of course, lay somewhere in between.

Zhvania's tenure as prime minister was not easy. In addition to the extraordinary challenges of reforming Georgia's government and rebuilding its economy, his rivalry with Saakashvili never really ended. Tensions between the two remained strong throughout the year Zhvania served as prime minister.

It was apparent that the controversial constitutional reforms of 2004 were primarily a way to ensure that Zhvania, who did not enjoy a high level of popular support, but who was understood by both Georgian elites and the international community as uniquely capable of running Georgia's government, would have a key role in the new regime. However, placing Zhvania in the prime minister's position served another purpose as well.

The new constitution dramatically expanded the president's powers. With the new parliament weak and dominated by Saakashvili's party, the legislature was clearly not going to serve as a significant check on the president. There was no tradition of an independent judiciary that might have served in this role. Moreover, civil society and media were too weakened to play this role either.

The last remaining check on Saakashvili was Zhvania. He was the only person in Georgia who possessed political and administrative skills and international connections comparable or superior to Saakashvili's. Saakashvili, although far more popular with voters, needed Zhvania as least as much as Zhvania needed him. With Zhvania inside the government, it would be much easier for Saakashvili to demonstrate his maturity and seriousness to the rest of the world, as well as to many Georgian elites. While Saakashvili could have fired Zhvania from the prime minister's post at any time, Zhvania had leverage of a different kind.

Had Zhvania publicly criticized Saakashvili, left the government. or expressed serious concerns to policy makers in Europe or the United States, it would have sent a very powerful message that things were not right in Saakashvili's Georgia. Thus, Zhvania, by virtue of his personal skills and relationships, made the position of prime minister a de facto check on the president, but once he died, the position did not retain this status.

Zhvania's death created serious political and governmental challenges. His successor, former minister of finance Zurab Noghaideli, who was appointed by Saakashvili and approved by parliament, is viewed as a good executive but not comparable to Zhvania. Nogadeli's successor Vladimer "Lado" Gurgenidze, who took office in November of 2007, enjoys a similar reputation However, neither Nogadeli or Gurgenidze has independent political power either domestically or in the international community. Thus, the post-Zhvania prime minister's office is far less powerful than when it was created for him, in 2004.

Democracy in Georgia After the Rose Revolution

Upon coming to power in November 2003, Georgia's new government inherited a battery of daunting problems that included troubled relationships with Russia, the nagging presence of Aslan Abashidze in Ajara, a society and economy ravaged by massive corruption, in Abhazia and South Ossetia, a stricken energy sector, and an economy in ruins. Under the leadership of Saakashvili and Zhvania, who in the months immediately following the Rose Revolution and before his death helped create a functioning government and administration, the post-revolution government of Georgia has clearly been more efficient and less corrupt than during Shevardnadze's years in power. Saakashvili and his colleagues can point to real success in some areas, such as defeating Abashidze, beginning to rebuild the infrastructure, reducing corruption in the police department, increasing state revenues, and dramatically improving the budget process. While there have been shortcomings in Georgia's democratization, an exclusive focus on this paints an unfair picture. The accomplishments are real and have strong effects on people's everyday lives. Moreover, the strength of the current regime and the support it enjoys among the Georgian people is based upon these accomplishments.

One of Saakashvili's greatest triumphs was ensuring the retention of

Ajara. When Saakashvili took office in 2004, the fate of Ajara was a major question facing all of Georgia. For Georgians outside Ajara, the de facto loss of that territory to the bizarre dictatorship of Aslan Abashidze, which had occurred in the mid-1990s, was more than just another loss of a piece of their country. Ajara was the most favored vacation spot for Georgians, particularly after the loss of Abkhazia, and with Abkhazia no longer under Georgian sovereignty, most of Georgia's remaining coast, including Batumi, its biggest port, was in Ajara and not governed directly from Tbilisi. Additionally, Ajara has a large border with Turkey, so that most of Georgia's trade with one of its most important neighbors and trading partners was subject to theft, corruption, smuggling, and other shenanigans by Abashidze and his gang.

After the Rose Revolution, ordinary Georgians became more aware of the possibility of losing Ajara permanently as Abashidze's talk of secession became more aggressive. Losing this key piece of territory would have been a terrible blow to the new government and the Georgian state. Ajarans themselves became much more disgruntled with their leadership after the Rose Revolution. During the Shevardnadze years, Abashidze could plausibly tell the people of Ajara that they had it better than the rest of Georgia. But when it became clear that the excitement and hope of the Rose Revolution would stop at the Ajaran line, the Ajaran people began to be less pleased with Abashidze's regime.

Abashidze had long harbored a deep disdain for Saakashvili as evinced beyond a doubt during November 2003, when Ajara television, which Abashidze controlled, showed film of Saakashvili giving speeches at Tbilisi demonstrations interspersed with images of speeches by Adolf Hitler. Georgia's new president, for his part, harbored no great love for the Ajaran dictator. This combination of economic, political, and personal factors led to a very tense situation between Tbilisi and Batumi almost immediately after Saakashvili took office. As winter turned into spring, the brinkmanship became more intense and the likelihood of violence greater.[6] Then, on May 6, with Georgian troops amassed at the border of Ajara, after Abashidze had blown up the bridges leading into the region and thousands of Ajarans had taken to the streets to demonstrate against his dictatorial rule, Abashidze blinked first and fled to Russia. This was, by any measure, an enormous victory for the new government, one that meant a great deal to many Georgians. Since Abashidze's departure, a new Ajaran legislature has been elected through free and fair elections. Ajara still enjoys some regional autonomy, but has been integrated into the state more broadly and has become an engine for economic growth due to the resurgent tourist industry in that region.

In the years that Saakashvili has been in power, the country has changed tangibly in other ways as well. Roads have been rebuilt; the energy situation is better, there is greater access for most Georgians to water, heat, and electricity; infrastructure is improving as office buildings, schools, and playgrounds, particularly in Tbilisi, are being repaired; state revenues have increased; pensions and salaries are paid regularly; Armenian tourists are coming to Batumi for their summer vacations; there is a better business climate; and slowly the country is beginning to shake off the effects of fifteen years of post-Soviet deterioration. Tbilisi's old city, which in 2003 was a dusty collection of collapsing brown and gray wooden buildings with a handful of rug shops, largely unimpressive restaurants, and the odd artists' boutique surrounding a few old churches, a mosque, and a synagogue, now contains several beautiful walking streets where the buildings have been repaired, the streets are recobbled and well lit, and numerous cafés and restaurants are filled with tourists and Georgia's nascent middle class.

Saakashvili's success can be largely attributed to the radical approach he has taken to foreign assistance. Georgia's president has insisted that money given to Georgia to rebuild infrastructure or develop the economy should be used for those purposes, not stolen and put into dachas, new SUVs, and Swiss bank accounts. He has held his government accountable on this issue, and the results are unmistakable. Indeed, the government has taken a hard line on official corruption, reformed the police department, enforced anticorruption legislation, and sought, at times a bit too enthusiastically, to arrest some of the most corrupt figures from the Shevardnadze years.

Under Shevardnadze petty corruption in the traffic police was rampant. Driving on the country's main highway, it was not unusual to get shaken down for a bribe every 30 miles or so. Under Saakashvili, the police are decently paid and this kind of corruption has been reduced dramatically. Fighting corruption has been one of the signature goals of the regime, and this is just one example of how this fight has improved the life of ordinary Georgians.

Nonetheless, on specific democracy related issues such as building democratic institutions, ensuring government accountability, and cultivating a strong and free civil society, the record of the new government has been more uneven. A brief look at the current political environment as well as some of the major advances and current shortcomings of Georgian democracy should make this clear.

The Post-Rose Revolution Political Landscape

The events of late 2003 and early 2004 dramatically changed the political landscape and the electoral and the political party environment in

Georgia. With Shevardnadze removed from the political scene, the primary force around which Georgian politics had been organized for over a decade was gone. Shevardnadze's CUG seemed to disappear almost immediately after he left office. Within weeks of his departure the party all but ceased to exist. Abashidze's Revival Party briefly stayed in place as the last holdout of the old regime. It was able to maintain this position for about six months before falling victim to Ajara's smaller scale Rose Revolution in May 2004.

The political party alignments and rankings from 2003 were completely reshuffled as the Rose Revolution became the new defining moment for Georgia's politicians and political parties. Although the Rose Revolution was primarily the work of two parties, the NM and the BD, it was broadly, almost universally, supported by the Georgian population. This is demonstrated by the failure of anybody but completely unknown fringe candidates to run against Saakashvili for the presidency in January 2004. The parties from the previous system saw their fortunes rise or fall based on their relationship to the Rose Revolution. The old party system was finished, and the new system that would emerge would be centered on the Rose Revolution and Mikheil Saakashvili, not Eduard Shevardnadze.

Almost all the smaller parties from 2003 disappeared after the Rose Revolution. Some, such as the People's Party or the Traditionalists (which had merged with the BD in fall 2003), were absorbed into the new ruling party. Vano Khokhonashvili, colorful leader of the People's Party, who had joined the demonstrations in November, was put on the NM list for parliament for the March 2004 elections and became chair of the committee on local government, a key committee in the new parliament. Akaki Asatiani and Gubaz Sanikidze, leaders of the Traditionalists Party, were initially included in the new leadership, but left the government in early 2004 because they refused to support the constitutional reforms. The remaining small parties that had not supported the Rose Revolution, such as the Greens, Socialists, National Democratic Party, and Christian Democrats, faded even further into oblivion or ceased to exist altogether.

The political landscape with regard to the major parties, which had been important players in the 2003 elections, changed as well. Revival and the CUG, as discussed above, had completely disappeared from the political scene by late 2004. Shalva Natalashvili's Labor Party paid dearly for misjudging the political situation in November. According to both the PVT and the exit poll, Labor had finished in second place in November behind only the National Movement. However, as we have seen, Natalashvili did not join the demonstrations or make any public statements in support of the demands of the Rose Revolution. By the time

Shevardnadze had resigned, Natalashvili's and Labor's popularity was falling rapidly. His support continued to decline in 2004 so that by spring his party was a political also-ran.

The BD- and NM- led street demonstrations put Labor in a no-win situation. Had it supported the demonstrations, Labor would have looked appeared to be throwing support to what Natalashvili had previously called the "new CUG." Not supporting the demonstrations would have made it appear pro-Shevardnadze. Faced with this situation, Natalashvili decided not to participate in or support the demonstrations. However, many people who had voted for the Labor party chose to support and even join the demonstrations and the revolution.

Natalashvili felt betrayed by the West, particularly the United States, during this period. He had never enjoyed the close relationship with the Western political leaders and others that Zhvania and Saakashvili had, and felt that Western governments supported these politicians while overlooking him. However, during the pre-election period Natalashvili had made an agreement with Western embassies not to go to the streets after the election. He was furious when he saw other parties doing so and being, as he saw it, supported by the West in these efforts.

I encountered this anger during a phone call with Natalashvili in mid-November 2003 when demonstrators were protesting in front of parliament in the early days of the Rose Revolution. During this call Natalashvili was very upset with me because of the role he perceived being played by NDI, the organization for which I was serving as Chief of Party. He told me, referring to the demonstrations, "You are responsible for this—you and George Soros." By "you" Natalashvili meant me individually as well as the U.S. government, of which he saw me as a representative, although I was not.[7]

Although the party's popularity continued to fall after Saakashvili became president in January, Labor decided to contest the new parliamentary elections in March 2004. It ended up narrowly missing the 7 percent threshold and for the second time in a row was shut out of parliament. In Natalashvili's mind, little had changed; he viewed his party as unfairly kept out of parliament yet again by the manipulations of Zurab Zhvania, who was by then the prime minister and an important figure in the UNM election campaign. However, this time Labor had lost on its own and was not a victim of election fraud.

After the parliamentary election, Labor continued its collapse and is now something of a minor party, with some support but increasingly rumored to be backed by Russia. Although there is no real proof of this, there is some evidence, including funding issues and positions taken by the party. In November 2007 when the Georgian government sought to blame a pro-Russian plot for large street demonstrations that they broke up with tear gas and rubber bullets, the government again suggested that Natalashvili was part of this Russian plot. After initially being forced into hiding, the government dropped the charges, presumably to ensure that Natalashvili would run against Saakashvili and lose badly in the snap presidential election of January 2008. Labor has positioned itself as a strong critic not just of the president and his party but of the regime and the state as well. This is a strategic mistake, as the state and regime still enjoy support and legitimacy in Georgia. There is a very important role for a pro-state, anti-government party in today's Georgia. Unfortunately, Labor has not stepped up to fill this niche.

Neither the Industrialists nor the New Rights, the other major parties from the 2003 elections, have stepped into this role either. These two parties have been closely linked since the Rose Revolution. As noted in Chapter 3, neither participated in the demonstrations after the stolen parliamentary election. This was a bigger mistake for the New Rights because, while many Georgians at the time believed the Industrialists to be pro-government, they were not so certain about the New Rights. Failing to participate in the demonstrations convinced many to believe that the New Rights was not a true opposition party either.

The Industrialists and New Rights decided to run together in the March 2004 parliamentary elections, forming a coalition called the Right Wing Opposition (RWO). The RWO narrowly achieved the 7 percent necessary to get into parliament and became the only opposition party in the NM-dominated parliament. It became formally the leading opposition party, with David Gamkrelidze the leader of their parliamentary block. However, its policies and political decisions have proven to be very unpopular, relegating it to a peripheral role in Georgian politics. Again, the inability to find a pro-state, anti-government position has hurt the RWO with voters. In mid-2006 the coalition broke apart, so the New Rights and Industrialists were no longer one parliamentary faction. The New Rights supported but did not join the November 2007 demonstrations, and Gamkrelidze lost badly to Saakashvili in the presidential election of January 2008.

Thus, the NM and the BD, because they were leading parties during the Rose Revolution, were the only parties left standing by early 2004. However, while their rivalry initially continued, particularly at the leadership level where cabinet ministers, powerful MPs, and other senior political figures were known to be affiliated with either Saakashvili or Zhvania, the two parties supported the same candidate for president in January 2004, ran on a single list in the parliamentary elections that March, and by mid-summer had formally merged into a single party. The reality was that the NM, as the dominant partner in this merger, essentially took over the BD.

It was apparent by early 2004 that the previous party system had been destroyed and a new one, centered around the UNM with a number of minor opposition parties, was beginning to emerge. Because of their actions during decisive moments in November 2003, as well as their failure to recognize the legitimacy of the Rose Revolution and the new government, the remaining opposition parties had little support or credibility with the Georgian public. It had become clear that for Georgian democracy to advance to the next level, new opposition parties that recognized the Rose Revolution and the new leadership needed to emerge.

So far no party has emerged to fill this gap. This is due partly to the manipulations of the ruling party, but also to the successes of the new government in fighting corruption and improving service delivery, poor political judgment on the part of the leadership of the New Rights and Labor, and failure of any of the parties formed after the Rose Revolution to strengthen themselves sufficiently to play this role.

The two parties that might have done so, the Republicans and the Conservatives, broke off from the NM in 2005 and sought to position themselves as pro-revolution but anti-NM and, ultimately, anti-Saakashvili. The Republicans were led by longtime civil society activists and Saakashvili supporters David Usupashvili and Koba Davitashvili. The Conservatives were led by another erstwhile Saakashvili supporter, Zviad Dzidziguri. Parties like the Conservatives and the Republicans were precisely what were needed in Georgia after the Rose Revolution. Their leaders believed in the legitimacy of the new government and had played important roles in the events, so they could not be easily accused of being sympathetic to Russia or supporters of the old regime. However, neither of these parties has evolved into a major political actor.

Although they originally sought to be moderate opposition forces, both parties became very critical of the government. This was due in some degree to the very aggressive government responses to any of their criticisms. Additionally, neither party was able to build strong political support. The Republican leadership, while smart and politically sophisticated, proved to be Tbilisi-based and unable to build much beyond their base of mostly well-educated young people who were disgruntled with the Rose Revolution. The Conservatives, without any prominent national leaders, also remained a relatively minor party. Both showed some political strength in being part of the coalition that mobilized thousands of demonstrators on the streets of Tbilisi in November 2007. The long-term political impact of that is not yet clear.

The political environment during the first few years of the new regime was dominated by the governing party in a way that Georgia had not seen since before Shevardnadze was president. The new government faced no serious opposition as it sought to implement its agenda of reform, but there were also no political checks on the government, other than internal dynamics among the leadership.

The dominance of Saakashvili's party is a serious and complex threat to democratic development in Georgia. There is a real threat that the regime will begin to evolve into a one-party system. Even if this one party is popularly elected, as it has been so far, the absence of a competitive multiparty system will inevitably curb democracy. The problem is complex because the governing party has generally been genuinely popular and well liked. Moreover, the opposition is weak and clearly lacks the political skills and sophistication possessed by the government.

The failure of New Rights and Labor to recognize that the Rose Revolution is a political fact that is not going to change has severely limited their popular appeal. The tendency of the Republicans and Conservatives to rely on personal attacks and their failure to understand the need to develop a longer term and more modest strategy have cost them support among voters. However, the UNM is not without blame here either, as it has not taken adequate steps to ensure a fair opportunity for the opposition.

Democratic Development in Post-Rose Revolution Georgia

The primary area where democratic advances have been made in Georgia since the Rose Revolution is in elections. Elections in the later years of Shevardnadze's presidency, as described in previous chapters, were characterized by fraud, violence, and cheating. Fair elections were the rule until 2008, when presidential and parliamentary elections of questionable quality were held. Official reports by both foreign and domestic observers show the contrast between elections in the Shevardnadze and early Saakashvili periods. Elections in the latter are generally described as free and fair, while those in the former never were. Elections are rarely perfect, and some problems remain, but now voters know their votes will most likely be cast freely and without interference and will be counted fairly as well. This is an enormous change in Georgia, one that goes to the very core of democracy and for which the Saakashvili administration should be given recognition.[8] Because of their visibility, elections often take on an outsized role in perceptions of democratic development. This is certainly the case in Georgia, where important pieces of the democratization puzzle are occurring outside of the context of elections.

In many other respects democratic consolidation in Georgia has stalled. One election related area where this can be seen is with regard to political parties, where the ruling UNM party has made little effort to strengthen the distinctions between ruling party and government which are essential in a democratic state. Party membership, or at least support, albeit in a new party, is still viewed as a prerequisite to any position of power. UNM leadership speaks of itself as the only democratizing political force in Georgia and has openly questioned the need for opposition from outside the UNM. The UNM also dominates parliament, controlling well over two-thirds of the seats. The UNM members in parliament are loyal to the president as many were hand picked by him to be on the party list for the 2004 and 2008 elections. As a result, there is little opposition in parliament. Even parliamentary chairs Nino Burjanadze and Davaid Bakradze served at Saakashvili's pleasure, as the president controls enough votes to force her out of the post if, for example, she is too critical. The adaptation of the UNM party's flag as the new Georgian flag shortly after Saakashvili came to office nicely encapsulates the blurring of the lines between ruling party and state, as well as the threat of one-party hegemony.

Shevardnadze's Georgia was a place where civil organizations and vibrant free media played valuable roles in the country's political life. This too has changed somewhat under Saakashvili, as NGOs no longer play a leading role as government watchdogs and critics. Ironically, in some respects Georgia had less independent media and fewer opposition voices than it had under Shevardnadze. Many of the leaders of Georgia's civic and NGO community during the Shevardnadze years have been brought into government as cabinet ministers, MPs, or in other positions. Their replacements generally share a pro-government outlook and have been reluctant to criticize the new government.

The change in Georgia's media has been more disturbing. Shortly after Saakashvili assumed the presidency, a number of lively, often critical, political television programs were taken off the air. When they were reinstated, many Georgians found them substantially watered down from their previous form. The hosts are less outspoken and there are fewer guests who are critical of the government. Similarly, a number of formerly independent media outlets, most notably television station Rustavi Two, have become far less critical and independent in their reporting since the Rose Revolution. Shifts in U.S. democracy assistance strategy in Georgia have contributed to this as USAID support for independent media has all but disappeared since the Rose Revolution. The state of emergency declared after a few days of protests and a violent crackdown by the government in November 2007 was a more dramatic example of this, as was the government's decision to shut down Imedi, Georgia's last remaining national independent station, during this period.

Freedom House's 2005 evaluation of Georgia based on information from 2004, raised the issue of media freedom as well.

Before the Georgian leadership change, the country's independent press was able to publish discerning and critical political analyses . . . During 2004, some critics of the new government leveled charges that media outlets unfriendly to Saakashvili were pressured and that a new round of self-censorship had begun. There were also some indications that a wider effort to manage news media was being undertaken by the authorities.[9]

The 2007 Freedom House Report makes a similar point two years later: "While a diversity of political opinions and perspectives flourish in the print media, broadcast media in 2006 continued to suffer from some self-censorship. . . . To the extent that there is political debate in the broadcast media, it rarely amounts to a thoughtful discussion of public policy."[10]

A number of these concerns were expressed in an open letter to President Saakashvili from some of Georgia's leading intellectuals in October 2004, only eleven months after Shevardnadze's resignation. This letter addressed the threat of one-party dominance and asserted that the "ruling party" expressed "intolerance of people with different opinions," adding that "leaders and officials of the ruling party constantly use the labels . . . such as the enemy of the nation, traitor, the fifth column etc." Concern over freedom of expression was addressed as well: "your [Saakashvili's] recent public speeches . . . are more and more humiliating and insulting towards the opponents." The letter goes on to warn against "attempts to establish and intellectual dictatorship and the dominance of one opinion."[11]

The issue of judicial independence, essential to a strong democracy, has also been a challenge for the new government. Under Shevardnadze, the judiciary was highly corrupt and dominated by old Soviet era judges. Saakashvili has sought to reform the judiciary by firing a substantial number of judges and creating a system of exams for future judges.

The new judges, however, have been frequently criticized, both domestically and abroad, as being too close to Saakashvili and, in some cases, consulting with him or members of his government before issuing key decisions. Concern has also been raised about the length of pretrial detentions and the aggressive approach the government has taken in efforts to force officials accused of corruption to forfeit their assets.[12]

Although the conduct of elections in Georgia since the Rose Revolution has been much better, there are still some serious concerns surrounding these elections. Elections in Saakashvili's Georgia from 2004–2006 were free, fair, and uncompetitive. Competition is, of course, an absolutely central component of democracy. Dahl (1971), Sartori (1976), and others have argued that competitiveness is a central way to measure elections and democracy. Sartori, for example, notes a distinction between hegemonic and predominant party systems. In the former, the ruling restricts the functioning of the other parties; in the latter, the ruling party simply continues to win elections. The danger in today's Georgia is that the UNM will gradually mover from the latter to the former type of ruling party. Thus far, the signals have been mixed.

Part of the reason elections in the first few years following the Rose Revolution were uncompetitive was the failure of a strong opposition to Saakashvili's National Movement Party to emerge. But this is only a partial explanation because the ruling party has manipulated elections in very clever, and legal, ways to ensure victory. The government has frequently bemoaned their lack of opposition recognizing that a strong opposition is necessary in a democracy. In a speech to the European Parliament on November 14, 2006, Saakashvili commented:

Perhaps one of my biggest regrets to date is the fact that Georgia still does not have a robust and constructive opposition. . . . Nothing would be more dangerous to a fledgling democracy that to artificially manufacture an opposition. I can only hope that Georgia's opposition parties will become more vigorous, as well as more responsible and competent, testing the government, and one day (but not that soon!) prevail in open and fair elections.[13]

These have proven to be crocodile tears on the part of Saakashvili since the government has also undermined the opposition's chances through electoral manipulation, particularly in advance of the local elections to which Saakashvili referred in this speech. Remarks like these are also, of course, thinly veiled attacks on the existing opposition parties, implying they are not constructive, responsible, or competent.

The electoral system that was introduced and created specifically for the October 2006 local elections was viewed by the opposition and many independent civic organizations as an effort to ensure a large majority for the UNM in local government councils throughout Georgia, most critically in Tbilisi. Rather than having district-based elections, which would have allowed some candidates not affiliated with the UNM, but popular in their community, to get elected, or having a straight party list system, which would translate votes more or less directly into seats, the new electoral system, passed by parliament in spring 2006, called for a mixed system for electing the Tbilisi city council.

According to the new system, the Tbilisi city council would be drawn partly from a party list and partly from a single vote multi-member system, where the party winning a plurality of votes in a large area of Tbilisi would get all the seats, usually 2–3, in that district. This allowed the UNM to run prominent citywide figures in each large district and restrict the influence of popular local figures. The UNM defended this system by asserting that it was the best of both systems, but few outside the party saw it this way. The result of this manipulation was that while the UNM only got 67 percent of the vote in Tbilisi, it ended up with 92 percent of the seats.

Another key element of the new election law was that it did not call for direct election of the mayor of Tbilisi. This had been a concrete demand of the opposition, including Saakashvili himself, during the months and years preceding the Rose Revolution, but one the new government did not seem to consider seriously. Instead, the election law called for the mayor to be selected by and from the newly elected council members. The mayor of Tbilisi is an extremely visible and important position; between 35 and 50 percent of Georgia's population live in this cultural, political, and economic capital. Not only would a directly elected mayor be a key policy maker, but it would be a visible position from which a politician could build a strong electoral base for a presidential campaign. The UNM strategy, it must be presumed, was that an opposition candidate with high popularity and political skill could win a direct election but would not be able to put a party together and organize well enough to compete under the new system. Potential candidates who might have run for mayor had there been direct elections included former foreign minister Salome Zurabishvili and the late media tycoon Badri Paterkatsishvili.

The government, again in a legal but not altogether democratic way, used the timing of the local elections to their advantage. After suggesting all year that the election would be held in early December, the government announced on August 26 that the election would be held in early October. This announcement came late at night precisely forty days, the legal minimum for announcing a date, before the proposed October 5 date for the election. Assigning a date in early October caught the opposition off guard, making it more difficult for them to plan their campaigns and other preelection activities. There was not sufficient time for ODIHR to field a full election monitoring mission for the local elections. The elections also were timed to coincide with a period of high tensions with Russia so that the NM could take advantage of a rally-around-the-flag-effect.

Shortly after the local elections, Saakashvili's government turned their attention to the next round of national elections, as parliamentary elections were due in 2008 with presidential elections due in 2009. The government again altered the constitution so that the president and parliament would be elected together. This was presented as a way of allowing the voters a clearer way to determine a course for Georgia and deliver a more unambiguous judgment regarding the government. However, most observers both inside and outside Georgia saw it as an attempt to help UNM parliamentary candidates by allowing them to ride a bit on Saakashvili's electoral coattails, because, as polls consistently showed,

Saakashvili is more popular than the parliament or any of its members. The government also began exploring the electoral system for electing the new parliament. There has been a fair amount of European pressure to lower the threshold for getting into parliament from 7 percent, which was initially resisted by the Georgian government. After the demonstrations of November 2007 and the subsequent turmoil in Georgia, the government finally agreed to lower the threshold to 5 percent for the May 2008 parliamentary elections.

These types of manipulations, which are not election fraud but not precisely fair democratic practices, can be particularly harmful in a democratizing country. Constantly changing the rules of the election makes it hard for opposition parties and candidates to create a long-term strategy and also created a sense that elections are still tools for the government to manipulate rather than a fair way to choose the country's leadership. Even if the government's motives are to be taken at face value, which is not obviously the case, it is making the mistake of making the perfect the enemy of the good. There is no perfect electoral system, as has been shown by countless scholars.[14] It would be far more helpful to Georgia's democratic development for the government to stay with a simple and reasonably fair system.

The decision to push through constitutional changes and explore further manipulation of the electoral system was one of the primary factors contributing to the demonstrations of November 2007, which led to the government's most flagrant antidemocratic behavior. Interestingly, once the dust had settled somewhat after the violent repression of these demonstrations, Saakashvili's response was to continue to play electoral games by calling for snap elections in an environment where free and fair elections were impossible.

Importantly, since those demonstrations elections in Georgia can no longer be classified so neatly as free, fair, and noncompetitive. The January 2008 presidential election was the most competitive ever. President Saakashvili only received 53.6 percent of the vote and barely passed the 50 percent mark needed to avoid a runoff. Opposition coalition candidate Levan Gachechiladze finished a strong second with 25.6 percent of the vote while other minor candidates including Gamkrelidze and Natalashvili split the remaining votes.

These elections were also not viewed as unambiguously positive by international or domestic audiences. The ODIHR report was lukewarm at best:

In its Statement of Preliminary Findings and Conclusions of 6 January, the IEOM [International Election Observation Mission] stated that while the election was in essence consistent with most OSCE and Council of Europe commitments and standards for democratic elections, it also revealed significant challenges which need to be addressed urgently. Although this election represented the first genuinely competitive post-independence presidential election, shortcomings were noted. The campaign was overshadowed by widespread allegations of intimidation and pressure, among others on public-sector employees and opposition activists, some of which were verified by the OSCE/ODIHR EOM. The distinction between State activities and the campaign of the ruling United National Movement [UNM] party candidate, Mr. Mikheil Saakashvili, was blurred. In addition, as referenced in a Post-Election Interim Report issued by the OSCE/ODIHR on 18 January, other aspects of the election process, notably vote count and tabulation procedures, as well as the post-election complaints and appeals process, further presented serious challenges to the fulfillment of some OSCE commitments.

The election was followed by demonstrations in Tbilisi as the opposition, not without evidence, viewed Saakashvili as relying on fraud to get over 50 percent and avoid a runoff. The May 2008 elections, which had not yet occurred when this was written, promised to be similarly competitive, raising the same questions about the degree to which they would be free and fair.

One reason these electoral manipulations are so surprising is that they not only are somehow undemocratic, but are so politically unnecessary for Saakashvili and his party. The government is quite popular and would have won the local election system in Tbilisi and nationally with almost any electoral system. Losing a few seats in the local legislatures, or even the national parliament, would not significantly hurt the government. It would more likely show its strength, as even if the playing field were uneven in favor of the opposition, the government would still win. The failure of the government to recognize this demonstrates that democracy, in its view, takes a back seat to the need to continue to move forward with their program with as few impediments as possible.

The government treatment of the opposition has also raised disturbing concerns regarding the direction of democratization more broadly in Georgia. The tone of political discourse is often quite personal on both sides. However because of the asymmetry of power, the government treatment of the opposition is more damaging to the country's fragile democratic balance. Moreover, the government has frequently attacked the motives and affiliations of the opposition. Opponents have, for example, been attacked as being Russian operatives.[15] This charge sticks easily and destroys the credibility of the accused.

In another case, in March 2006 media tycoon Badri Paterkatsishvili gave a speech in which he asserted that his television station, Imedi, was the only one sufficiently independent to do quality investigative journalism looking into the death of Sandro Girgvliani, a young bank employee who was killed following an altercation with the wife of the minister of the interior. Girgvliani's death, in which the Ministry of the Interior had been rumored to be involved, had led to several resignations within the Ministry, but not of the minister himself, longtime Saakashvili supporter Vano Merabishvili. Paterkatsishvili's assertion was far from controversial as it was apparent that his station had been ahead of the rest of the media in the investigation of Girgvliaini's death.

Patarkatsishvili's speech immediately drew a stinging rebuke from the government, as MP Giga Bokeria attacked Patarkatsishvili personally. In addition to attacking his integrity and motives, Bokeria claimed that Patarkatsishvili was very angry at the government for thwarting his efforts to "establish himself as the Don Corleone of Georgian business."[16] Bokeria also alluded to Patarkatsishvili's history in Russia:

It appears that he [Patarkatsishvili] cannot forget his past—Russia during [ex-President Boris] Yeltsin's presidency, when he and his friends controlled everything—the authorities, business and seized huge amounts of property. However, present-day Georgia is not Yeltsin's Russia. . . . Mr. Patarkatsishvili can be engaged in politics, business—but he will not be able to blackmail the authorities through his own television or influence.

Attacking Patarkatsishvili, who is alleged to have been linked to criminal activity in Russia, but is a law-abiding, well-liked, and important figure in Georgia, in such a way made the government seem defensive and hostile, but it also continued to send the message that the government would not take criticism well. Moreover, Bokeria's suggestion that Patarkatsishvili was trying to blackmail the government was strange and unfounded. This example is one of many cases of remarks critical of the government being met with disproportionately strong attacks.

Needless to say, the events of November 2007 demonstrated very clearly the government's lack of tolerance for any opposition. The violent crackdown and accusations of being Russian operatives leveled against most opponents was further evidence. Paterkatsishvili himself was a key player, as he openly funded the demonstrations and made public statements that he would seek to bring down the government. Not surprisingly, the response was to call him a Russian operative.

Saakashvili's government remains far more politically sophisticated, experienced, and savvy than any other political force in Georgia. This disparity has helped it to remain the dominant political force, while deflecting and avoiding criticism. The government has demonstrated an ability to use this advantage to manipulate the political and electoral rules, set the political and media agenda, frame international perceptions, and undermine the opposition.

Political skills and savvy were among the key factors in the new regime's ascendance to power. However, these advantages must be wielded differently by a governing party in a democratizing country than by an opposition party in a stagnant semidemocratic country. This difficult distinction seems to be lost on the government as it has continued the aggressive, no holds barred approach which served so well in 2002–3.

Some of the issues touched on above, such as those concerning the media, could be ameliorated through relatively straightforward government action. The government can, without much difficulty, create a climate of free media by encouraging debate, allowing media and political criticism of the government to go without a response, and exerting less influence over the media. Similarly, the government could revisit some of Georgia's constitutional arrangements to create more balance between the legislature and the executive and limit the power of the president.

Georgia's government has not done these things. Nor has Saakashvili's administration sought to create strong and clear barriers between party and state, which might begin to break down that problem. The question why this has not happened is critical to understanding both the future of Georgia and the nature of American democracy promotion policy.

The answer is not that Georgia's new government is essentially the old government with a few different faces, nor is it that the problems are so entrenched that no government can change them. The success of the post-Rose Revolution government in both instituting fair elections and reducing government corruption demonstrates this. The reality is somewhat less dramatic. While there is some commitment to democracy in Georgia, one the government stresses, particularly when speaking with Western media and governments, it is not a top priority for the new government. Given all the problems Saakashvili inherited from the Shevardnadze regime, it is not surprising that he would have competing priorities.

President Saakashvili

It is impossible to disaggregate Georgia's current efforts toward democratization from the person of Mikheil Saakashvili. He is more than just Georgia's president, elected in January 2004 with 96 percent of the vote in an election broadly seen as free and fair. Saakashvili was the unquestioned leader of the Rose Revolution. His party polled higher than any other party in the flawed elections of 2003 that Shevardnadze tried to steal. It was he who gave the Rose Revolution both its symbol and its name; and he who burst into parliament on November 22 and dramatically drank the cold unfinished tea, left by Shevardnadze when hustled out of the room, in a primal and unambiguous gesture of triumph.

In the international setting, Saakashvili's fluency in English and French, Ivy League credentials, personal charm, humor, courage, intelligence, and passion have made him the most visible and engaging reformer in the former Soviet Union. While Ukraine may have eclipsed Georgia in the eyes of some, Saakashvili has not been eclipsed by Ukrainian president Viktor Yushchenko. Therefore, understanding Saakashvili's goals and actions is central to understanding the priorities and goals of Georgia's reform government.

Even a cursory look at Saakashvili's presidency demonstrates that he has been a state builder first and a democrat second. At this moment, Georgia needs both democracy and a modern state, and Saakashvili has made substantial steps with regards to the former. Ousting Ajaran strongman Aslan Abashidze and bringing Ajara back under the authority of Georgia's government in Tbilisi, and working, albeit with less success so far, to do the same in Abkhazia and South Ossetia, have helped create a stronger and more able Georgian state. Under Shevardnadze, all three regions were essentially written off as lost to Tbilisi. Saakashvili's efforts to create a strong central government able to act decisively and with far less corruption than before in areas such as building infrastructure, creating educational standards, and economic development have also helped strengthen the Georgian state.

Domestically, Saakashvili often cultivates a comparison between himself and David the Builder,[17] who is viewed as the greatest of Georgian kings and the unifier and builder of the Georgian nation. Saakashvili has also, for a foreign audience, said that his role models were Ben Gurion, Ataturk, and De Gaulle.[18] His choice of people famous for building modern states rather than for being democrats is very revealing. Saakashvili could have mentioned Havel, Walesa, Jefferson, or others who are viewed as important figures in the history of democracy. Instead, he expressed his preference for state builders.

The somewhat dramatic changes to the Georgian constitution described above, which were pushed through by Saakashvili and his supporters shortly after he took office, also reveal much about the priorities of the new Georgian government and its president. It is not easy to determine whether the goal of constitutional reform was to weaken the parliament and its leader, Nino Burjanadze, while giving more power to the president and prime minister, but that was undeniably its effect. Politics notwithstanding, the constitutional changes of February 2004 reveal a clear preference for state building over democratizing. Concentrating power in the executive, creating an appointed prime minister, weakening the legislature are what governments do when they want to get things done more quickly and efficiently, not when they want to democratize.

Saakashvili's presidency has been marked by the president's impatience. In some respects, this impatience has served Saakashvili, and Georgia, well. Saakashvili is indeed impatient by temperament. He has been a young man in a hurry since leaving his law career in New York to return to Georgia in 1995. His impatience with the corruption and dishonesty of Shevardnadze's regime led him to be an aggressively reform oriented MP and justice minister. His unwillingness to wait for the presidential elections scheduled for 2005 led him not to accept the stolen 2003 parliamentary elections, but to demand fairness for his party and the Georgian people.

As president, Saakashvili's impatient temperament has been buoyed by the reality that the clock has always been ticking for his reform agenda. He has had to show results quickly to keep the people from being disillusioned with the revolution and the new government. Moreover, it has been good policy to attempt reforms in numerous fields at the same time and to demand the government agencies respond quickly so as to send the unequivocal message that there is a new era. There is a window in which these reforms need to be done in order for Georgia to be able to show the world that the Rose Revolution has truly been a turning point in the country's history, so quick decisive reforms have been very helpful.

This is also true, however, with regard to democracy. The window for meaningful democratic reform is also relatively small. It is critical for the government to make these democratic advances before the new leaders grow accustomed to a style of governance that is undemocratic in nature. If, for example, cabinet ministers, government bureaucrats, and others grow accustomed to not always seeking parliamentary approval or public input, or if election officials and strategists understand that some electoral corners can be cut, it will be very hard to retrain them to do things more democratically when the government refocuses on reforms in this area. Similarly, if government officials get in the habit of responding inappropriately harshly to dissident voices in civil society and the media and forcefully breaking up demonstrations, this will also prove a difficult habit to break. It is unfortunate that the impatience that serves Saakashvili and his government so well in other reforms areas, and which would be such a strong asset in efforts to consolidate democracy, seems to be absent in this sector.

Why the Rose Revolution?

The question of the priorities of Saakashvili and his government is part of the broader question of what the Rose Revolution was for. This is not a simple question to answer because the Rose Revolution meant, and continues to mean, different things for different people. The governments of the United States, European countries, and Russia, as well as the new Georgian leadership, opposition, and various segments of the Georgian population all have different interpretations of the Rose Revolutions. In this regard, it was something of an international political Rorschach test.

To the American government, the Rose Revolution meant that Georgia was looking westward, embracing democracy and was willing to cooperate with the U.S. on numerous foreign policy goals. One example is the comments by then deputy secretary of state Richard Armitage on May 17, 2004: "The people of Georgia ultimately prevailed in their peaceful desire for democracy. And because of our solid diplomacy, they see America as a friend in that endeavor."[19] For Europe, it meant that the Georgians were taking another step toward Europe, and issues of European expansion and European borders would need to be reexamined. Many Russians have interpreted the Rose Revolution as an American CIA plot to make sure that pro-American leaders get into power and to further encircle Russia with American allies.

In Georgia, the interpretations were different still. Among ordinary Georgians, expectations were quite high in the months immediately following the Rose Revolution. The end of the Shevardnadze era was greeted with almost universal excitement as people believed their country was going to have a new beginning. Expectations were varied and broad, but most were centered around economic growth, jobs, and a reduction of poverty. People believed that the new government would be able to get the country running again.

Thus, for most Georgians expectations focused on economic rather than political issues. Although the origins and direction of the Rose Revolution itself were very political in nature, oriented around fair elections and democratic change, for many ordinary citizens these demands were peripheral to their primary interest in change, finally getting rid of Shevardnadze and improving their economic lot.

Interestingly, in the years following the Rose Revolution, the new government, particularly Saakashvili himself, has done little to reduce these expectations. On the contrary, Saakashvili's rhetoric has been dramatic, promising rapid change in all sectors, asserting that Georgia has genuinely turned a corner and has become a functioning democratic state. Saakashvili's comments on Georgian Independence Day (May 26), 2004 show his high expectations for the country and his administration.

Today we witness the first results of our beliefs. Four months ago skeptical people prevailed among us as well as among those residing abroad. Pessimists were predicting that we would fail from the very first moment; they could not imagine that it was possible to improve the situation in Georgia. But still, today I am standing in front of you. Georgia is on its right way and no one can deny it. Today, our people are becoming stronger. Our faith instead of diminishing becomes even stronger. Today our beliefs stand on actual achievements.

Saakashvili has promised rapid and concrete improvements in the lives of ordinary Georgians. This strategy of keeping expectations high, rather than trying to manage expectations so that voters are less likely to be disappointed at the pace of change, is potentially explosive for the government. This discrepancy between rhetoric and reality was one of the reasons so many demonstrators came to the streets to protest against the government in November of 2007.

The new Georgian government has interpreted the Rose Revolution as a broad mandate to do whatever they think is best for Georgia. This mandate has been reaffirmed, in their view, by the overwhelming victory at the polls for Saakashvili in his bid for the presidency in January of 2004, as well as resounding victories for his party in the redo of the parliamentary election in March of 2004, the Ajaran election in June of that year and the local elections held throughout Georgia in October of 2006. These elections have demonstrated the Saakashvili and his government were popular and enjoyed the support of much of the Georgian population. Clearly, the far smaller margin of victory in 2008 weakened the mandate of Saakashvili and his government.

It is still important, nonetheless, to look closely at how the government has interpreted this mandate, and what they have done with it. As mentioned above, the government has interpreted this mandate to mean that they are empowered to decide what is best for Georgia and to implement those ideas. To a substantial extent, the policy decisions made by Saakashvili's government are quite reasonable. Their priorities have included rebuilding the country's destroyed infrastructure, seeking foreign investment, reducing corruption at high and low levels of government, and reforming the education system so that degrees are no longer simply bought and sold by professors and students. The new government has made sure that foreign assistance is no longer stolen and has sought to pass a broad reformist agenda. The reform agenda includes passing a body of legislation aimed at making Georgia a more appealing place for foreign investors.

Based on these actions, it seems as if the government has interpreted their mandate to be one of modernizing Georgia and building up the Georgian state. However, reforming education and passing laws to make the business climate better have little bearing on ordinary Georgians still struggling economically. The combination of high expectations and a program which, while clearly improving conditions and governance in Georgia, has yet to have a substantial enough impact on the lives of many ordinary Georgians, is a dangerous one for Georgia's government.

The government has been successful in ameliorating some of this potential source of opposition and disappointment because they have delivered on some promises such as improved infrastructure and less corruption and because they have stressed a number of international, territorial and ethnic issues as well. Saakashvili's government has placed a strong emphasis on resolving frozen conflicts and restoring Georgian sovereignty to the areas lost to the country during the Shevardnadze years, and sees these issues as a core part of their mandate. It is important to recognize that while these goals have created a great deal of international controversy for Georgia, and have placed great stress on their relationships with Russia, they are extremely popular in Georgia.

The issue of "territorial integrity," as it is known in Georgia, is of crucial import to many Georgians. Although the issue was in no way central to the politics or demands of the Rose Revolution, voters in Georgia strongly support the new government in its efforts to restore Georgia's territorial integrity.[20] Prioritizing this issue has been a way for the government to increase support whenever it is needed. The heated rhetoric of Saakashvili and others in the government has almost always met with enormous support from the electorate. Saakashvili's appeal to the nationalist sentiments of the Georgian people in this regard has caused critics to compare him to Zviad Gamsakurdia. While this criticism is largely unfair, the similar appeal to national sentiment that distracts from more difficult economic realities is certainly accurate.

It is no coincidence that during the weeks preceding the local elections of October 2006, which for months had been described as the first true test of the popularity of Saakashvili and his government, tensions with Russia, specifically around Abkhazia and South Ossetia, were as high as they had ever been. After the elections, in which Saakashvili's party scored a resounding victory, there was something of deescalation, as statements of the Georgian government became notably calmer. As noted earlier, the government moved the date for the local election forward from early December to early October, presumably to take advantage of the period of highest tension between Georgia and Russia.

Georgia's relationship with Russia has been one of the most pressing concerns of the new government. It has come to dominate politics and policy in Georgia. The larger picture surrounding this issue has been addressed elsewhere.[21] For Georgia, the Russian threat seems real and powerful. Saakashvili believes that the best way for Georgia to confront this threat is an accelerated program of reform and state building, because without a strong Georgian state, demands regarding Abkhazia and South Ossetia are laughable. It is too early to tell whether this is another case where Saakashvili's natural impatience will again dovetail nicely with the country's needs.

Focusing on the issue of territorial integrity has been a way for the government to subtly use nationalism to reduce demands for more jobs and economic growth. Snyder and Mansfield (2005) describe how elected governments in democratizing countries often use nationalist appeals and even start wars to consolidate their power. This is somewhat applicable to Saakashvili, but in this case the Russian threat to the Georgian state is very real. The emphasis on territorial integrity is more than just a political ploy by the government. It is consistent with the government's state building goals because the government's view is that a strong Georgian state cannot exist if it only has sovereignty over about 80 percent of the country. It is also something that for many Georgians is far more important than, for example, democracy. The government's tendency to attribute opposition political behavior to various Russian plots is, of course, considerably more disturbing.

It is reasonably apparent from both the actions of the government as well as some of the more honest public statements of its leadership that democratization is not one of its core goals. Moreover, while concern in Georgia over jobs and the economic situation remain quite high, among the general population there is mixed evidence that the pace of democratization is a great concern. While this issue is important to many political and civic elites, it is not widespread throughout society. In short, the demand for democratization remains relatively low so the government does not have much real pressure to make it a priority.

Demands for democratization that might have come from the international community have not been very strong either. This is partly because elections, the most visible component of democracy, have been much better under the new government. Moreover, the government's statements and presentations toward the West have been very good, consistently sending the message that it is democratizing Georgia. This image was somewhat compromised in November 2007, but the longer term effect of the government's actions then are not yet clear. Most important, the government has been successful in blurring the issues of reform and democratization.[22] It is not clear to what extent this is deliberate, but it has had a strong impact.

For many, reform and democratization are interchangeable, but while the two notions are quite similar, they are not the same thing. The Georgian government has sought to pass laws to improve the business climate, strengthen the rule of law, make education and public security policies more rational and fair, and for numerous other important reforms. But it has generally done this in a way that is not participatory, is often very fast, and leaves little room for public debate. As I have shown above, democracy has often been sacrificed to the notion of expedience in all areas, including, perhaps ironically, political reforms. Thus, Georgia's reform agenda has been pushed through by an elected government but is not really the product of deliberation, participation, or citizen input.

For the Georgian government, then, the Rose Revolution has been largely for rebuilding the Georgian state, reasserting Georgian sovereignty over areas lost during the early years of independence, and reforming the government. Thus far, the government has been successful in two of these areas, while restoring territorial integrity remains a vexing problem. Democracy, it seems, may only be an important goal of the Rose Revolution for a handful of foreign and domestic elites.

Nonetheless, among foreign observers and policy makers the Rose Revolution has generally, including in this work, been discussed and analyzed in the context of democracy and democratization. This discrepancy underscores the problems with U.S. policy toward Georgia since the Rose Revolution. Previously, Georgia was governed by a semi-democratic, corrupt, and very unpopular government with which most of the rest of the world had finally lost patience and hope. Since the Rose Revolution, Georgia has been governed by a far less corrupt and well liked government with a questionable commitment to democratization. While the U.S. and Europe still view the Rose Revolution as a demand for democratization in Georgia, that has never been the interpretation of Saakashvili's government.

The New Georgian Regime

As discussed in Chapter 2, understanding the nature of the Shevardnadze regime provides valuable context for studying the Rose Revolution. More simply, it is useful to understand with some nuance from what Georgia under Saakashvili's leadership has been transitioning. Similarly, examining the new Georgian regime through the lens of recent work on regime types helps us understand into what the new Georgia has transitioned, or is transitioning.

Some in both the Georgian and American governments would view Georgia as a consolidated democratic regime. This has certainly been the official view of the Bush administration, which has held Georgia up as a beacon of democracy in the post-Soviet region. However, even the most cursory, and most friendly, look at political reality demonstrates that democracy in Georgia today is a work in progress.

Saakashvili's critics, primarily in Russia, but also in Georgia and elsewhere, would describe the regime as dictatorial, populist, or Peronist. Russian hatred for Saakashvili is intense and at times almost palpable.

Dmitry Sedov, writing for the online pro-government Russian magazine *Strategic Culture Foundation*, argues that "Saakashvili's inability to conduct reasonable politics and his inclination to armed violence make the present regime in Georgia extremely vulnerable. Saakashvili's Americanized and robotized guards will not rescue him in case one day hungry masses storm his residence."[23] Responding to the arrest of several Russians in Georgia accused of spying, Russian president Putin stated that "It is a sign of the legacy of Lavrenti Pavlovich Beria's policy," comparing Saakashvili to Stalin's vicious KGB chief who, like Stalin, was Georgian.[24]

The strongest domestic critics have proven no less colorful in their critiques of the new government. After the local elections of October 2006, Labor Party leader Shalva Natelashvili offered that "Saakashvili has proved once again that he is a pathological, bloody dictator, whose leadership [depends] solely on unquestioning support from President Bush."[25]

In reality, Saakashvili, like his predecessor, presides over a regime that is somewhere in the large gray area between democracy and authoritarianism. However, within this gray area, Georgia has moved quite a bit in the years since the Rose Revolution. For example, while Shevardnadze's Georgia was something of a hybrid between Carothers's (2002) "feckless pluralism" and "dominant power politics" models, Georgia under Saakashvili looks much more like the latter model. Although elections still occur in Georgia, there is less political freedom and less involvement by those outside of the ruling party, making the feckless pluralism description seem less apt for today's Georgia. Carothers's "deep seated intolerance for anything more than a limited opposition" and the lack of credibility enjoyed by opposition parties, which characterize dominant power politics, fit Saakashvili's Georgia much better than pre-Rose Revolution Georgia.

The electoral authoritarianism model clearly does not apply to Saakashvili's Georgia because elections are not stolen under the new government. Schedler (2006) describes manipulating and stealing elections as a key component of electoral authoritarian regimes. Elections in Georgia are manipulated, but not stolen. Some critics have suggested that Saakashvili behaves like an elected dictator, but while he does at times overstep the boundaries of his office, he and his party do not steal elections. The test for this model will come when the popularity of the UNM declines, a process that seems to have begun but not yet been completed in the two 2008 elections, because until that time the ruling party has not needed to steal elections to win them.

Georgia under Saakashvili does not seem to be a competitive authoritarian regime, as described by Levitsky and Way either. While there are abuses under Saakashvili, violation of the basic rules of democracy is not widespread as elections are reasonably fair and rule of law is considerably stronger than it was under Shevardnadze. Nonetheless, Levitsky and Way categorize Saakashvili's regime as competitive authoritarian accusing Saakashvili of "harass[ing] antigovernmental media and manipulate[ing] the March 2004 parliamentary elections."[26] This categorization seems somewhat hasty and overstated. The manipulations in the March 2004 elections were relatively minor as the UNM was extremely popular at that time. This description may fit the 2008 election cycle better.

Ottaway's (2002) category of semi-authoritarian regimes matches Georgia somewhat because Georgia today does have some "authoritarian traits" such as lack of tolerance for opposition, restricted media freedom and a tendency to push legislation through very quickly as power is centralized in the person and institution of the presidency. However, this category seems something of a stretch because Georgia today is not an authoritarian regime comparable to Azerbaijan, Egypt or any of the other examples of semi-authoritarian regimes which Ottaway presents.

The transition paradigm as Carothers (2002) describes it has been much maligned in the transition literature, but it provides a framework for understanding Saakashvili's Georgia which is at least as valuable as some of the others.[27] It is not possible to know in what direction Georgian democracy will move in the future, but the events of November 2003–January 2004 look a great deal like democratic breakthrough. A fraudulent election mobilized thousands of people, forcing the corrupt regime to collapse and ushering in a new democratically elected, reform oriented government. The advance of democracy during this period has been uneven and slow, but it is certainly possible that this is difficult period of consolidation rather than a move toward a different regime type entirely.

Saakashvili's regime, at this time, shows indications of being both semidemocratic and semi-authoritarian. However, it is very different mix of these two regimes than its predecessor. Elections are, for the most part, fair, corruption has been substantially reduced and rule of law seems to be slowly gaining strength. However, there are almost no voices in government other than those of the governing party, a weaker parliament and less of a sense of associational and media freedoms. Additionally, there seems to be little chance of an alternation of power in the immediately foreseeable future.

Thus, to some extent Saakashvili's regime is a mirror image of Shevardnadze's. If, as argued in Chapter 2, the central feature of Shevardnadze's regime was weakness, the central feature of Saakashvili's regime is strength. The regime's commitment to building the Georgian state is consistent with this. It is also reflected in the approach to the issue of territorial integrity, which the government also sees as central to its mission. However, this sense of strength spills over into intolerance for opposition and a strong relationship between the state and the governing party which is not healthy for democracy.

It will be easier and more fruitful to define the new Georgian regime as more time goes by. If the regime is indeed moving through the transition paradigm, the ruling party will allow more opposition voices, restrictions on media will fall away, associational life will return to its previous levels, and other reforms will continue. If the regime is moving away from democracy, electoral manipulations will continue and perhaps bleed over into more clear cases of fraud, restrictions on media and other freedoms will increase, and the relationship between state and party will become stronger.

Following the ongoing democratic developments in Georgia will likely yield a mixed picture of democracy there, as it has so far. However, there will be some indications and potential benchmarks in the upcoming years which will be somewhat indicative of the direction of Georgian democracy. Some of these will involve electoral politics.

In the May 2008 elections the UNM maintained its position as the largest block in parliament. However, while the UNM was viewed as the heavy favorite to win the parliamentary elections, these elections bacame a missed opportunity for far more substantial opposition presence in the parliament and to ensure that these voices have more impact on policy and are more able to act as a check on the governing party.

Nonetheless, the temptation to manipulate the election to increase the UNM margin is already quite strong and will likely get stronger as the election approaches. I have already described how shortly after the 2006 local elections the UNM began to float the idea of altering the schedule so that parliamentary election and presidential elections would be held at the same time in 2008. By early December 2006, these and other amendments had been approved by the parliament in a first but not final reading; they were finalized shortly afterward with little real debate at any stage. Of course, the snap presidential elections in January 2008 meant that the parliamentary and presidential elections would not occur simultaneously.

Similarly, future efforts to change the electoral system, or structure of parliament, particularly if it is done unilaterally by the UNM or during the period immediately before an election, will likely be perceived, probably with good reason, as efforts to manipulate the election in favor of the UNM. This is not to say that the electoral system and structure of parliament must remain the same. Many in Georgia agree that the parliament should be reduced in number from its currently 150 members, which will occur with the next parliament. Others, both inside and outside the UNM, believe that the current structure of parliament is not the right one. Advocates for lowering the threshold. introducing a second chamber, and other reforms believe that changing the structure is necessary. However, this process must be done in an inclusive and democratic manner, not the way previous changes to the election law and even the constitution under this current regime has occurred in recent years.

Linz and Stepan (1996) argue that one of the indicators of a successfully consolidated democracy is when the ruling party associated with the democratic breakthrough finally loses an election. A further indicator is when the first democratically elected leader leaves office through a smooth transition. In other words, when the Havels, Mandelas, or Walesas leave office is at least as important a step for democratization as when they come into office. The same is true of Saakashvili.

Saakashvili will serve at least one more full term following his reelection in 2008. The question of what post-Saakashvili Georgia will look like, while still a few years off, is an intriguing one, particularly with regard to democratization.

If there are no further major disruptions, Saakashvili's second and final term in office will expire in 2013 when he will be only forty-five years old. A smooth transition from Saakashvili to the next president will be absolutely essential for the further advance of democracy in Georgia. By simply leaving office and only remaining involved in Georgian politics as an elder statesman, albeit a very young one, Saakashvili would be doing a tremendous service to his country.

Should Saakashvili pursue possible ways to extend his tenure and his dominant role in Georgian politics, it will be a clear signal that his regime is better understood as a hyphenated authoritarian, rather than hyphenated democratic regime.[28] This will be a test for Saakashvili because his personal ambition and his country's democratic future will, for the first time, be at odds with each other. The temptation to alter the constitution, remain the power behind the new president, or otherwise tamper with the transition may be a strong one. It will be exacerbated by Saakashvili's extreme youth and the real possibility that even in 2013 he will still be a popular president.

If Saakashvili does make it clear that he will not seek to remain at the center of power in Georgia after his second term, this decision will create a very complex political scenario both inside and outside Georgia's governing party. It is far too early to speculate as to Saakashvili's eventual successor, but it is not hard to imagine that there will be a great deal of competition within the governing party that could lead to fracturing that party. It is also likely that a number of politicians outside the UNM will seek the presidency. The resolution of all this will reveal a great deal about the direction of the regime and will have to be watched closely in upcoming years.

Chapter 6
The U.S. Role in the Rose Revolution

Democratic consolidation in Georgia has proved difficult, and substantial challenges remain. Additionally, the government of Georgia, while making strong advances in fighting corruption and reforming governance, has not made democracy a priority or seen it as a central part of its electoral mandate. Nonetheless, the Rose Revolution is still understood by many, not altogether inaccurately, as an important breakthrough for democracy. Additionally, because it has been highlighted as one of the Bush administration's most significant success stories in foreign policy generally and in democracy promotion in particular, the Rose Revolution has also become an important chapter in the story of American democracy assistance.

The precise role of the U.S. in the Rose Revolution has been a subject of some controversy and dispute. Opponents of democracy throughout the former Soviet Union have, in many cases, viewed it as an American plot. In its extreme form, this view asserts that Saakashvili was an American creation who was trained in the U.S. and sent back to Georgia with directions to overthrow the Shevardnadze regime. Proponents of this view also assert that American democracy promotion organizations not only worked closely with Saakashvili and his supporters but guided their efforts and pushed them to demand Shevardnadze's resignation.

These views are, of course, nonsense. But they are nonetheless widespread not only in Russia and other parts of the former Soviet Union but increasingly among critics of U.S. foreign policy in the West as well. One of the more moderate and scholarly sounding examples of this perception comes from Gerald Sussman, who writes, "Clearly, the White House's first choice to replace Shevardnadze was Saakashvili, a George Washington University and Columbia University law school graduate. The United States supplied his campaign with pollsters, strategists, and consultants."[1] In a more extreme example, John Laughland of the UK-based British Helsinki Human Rights Group (BHHRG), an organization that is an apologist for numerous nondemocratic regimes, wrote shortly after Saakashvili's election that

There can be no doubt that the change of regime in Tbilisi is the result of U.S. secret service operations. The allegations that the elections on 2nd November were flawed was based exclusively on exit polls conducted by an American "polling agency"; the students activists from the "Kmara!" organisation are modeled on, and trained by, their U.S.-backed opposite numbers in Serbia, Otpor.[2]

Saakashvili is also aware of this perception regarding his ascendancy to power. He noted in 2006 that "We are perceived [by Russia] as some kind of forefront in a world-wide plot of the CIA and the Western world against [Russia's] greatness."[3]

Ironically, American efforts to claim credit for the Rose Revolution, while not comparable to the assertions made by Russians and others, also have occasionally overstated the role and intention of democracy assistance in Georgia preceding the Rose Revolution. During his confirmation hearings in front of the Senate Foreign Relations Committee in May 2005, U.S. ambassador to Georgia John Tefft summed up this view of the Rose Revolution by stating that Georgia "is a country at the forefront of the President's democracy agenda. It is an example of what transformational diplomacy can achieve." Tefft added that "Georgia is a tremendous success story."[4] While this statement is not altogether false it implies a much more central role for the U.S. in the Rose Revolution than was actually the case. Georgia was also highlighted in a short-lived USAID online magazine *Democracy Rising* in 2005 as one of several recent U.S.-supported democratic breakthroughs. The words of President Bush, throughout this work also show the extent to which the U.S. has sought to take credit for the Rose Revolution.

It is certainly true that a broad range of American programs, including explicit democracy assistance through various Georgian and American NGOs, support for civil society and election monitoring, as well as less overt democracy-oriented programs such as the Muskie Fellowship program and other exchange programs for students and young leaders, contributed to the conditions that made a democratic breakthrough in Georgia possible. However, to conclude the Rose Revolution was in any way the goal of these U.S.-supported programs would be inaccurate. In reality, the goals of American democracy assistance in Georgia were less extreme and less clear.[5] Moreover, they played a secondary and indirect role. The primary and most immediate causes of the Rose Revolution were clearly the weakness and unpopularity of Shevardnadze's regime, the strong and vibrant Georgian civil society, which was, perhaps ironically, facilitated by the relatively open and free nature of Shevardnadze's

Georgia, and Shevardnadze's unfortunate decision to try to steal one more election.

By 2003, U.S. policy toward Georgia was driven by several different considerations. First, Shevardnadze still enjoyed more support and respect than he deserved based on his disastrous tenure as president of Georgia. These feelings were strengthened by Shevardnadze's general support of the U.S. war on terror following September 11, and further buoyed by his support for the U.S.-led invasion of Iraq in March 2003. Since so few world leaders approved of the invasion, it is hard to imagine that the Bush administration would have contributed to or participated in the overthrow of one of them.

Second, there was a growing sense of "Georgia fatigue" in Washington. In the decade since Shevardnadze had returned to Georgia, total U.S. foreign assistance to Georgia had been an estimated $1 billion, and policy makers in Washington were beginning to think they had very little to show for it.[6] The Georgia economy, after a brief burst of growth in the mid-1990s, had stopped moving forward; corruption had not been curbed, and there was little indication of any democratic advances.

Third, U.S. views of the Georgian opposition were ambivalent. Shevardadze's democratic opposition was viewed as disunified and not quite ready for prime time. The rise in popularity of both Natalashvili and Saakashvili caused discomfort among many who viewed both these politicians as too impulsive and radical. Their strong critique of Shevardnadze did not always sit well with U.S. policy makers. Moreover, the days when Saakashvili or Zhvania could impress a U.S. senator or State Department official simply by speaking about Western democracy in English had also passed as Washington was increasingly looking for results.

It is worth stressing again, as mentioned in chapter three, that during the summer and fall of 2003, there was no consensus on the American or European side that Saakashvili was the best choice to lead Georgia after Shevardnadze's term as president expired in 2005. Many were put off by Saakashvili's aggressive and uncompromising style and refusal to be flexible in his opinions and positions and preferred the calmer more thoughtful approach of Zurab Zhvania or Nino Burjanadze. Saakashvili certainly had his supporters in the U.S. government, but there was a genuine diversity of views about him.

Thus, during the period leading up to the election, American views on both Shevardnadze and the opposition were mixed. There had been increasing disillusionment with the Shevardnadze regime, but rarely was the blame placed directly on Shevardnadze. It was clear that the reformers around Shevardnadze had mostly abandoned him; and many policy makers outside Georgia believed that Shevardnadze was receiving bad advice from his remaining aides and cronies. As people like Zhvania and Saakashvili left Shevardnadze's side, they were replaced by people like the corrupt state minister—and rumored drug addict Avtil Jorbenadze, the thuggish governor of Kvemo Kartli, Levan Mamaladze, and others who had a great deal to lose should the Georgian government fall into the hands of reformers who opposed corruption.[7]

Saakashvili and Zhvania still had their supporters in Washington and elsewhere, but the increasingly heated rhetoric from the Georgian opposition was off-putting to Americans who were not yet ready to concede that Shevardnadze was such a major part of the problem. The increasingly visible division with the opposition had a similar effect. Overall policy to Georgia was also driven by concerns about stability, as many feared that a change in government in Georgia would destabilize the country. Shevardnadze understood this and frequently alluded to the need to maintain stability in Georgia and his indispensability with regard to this goal. Moreover, as described earlier, the 2003 election was seen as a warm-up for 2005, when post-Shevardnadze Georgia would select a new leader, not as an opportunity to change Georgia's leadership.

Democracy Assistance in Pre-Rose Revolution Georgia

Overthrowing President Shevardnadze was not the goal of democracy assistance in Georgia during the decade preceding 2003. Georgia had, however, received more than its fair share of democracy assistance resources during that period. What then was the purpose of this support and how, if at all, did it contribute to the Rose Revolution?

In the decade preceding the Rose Revolution, Georgia was something of a prototype for American democracy assistance in the former Soviet Union. Shevardnadze's government seemed to be interested in democratizing and welcomed democracy assistance of virtually all kinds. Moreover, the legal and political environment in the country was such that civil society, media and civic education programs were allowed and not threatened by the government. For much of the late 1990s, Shevardnadze was viewed, by U.S. democracy assistance organizations as one of the leading reformers in the former Soviet Union.[8]

Democracy assistance to Georgia thus had a broad scope. There were programs to strengthen the parliament, support local government, encourage civil society, teach citizens how to advocate, push for women's equality in politics, work with political parties, increase the rule of law, and create free, competent, and responsible media. The biggest funder of these programs by far was the U.S., who financed these programs through contracts and grants to Georgian and international NGOs and a few U.S.-based private businesses.

By 2003, these programs had become a permanent part of Georgian society as well as its economy. A middle class, albeit a very small one, of English-speaking NGO professionals had emerged. These organizations also employed hundreds more Georgians as drivers, security guards and in other less skilled positions. During the late Shevardnadze years working for an NGO was one of the few ways a Georgian could make a decent and honest living. Additionally, a parallel class of foreigners quickly emerged. These people, charged with the implementation of U.S. funded programs, generally shared a commitment to trying to help strengthen democracy in Georgia, but had institutional loyalties and interests as well.

Democracy assistance in Georgia during the first few years of the 21st century was strong, entrenched and viewed as a fixture in the economic and political landscape of Georgia, but it was also, at times, confused and directionless. The goals of this assistance were largely incremental, aimed at raising the skill levels of a few city councils, pushing the government to conduct better elections, informing the parliament of the rules of legislative procedure, increasing the capacity of people outside to Tbilisi to advocate for their needs and the other similarly modest goals. Moreover, the degree to which Shevardnadze was an obstacle to reform never was fully internalized by many policy makers, outside of Georgia, who were involved in democracy assistance to Georgia.

There was no underlying goal driving democratization policy in Georgia as the elections approached, but rather a more general sense that development toward democracy would probably be slow, but needed to be in the right direction. This can be seen in a USAID strategy document calling for "New Program Directions and Emphasis," which was finalized less than four months before Shevardnadze's resignation:

Georgia in many ways is more evocative of a "developmental" state rather than a "transitional" one . . . institutions to be built "or rebuilt" from the ground up. . . . The realization that Western economic/political models cannot necessarily be grafted onto Georgian organs of economy and governance has resulted in a strategic, and tactical, reappraisal of at least some assumptions.[9]

The language is a little murky and bureaucratic, but it is relatively clear that the "new program direction" for which the U.S. was calling was one of caution and reduced expectations.

It seems, then, that the American pre-Rose Revolution strategy regarding democracy in Georgia and the post-Rose Revolution spin are in conflict with each other. Not surprisingly, the real story lies in between and requires a more nuanced look at the events in Georgia and the U.S. role in them. While it was not the intention of the United States or any of the organizations it supported in Georgia to overthrow the Shevardnadze regime or to make a revolution in Georgia, it is probably the case that without the ongoing efforts of the U.S. government to support democracy in Georgia, from shortly after the collapse of the Soviet Union in 1991 through 2003, the Rose Revolution would not have occurred in the form that it did. In this sense U.S. democracy assistance can be described as a necessary, but far from sufficient, condition which made it possible.

Ongoing U.S. programs such as financial and technical support for civil society organizations, media outlets, and even less politically oriented programs like the Muskie fellowship and other exchange programs, which had existed for years, contributed to the political environment in Georgia that made the Rose Revolution possible. Additionally, there were some explicitly political and more immediate programs during 2002 and 2003 that played roles in the events. However, this is not to say that American democracy assistance programs were the primary mover in the Rose Revolution. Had it not been for the other conditions in Georgia at the time, these American programs alone would not have added up to anything close to the Rose Revolution.

Almost all the major Georgian civil society leaders who made important contributions to the Rose Revolution—David Usupashvili from IRIS, Ghia Nodia from the Caucasus Institute for Peace, Democracy, and Development, Zurab Tchiabarashvili from ISFED, Kaha Lomaia from OSI, Giga Bokeria and Levan Ramishvili from the Liberty Institute, the leadership of Kmara, and others—worked for organizations funded by the U.S. government or by the U.S.-based OSI funded by George Soros. The years these activists spent building networks, developing expertise, and strengthening their political influence had been supported largely by the U.S. government. Washington had been seeking to create democrats and civil society, not revolutionaries, but as Shevardnadze's regime continued, this distinction became less possible or useful.

Funding for these civil society organizations was exclusively international, largely American, but with some European money as well. American taxpayer dollars in Georgia during this period, as in most other countries that receive democracy assistance, came from several different sources. USAID, through its democracy and governance programs, provided the most funding. NED also provided some direct funding to Georgian and international NGOs. Additionally, some American NGOs that received U.S. money funded Georgian NGOs through various subgrants. The most notable example of this was ISFED, the nonpartisan election monitoring group, which received almost all its funding for this election through subgrants from NDI. Moreover, although George Soros is a U.S. citizen and OSI is based in New York City, support from OSI is, in fact, quite different from support from the U.S. government.

Thus, the highly regarded Georgian civil society, with its free media, strong watchdog civic organizations, national and international networks, and strong communication and technical skills was, at least, partially, the result of many years, and many thousands of dollars of investments in Georgian civil society by the U.S. and Europe. Without this financial support from overseas, these civil society organizations would have had a very difficult time surviving in Georgia, since there was no government or private support available for NGOs. Clearly, individual Georgian civic activists such as those named earlier brought great dedication, commitment, and talent to their work, but Western resources made it possible for these contributions to be maximized. Support for civil society during the Shevardnadze regime included training activists in advocacy, strategic communication, organizing, planning, and fundraising. It also included directly funding groups to function as think tanks, election monitors and government watchdogs.

In addition to this work with civil society, exchange programs, including programs for high school, college, and graduate students, members of parliament, civic activists and other young leaders helped the Georgian government build a nucleus of leaders who spoke English, making it possible to communicate effectively with Western governments and seek support directly. Many of these people also understood Western political systems and strategies and developed a network of relationships with Western leaders and colleagues both inside and outside government. Importantly, many of the individuals involved were first brought into these programs through Shevardnadze and his CUG, but took these skills with them to the opposition when they split with Shevardnadze. All these skills became essential elements in the success of the Rose Revolution.

Other more explicitly political programs over the course of the decade preceding the Rose Revolution had an impact on Georgian politics as well. Years of support to the Georgian parliament helped the national legislature develop into an institution where multiple voices could be heard, issues could be addressed, and criticism of the government could be given some official imprimatur, even in the context of a national government strongly dominated by the executive branch. For many of these years, the reform wing of the CUG in parliament, led by Zurab Zhvania, played this role, but beginning in 2001 the opposition began to take on this role. The strength of the Georgian legislature during Shevardnadze's presidency is often overlooked, but it is a key difference between Georgia and many other former Soviet countries.

The parliament of Georgia had been the recipient of years of training, workshops, exchange programs, study tours, and advice from the U.S. and Europe, beginning in the 1990s. These programs sought to help the legislature establish rules of procedure, increase professionalism among parliament members and staff, and provide opportunities for citizens to have access to parliament. Zurab Zhvania, who led the parliament in 1996–2001, worked closely with American democracy assistance organizations, initially NDI, to build the parliament into a respectable and by, post-Soviet standards, serious legislative body. This international support also made it possible for the parliament to evolve politically as well. By 2003 parliament, while not a powerful legislative body or true partner in governance with the executive branch, had become a democratic space where issues could be debated, criticisms of the government could be made, and attention could be drawn to problems and potential solutions.

Members of parliament were able to use their status to gain access to colleagues in Europe and the U.S. and to build relationships that became extremely useful in 2003. Again, many of these people began their careers in the government party, but joined the opposition as Shevardnadze's regime became more incompetent and corrupt. Members of the parliament in general traveled widely, participated in exchange programs and began to convince contacts in the West about the depth of the problems of democratization in Shevardnadze's Georgia. Domestically, Georgians grew accustomed to lively parliamentary debate. Criticisms of the government were more powerful because they came from members of parliament who, in many cases, had been elected as part of Shevardnadze's party.

Further evidence of the import and relevance of the parliament in Georgia is the amount of emphasis both the government and opposition placed on the 2003 elections. These were parliamentary, not presidential elections, and Shevardnadze was not even on the ballot. Even if the opposition had been allowed to sit in the new parliament, it would have only had a limited amount of formal power. But the political value of the parliament was lost on nobody, and the import of these elections was understood by everybody involved in politics in Georgia.

Similarly, almost a decade of U.S. funding for domestic election monitoring created a context that accustomed Georgians to the evaluation of their elections by well-respected domestic observers such as ISFED, whose views by 2003 carried real weight with the media, civil society, and ordinary Georgians.

In the bigger picture, describing the Rose Revolution as a success story for U.S. foreign policy and democracy promotion is not inaccurate, but it is too vague and does not explain why, how, or to what degree

Georgia is a success story. This analysis should be refined to make it clear how U.S. assistance contributed to this democratic breakthrough and to what extent various aspects of this transition were augmented, underpinned, or strengthened by U.S. support. Moreover, the distinction between programs that have an impact and programs that are part of a strategy is critical. Clearly, the myriad U.S.-supported democracy assistance programs in Georgia had an impact, but this does not mean that U.S. government decision makers or NGOs involved in democracy assistance viewed this as part of a strategy for revolution in Georgia.

The most important contribution that U.S. democracy promotion made to this transition was not, contrary to what Russian propaganda and various conspiracy-oriented Westerners might think, to create a blueprint for the overthrow of the Shevardnadze regime. The present volume has shown that there was little incentive for the U.S. to do this, that the U.S. view of Shevardnadze and his eventual deposal was far from unambiguously negative, and that during November 2003, while demonstrators in Tbilisi were calling for Shevardnadze's resignation, the U.S. did not ask or put pressure on Shevardnadze to resign.

The primary U.S. contribution was to strengthen and support a new generation of leadership for the inevitable post-Shevardnadze period, which was, for the most part, democratically oriented and, yes, which viewed the U.S. and the West in general as the direction in which Georgia needed to move. This was the general theme around which the battery of varied U.S. programs discussed in this section centered, including study opportunities, financial and technical support for civil society organizations, support, training, and advice for political parties, and working to strengthen the Georgian parliament.

The success of the Rose Revolution, and the U.S. role in it, did not lie in bringing down Shevardnadze. This was easy, and perhaps inevitable, due primarily to the extreme weakness, corruption, and incompetence of that regime. The success, for both Georgia and the U.S., was that the people who finally overthrew Shevardnadze did it through largely democratic means, and saw democracy as the key to the success of post-Shevardnadze Georgia.

The 2003 Election and Democracy Assistance

Because the 2003 parliamentary elections were viewed by many outside Georgia as potentially extremely important, funding for election and democracy related programs created a number of programs that had substantial short-term effects on the political developments in Georgia after the election. In 2003, democracy assistance to Georgia continued to support civil society in the ways that it always had, but it took on other dimensions as well. A broad and multifaceted strategy was put in place that sought to reduce election fraud. It included support for the creation of a good voter list, a number of voter education campaigns aimed at explaining to voters the election law, election procedures, and their rights as voters, support for the reform of the election law itself, and a substantially larger grant to ISFED, which included money to implement a national PVT.[10] Most of these programs were supported by assistance from European and American governments.

Additionally, political pressure was put on the Shevardnadze government as high-level visitors from the U.S. and elsewhere arrived to try to persuade their old friend from the last days of the Cold War to conduct these elections fairly. American visitors included former Secretary of State James Baker as well as former Deputy Secretary of State Strobe Talbott, former chairman of the Joint Chiefs of Staff John Shalikashvili, and Senator John McCain.[11] Ultimately, none of these trips made a lasting impact on Shevardnadze. While it is impossible to know for certain why these old friends and partners were unable to make an impression on Shevardnadze, it can be speculated that Shevardnadze himself was perhaps not aware of the depth of his unpopularity and poor governance. Moreover, it was not clear what Shevardnadze could have done as the leader of Georgia's very weak state.

The U.S. also continued to fund political party development in Georgia in the months preceding the 2003 election. During this period political party work in Georgia took several different forms. Training in a variety of campaign-related topics continued as candidates and political operatives participated in dozens of workshops aimed at enhancing their skills in these areas. These workshops were similar to the work the U.S. had supported in Georgia for years, and were conducted with all major political parties in Georgia including Shevardnadze's CUG. This work had already had a significant impact on politics in Georgia. Several political parties, most notably the National Movement and the United Democrats, had demonstrated impressive campaign skills during the 2002 local elections. Saakashvili, undoubtedly drawing on his years of living in New York City, actually campaigned with his wife in front of the stations for the Tbilisi metro. This may not seem unusual, but in the former Soviet Union, particularly at that time, this kind of activity counted as an innovative and Western campaign tactic.

Additionally, as discussed in Chapter 3, the U.S. began to support and encourage coalitions among the opposition political parties. This commitment to supporting coalitions among the Georgian opposition was strong, although the rationale for doing this was not entirely clear. Importantly, assistance to the CUG and other parties continued during this period as well. In spite of years of support to political parties in

Georgia, the country's political party system was weak and not entirely rational. There were numerous parties many of which were personality driven with little cohesive vision or program for Georgia. The inability of U.S.-supported programs to rectify this situation in the years leading up to the 2003 indicates the limits facing democracy assistance in countries like Georgia.

Coalitions might have brought some of these parties together, bringing some rationality and organization to the party system, but this seemed unlikely since any coalition would be largely the result of a political deal rather than a true coalition based on shared interests and goals. This had been the case in previous Georgian elections, notably the 1999 parliamentary elections, when several parties joined the Revival slate because Revival, due to its control of Ajara, was guaranteed to break the 7 percent threshold.[12]

There were, however, more political, often unspoken reasons as to why it was so important to the U.S. government and its related democracy assistance organizations to encourage coalitions. First, it was recognized that if the opposition, specifically the pro-Western English-speaking opposition consisting of the National Movement, United Democrats, and, to a lesser extent, New Rights, were to be in a position to put pressure on the government for fair elections, they would have to be able to work in concert. Many believed that Shevardnadze's ability to keep the opposition fighting with each other (which has been addressed in Chapter 3 in some detail) would make it impossible for the opposition parties to work together for the cause of good elections, either before or after the election.

Another reason coalitions were important to the U.S. government was that they would have been a way for the opposition to demonstrate that it was serious and prepared to govern. The constant squabbling between the opposition had helped undermine some of the good will that people like Zhvania and Saakashvili had built up over the years, even in foreign capitals. Uniting behind a common slate of candidates would have sent a message to decision makers overseas that members of the Georgian opposition were prepared to put personal rivalries behind them in the name of supporting democracy, sending an important message for the presidential elections scheduled for 2005. Most people in the democracy assistance community already understood that it was essential for Georgia's democrats to coalesce behind one candidate if progress was to be made after Shevardnadze left office

Another factor driving unification was an understanding among members of the opposition that they would be competing against each other for party list votes largely among the same pool of voters. Many of Georgia's younger, more educated voters were drawn to both the NM and the BD, but would not have considered voting for the government. As long as the parties were running separately, they would be competing against each other for these votes.

By encouraging and helping to develop coalitions through hosting roundtables between the parties, facilitating discussions, providing ongoing advice to leaders of key opposition parties, supporting study trips to Poland paid for by the NED, and to Serbia, paid for by OSI, and other means, U.S.-funded organizations were becoming involved in politics in a way that was went beyond simply providing technical support for fair elections, but still a far cry from promoting or inciting revolution. This upswing in U.S.- and to a lesser extent European-funded support for various democracy related programs in the months leading up to the election raises the question of what the strategy of the international community was for the 2003 election. Not surprisingly, this is not an easy question to answer.

Clearly, the 2003 election were extremely important to the U.S. and Europe. They saw the election as an opportunity to set the country on the right course leading into the first presidential election of the post-Shevardnadze period. However, to interpret these programs as an effort by the U.S. or Europe to foster regime change in Georgia is to interpret information selectively and inaccurately.

The programs the U.S. and Europe funded in the months immediately preceding the election do not demonstrate a commitment on the part of these countries to make dramatic change. To a great extent, the battery of election-related programs in Georgia preceding the 2003 elections voter education campaigns, support for domestic monitors, training and workshops for political parties, assistance with voter lists and other aspects of election administration was the same battery of programs the U.S. supports in most countries on the eve of an important election. With the exception of some of the coalition building work, these programs are part of the typical package of programs implemented around elections in semi-democratic countries. With regard to election assistance, Georgia in 2003 did not look substantially different than Georgia in 1999, Azerbaijan in 2003 or 2005 or other elections in the region where no regime change or democratic breakthrough of any kind occurred.

On balance, the U.S. and its diplomatic representation, led by Ambassador Richard Miles in Georgia, employed a cautious strategy with regard to these elections. Most election support money was provided for programs that aimed to improve the voter lists, encourage voter participation, train election workers, raise awareness of important campaign issues, and buy new election materials. Many of these programs were moderately useful, but without a political component that somehow put pressure on the government for fair elections, were sure to have only a minor effect. Ambassador Miles worked tirelessly behind the scenes to push the government into conducting fair elections in 2003, but he did not take a very publicly contentious position on this issue.

The role played by the Open Society Institute was an additional and complicating factor in the months leading up to the parliamentary election. As a private foundation, OSI was able to use its money as it wanted, in the context of both Georgian and American law, without the approval or consent of the U.S. government. Moreover, in a small and impoverished country like Georgia in 2003, a few million well-spent foreign dollars could make a substantial impact.

OSI did not share the essentially cautious nature of the U.S. government during this period. The more radical civic leaders who consistently articulated a very strong anti-Shevardnadze view—including Ramishvili, Bokeria, and Lomaia—worked for NGOs funded by OSI, rather than by European or American governmental sources. Additionally, OSI funded the radical youth group Kmara (discussed in Chapter 3) and brought members of Otpor from Serbia to help train them, provided the funding and much of the strategy for the effective use of the exit poll. OSI also paid for the trip to Serbia in February 2003 in which Zurab Zhvania, Mikheil Saakashvili, and David Gamkrelidze met with a number of the Serb political and civic leaders who had contributed substantially to the defeat of Slobodan Milosevic in 2000. OSI and George Soros also provided valuable advice and support to Saakashvili and Zhvania during 2003 and to their government beginning in 2004.

In general, OSI was more aggressive in their approach to the 2003 election and had a far keener sense of the need to push for democratic reform during these elections. They also borrowed from the Serbian model through their work with Kmara, and in seeking to bring the opposition into a coalition. In this respect, while it can be said that, with the benefit of hindsight, this organization may have pursued the foundation of what has become the electoral, or color, revolution strategy, it is critical to bear in mind that this view was neither fully articulated at the time or shared by the broader democracy assistance and diplomatic communities in Georgia in 2003.

There is further evidence to indicate that the U.S. government was not interested in regime change or ousting Shevardnadze. For example, as was noted earlier, when Saakashvili encountered violent opposition—his campaign convoy was shot at during an effort to campaign in the southern and heavily ethnic Azeri region of Kvemo Kartli—Western diplomats in Georgia, particularly U.S. diplomats sought to lay the blame on both the authorities in Kvemo Kartli, who had refused to let Saakashvili campaign there, and on Saakashvili himself, for his aggressive campaign tactics. Saakashvili was furious at suggestions that he was somehow responsible for this attack as he felt, correctly, that the right to campaign throughout the country is essential for democratic elections.

Additionally, once the post-election demonstrations began, the U.S. government did not act strongly and decisively in favor of the opposition, as might have been expected if the U.S. had been seeking regime change in Georgia. The U.S. government did not join the opposition demonstrators in asking Shevardnadze to resign, nor did they put any kind of pressure on him to do that. Instead, the position of the U.S. government was largely to seek a negotiated solution to the dispute while urging both sides to remain nonviolent. U.S. government-funded NGOs were significantly less involved once the demonstrations began and similarly did not seek to pressure Shevardnadze to resign, nor did they make any public statements calling for his resignation.

Democracy assistance generally relies on a relatively limited handful of tools, all of which were used in Georgia in the decade preceding the Rose Revolution. Because of the nature of the democracy assistance project, most of these tools are essentially some form of technical skill development, funding for civil society organizations, or advice for politicians. The U.S. approach throughout most of the world has largely been to employ as many of these tools as possible in each country and hope for the best. This is what its strategy was in Georgia.

The result, while ultimately not undesirable, was, from the U.S. view accidental. U.S. efforts to secure fair elections and create a positive climate for further democratization contributed to a major democratic breakthrough, surprising everybody except Saakashvili and his supporters. While this was a surprise for the U.S., Washington welcomed it and began to claim partial credit for it. Of course, without the context of the stolen election, the failed presidency of Shevardnadze, and the political savvy and courage of the Georgian political opposition, these efforts could not have amounted to anything resembling the Rose Revolution. Nonetheless, elements of U.S. democracy assistance played critical roles in it. The work done by ISFED, PVT, the efforts to bring unity to the opposition, the foundations of a strong Georgian civil society,and the OSI-funded projects described earlier were essential elements in the events. Equally important, the U.S. immediately embraced the new government and began to commit substantial resources to supporting it. It is easy, particularly for those who are looking to find a U.S. hand in these events, to conflate these realities with the notion that the U.S. created the Rose Revolution, but the truth, as we have seen, is far more complex. Ultimately, the role played by U.S. democracy assistance was modest— but indispensable.

The Rose Revolution has many similarities with electoral upheavals in

Serbia in 2000 and in Ukraine in 2004. All three of these democratic breakthroughs were centered on fraudulent elections and buoyed by heightened civic participation, street demonstrations, high-quality and well-publicized election monitoring, and a unified (in the case of Georgia only briefly) opposition. Moreover, the Georgians studied events in Serbia; the Ukrainians studied both the Serb and Georgian revolutions. However, to conclude from this that a similar U.S. strategy was in place is inaccurate. The U.S. strategy was neither consistent nor ambitious in Georgia in 2003, and to understand the Rose Revolution as an American phenomenon is to make a significant mistake.

Democracy promotion always exists in the context of broader U.S. foreign policy, which is why it is too simplistic to see the Rose Revolution as an American plot. American foreign policy, even toward a small and distant country like Georgia, encompasses a breadth of security and economic issues that often trump democracy promotion in the view of American policy makers. Shevardnadze's support of the U.S. on these issues made him an unlikely target of any U.S.-backed coup, revolution or plot.

While those who seek to criticize the U.S. for pushing for revolution in Georgia are misled, a more resonant analysis might be that the U.S. played both sides, and not only in Georgia. Democracy promotion in a number of countries, including Georgia, is a vehicle through which the U.S. can hedge its bets. Shevardnadze's government received millions of dollars in U.S. assistance. This money was, albeit inefficiently, in an important sense used to keep an undemocratic regime in place. However, by spending a significantly smaller amount of money on democracy assistance programs, the U.S. was able to ensure relative goodwill from the Georgian opposition, which turned out to be very valuable once it came to power.

Georgia is not the best case to demonstrate this issue, because it is one of the few countries where a close relationship with the U.S., for both the opposition and the government, is a strategic necessity and consistent with existing public opinion. However, this approach has been part of U.S. foreign policy in a number of countries. Another, perhaps better, example of this approach might be Kyrgyzstan, where Askar Akaev's nondemocratic government received ample support from the U.S. for years, but the U.S. democracy assistance community's relationship with the opposition before the Tulip Revolution helped make it possible for stronger ties to be established between the U.S. and the post-Tulip Revolution Bakiev-Kulov regime. This cynical view is not without its flaws, but it does reflect a more complex view of the interaction between democracy assistance and U.S. foreign policy more broadly.[13]

Chapter 7
Georgia and the United States After the Revolution

Democracy Assistance in Georgia Since the Rose Revolution

U.S. efforts to build and strengthen democracy in Georgia during the years between the collapse of the Soviet Union and the Rose Revolution yielded significant, but not entirely anticipated, results. Moreover, while the Rose Revolution and subsequent election of the pro-Western, explicitly reform oriented government of Mikheil Saakashvili set Georgian democracy on a new and reinvigorated course, it also raised a largely new and very different set of challenges for both democratization and democracy assistance in Georgia.

For years, as international confidence in Shevardnadze waned, hopes for democracy in Georgia were pinned on the post-Shevardnadze period. This, of course, came earlier than anticipated with Shevardnadze's resignation in November 2003. At that moment, the future was suddenly upon the new Georgian leadership. Expectations were high, and have remained high throughout Saakashvili's presidency. However, determining the most effective way to assist the democratization process through democracy assistance programs has not been easy or straightforward.

Democracy was just one of the areas in which the new government needed help. Shevardnadze had left the country in very bad shape. Similarly, democratization was only part of the ambitions of Saakashvili and the rest of Georgia's new leadership. The new government was focused, as we have seen, on Georgia's territorial integrity, its increasingly difficult relationship with Russia, economic problems, fight against corruption, and aspirations to join NATO.

After the Rose Revolution, the international community, and the U.S. in particular, still had a valuable role to play in Georgia to help the country consolidate its democratic gains. Because democratic institutions, ranging from national and local legislatures and political parties, cooperation and trust between citizens and understanding of the appropriate relationship between a state and its citizens in a democratic system, were so weak in Georgia, there was an obvious danger that the new government would at best not maximize this opportunity to meaningfully reform Georgian politics, or at worst become something akin to the old system with new faces.

Democracy assistance in Georgia was needed to help the UNM develop into a governing party that would become part of a multiparty system, rather than a state party; to facilitate the development of a new generation of civic and media watchdogs, since most of the previous leaders in this field were now part of the government;[1] and to create the demand side for democracy by continuing civic education programs to help citizens understand their rights, and the rights of their government in a democratic system. Perhaps most important, the international community had a role to play in holding the new government accountable to the promises they had made about democracy to both domestic and international audiences.

Unfortunately, democracy assistance, particularly on the part of the U.S. government, has taken a very different course in Georgia since the Rose Revolution. It has begun, to a substantial extent, with the assumption that the Rose Revolution marked the end, not the beginning, of the process of democratization and that Georgia under its new leadership was a mostly consolidated democracy.

American leaders, most prominently President Bush, have been effusive in their praise for Saakashvili and Georgian democracy. On a May 2005 visit to Tbilisi, Bush's words evinced the lack of ambiguity on his or the American government's part regarding democracy in Georgia.

We are living in historic times when freedom is advancing, from the Black Sea to the Caspian, and to the Persian Gulf and beyond. As you watch free people gathering in squares like this across the world, waving their nations' flags and demanding their God given rights, you can take pride in this fact: They have been inspired by your [Georgian] example and they take hope in your success. As you build freedom in this country, you must know that the seeds of liberty you are planting in Georgian soil are flowering across the globe. I have come here to thank you for your courage.[2]

While it is appropriate for Bush, and the United States, to support Georgia's nascent democracy through both policies and statements, a policy of not recognizing that Georgian democracy remains a work in progress, which needs the occasional appropriate criticism as well as support and encouragement of the American government, is not in the best interest of the U.S. or Georgia.

Statements like those Bush made in Tbilisi are bolstered by a U.S. approach to democracy assistance for Georgia that consists largely of direct support for a government viewed as the primary engine of democratization there. Since the Rose Revolution, there has been considerably less international money for civil society organization, media, or other nongovernmental aspects of democracy. Instead, there has been an increase in advisors and technical support for the government. This, of course, is important for the development of a modern, functioning Georgian state, but it is not necessarily democracy assistance.

Before looking more closely at U.S.-supported democracy assistance in Georgia since the Rose Revolution, it is important to remember the context. First, the U.S. continues to provide support in numerous other areas, such as economic development, energy, and infrastructure, so democracy assistance is a relatively small part of the overall U.S. assistance package.

Second, developing a post-color revolution democracy assistance strategy is not easy for the U.S. or international funders generally. For example, the civil society that had thrived under Shevardnadze was brought into government by Saakashvili, making it unavoidable that civil society would be weakened, but it is necessary for a new kind of civil society to emerge in Georgia, one that can do more than take radical antigovernment positions as much of civil society did during the Shevardnadze years.

Additionally, in the first few months and even year or two after a breakthrough such as the Rose Revolution, the new government will get, and probably deserves, the benefit of the doubt from international funders, as it tries to figure out the right way to govern. The question for Georgia is whether this honeymoon period has gone on too long. The events of November 2007 were a wake-up call for many policy makers and observers, but given all the problems of Georgian democracy between 2004 and 2007, it is puzzling why anybody was still asleep.

Democracy and governance assistance to post-Rose Revolution Georgia has, according to USAID, focused on reforming national governance which has meant "train[ing] the staff of the Offices of the President and Prime Minister in communications and outreach, provid[ing] IT equipment, and ma[king] recommendations to improve," improving the judiciary, primarily through "assisting the judiciary with structural reforms,"and strengthening parliament through "implementing a parliamentary strengthening project that responds to the priorities of the government of Georgia." There are also programs that work with local government and political parties. Nonetheless, almost all these programs work with branches of the government as the point of entry, rather than with independent civic or media actors.[3]

A major 2004 project, "Support to the New Government of Georgia," is representative of the U.S. government approach to democracy assistance in post-Rose Revolution Georgia. This program has been effective and well implemented in assisting the government in important tasks such as "more effective management of executive offices. . . . Improving intra-governmental consultation and information flow, both vertically and horizontally. . . . Working with the State Minister for Reforms Coordination in comprehensively reviewing and identifying ways to improve the GoG's [Government of Georgia] inter-ministerial process." This program also included money for upgrading computer and communications technology in government offices.[4]

The "Support to the New Government of Georgia" project is important work, but it is certainly a different approach to democracy assistance than seeking to build a strong independent civil society or concretely helping the development of a multi-party system. Programs like these have been implemented in Georgia since early 2004, yet IFES, the major U.S.-based NGO working on election administration and oversight, shut down its operation in Georgia in 2004 due to lack of funding. This occurred at a time when Georgia had three national elections scheduled for the next five years. Similarly, NDI, while continuing to work in Georgia, lost funding for a political party program while the IRI political party program has consisted largely of public opinion research.

Bob Evans who served as Chief of Party for the International Research and Exchange Board (IREX) on the biggest U.S.-supported media program in Georgia before and after the Rose Revolution, described the changed U.S. approach to democracy assistance following the transition:

We were told many times to fully support the new regime and not point out the shortcomings of the new government. "Watchdog" became "bad dog" in anticipation of some sort of counter-revolution. USAID seemed to almost simultaneously announce that we ran the best media program that they had ever seen and that they had no intention of offering a media program again. We were publicly told that we had done such a great job that media development was no longer necessary but behind the scenes we were hearing that they didn't need a media program because Georgia "had already had its revolution."[5]

Another American who has been involved in NGOs and civil society for over a decade summed up the U.S. approach even more succinctly:

For the U.S. in the late nineties political support for the government was paramount. By the end of 2000 it was becoming clear in Washington, as it had been in Georgia for some time that Shevardnadze and his remaining allies could not solve Georgia's problems. Pluralism and fair elections became all the rage. After he resigned, back we [the U.S.] went to helping out the government. The direction of effort of U.S. assistance in Georgia seems almost cyclical.[6]

Washington's unconditional support for Georgia's government, and its refusal to draw any attention to its shortcomings in the area of democratization, raises vital questions about how serious the U.S. is about democracy promotion, particularly in countries that have a semidemocratic but pro-American government. An approach to Georgia that recognizes remaining democratic challenges there and seeks to help Georgia solve these problems, will demonstrate that American democracy promotion really is concerned with democracy, rather than simply with supporting friendly governments. The continued failure to do this will send a message to Americans, democracy activists around the world, and other key players in international politics, that our commitment to helping countries develop deep and enduring democracies is less than genuine.

Another issue Georgia raises for American democracy promotion policy is that for these programs to be valuable and successful, rather than just the latest iteration of American self-interest, the goal should be to nurture and encourage the creation of strong democracies with an array of freedoms, institutions, protections and rights similar to those enjoyed in older, more established democracies. The challenge for the U.S. is to support Georgian democracy in a way that, while recognizing and supporting the consolidation of the initial democratic gains there, makes it clear that the U.S. wants and expects more democratic consolidation. Unfortunately, the U.S. relationship to Georgia does not reflect this nuance; the nature and tone of support seems to suggest that democratization is complete in Georgia and now we must support the new state as it strengthens itself. By not recognizing the challenges democracy in Georgia faces, the U.S. is not helping our new Georgian allies in their ongoing struggle for democracy. Striking this precise tone is not an easy task, but failing to do so will, in the long run, hurt Georgia and its nascent democracy. Georgia is far ahead of its neighbors and is the most democratic country, other than perhaps Turkey, in that part of the world. It is possible to recognize this and still push Georgia to resolve its remaining democratic challenges.

Moreover, the U.S. policy of strong unequivocal support and commendation of the Georgian government, with almost no public statements about shortcomings in democratic development, was very unlikely to lead to the Georgian government addressing any of these shortcomings.[7] Instead, quite reasonably, it assumed that the U.S., Georgia's most important ally and supporter, was pleased with the level of democracy. This contributed to Georgian democracy not achieving its potential in the first few years after the Rose Revolution. The Georgian government was also able to use American government support as evidence of its own democratic bona fides to defend itself from any criticism in the democracy realm. It is not yet clear whether U.S. policy toward Georgia will change significantly given the events in late 2007; a few days after the crackdown the U.S. State Department made a strong statement calling for fair elections and the immediate lifting of the state of emergency, but then returned to its largely uncritical assessment of democracy in Georgia.

It is worth repeating that, just as consolidating democracy is not a primary goal of the new Georgian government, it is similarly only one of several goals of U.S. policy toward Georgia or any country. Strengthening the new Georgian government so that it can continue its reforms and helping to somehow rebuild the still devastated Georgian economy are integral parts of U.S. assistance to Georgia. Georgia's ongoing conflicts with Russia, frozen or otherwise, also require attention from the U.S.

None of these goals are in conflict with the project of deepening Georgia's democracy. On the contrary, building the Georgian state and building Georgian democracy are largely overlapping goals. While some scholars still debate this point, among policy makers in Europe and North America, as well as multilateral organizations such as the UN and the EU, this is one of the fundamental bases of policy toward the developing world. Strong institutions of governance, which increase the role of ordinary citizens in decision making, the accountability of the government toward its people, and which give citizens a sense of their government and its institutions are an essential part of a strong state. This is the case whether the means for doing this are a strong governing party with deep roots in society, a deeply held ideology or worldview that the state uses to mobilize its citizens, or electoral democracy. Georgia, fortunately, has chosen the third of these approaches and needs the appropriate institutions to make it work.

If Georgia does not build these institutions, there will come a time when the adrenaline from the Rose Revolution finally wears off—which will probably be around the time Saakashvili leaves the presidency—and the state's strength will almost certainly dissipate. The constitutional reforms that sought to consolidate power in the president, and the efforts to increase the ruling party's strength in the parliament and more broadly in society, have been defended by the government as necessary for efficient governance and decision making. But these developments will be very hard to undo, particularly by a future president who may be less popular and clever than the current one. Additionally, Saakashvili's extraordinary political skills and his role as leader and hero of the revolution make his position within the government and the party beyond challenge or question. The next president will have a much harder time keeping the party and government unified. Democratic institutions will be essential for facilitating disagreement within and decision making outside the government. The absence of these institutions has been a central reason why Georgia's last three one-party regimes collapsed in 1991, 1993, and 2003, and why the state was so weak during its first thirteen years of independence. Ths is a crucial moment for the essential synergistic strengthening of the Georgian state and Georgian democracy. If this opportunity is lost, it will almost certainly not return for a quite a few years.

Technical Challenges to Democracy Assistance in Georgia

U.S. democracy assistance policy toward Georgia in recent years has also been affected by the renewed American emphasis on elections as the critical measure of democratization. By the late 1990s, the initial emphasis on elections in democracy promotion had begun to wane as most people working in the field understood that balloting alone is not enough to make a democracy. The consolidation of democracies in Africa, South America, and most notably Eastern Europe in the mid- and late 1990s occurred as institutions, rule of law and civil society in those countries was strengthened. U.S. democracy assistance during those years reflected that approach, with aid focused on those areas. However, during the Bush administration, this approach has become less central as the administration placed too much value on elections as evidence of democracy in places like Afghanistan and Iraq.

Elections have provided the starkest and most positive contrast between Saakashvili and Shevardnadze's rule, but they only tell one part of the story. Judging democratic development in Georgia simply on the quality of elections is a mistake which leads to a less than full understanding of the political environment and potential value of democracy assistance. Democracy assistance policy toward Georgia would benefit from a U.S. approach that understood elections to be one, albeit an important one, of several measures of democratization. This would lead to a view that Georgia has made some real strides toward democratization, but that democracy there is far from consolidated, and a to policy that offers both meaningful democracy assistance and the appropriate combination of U.S. support for and pressure on Georgia.

In addition to a different political approach, one that recognizes both the accomplishments and shortcomings of the regime and reflects U.S. willingness to be honest with our Georgian allies even when that means criticizing them, a different technical approach is needed as well. Democracy assistance in Georgia needs to help develop institutions both inside and outside government through which citizens can hold their government accountable and apply pressure for more democratic reforms. It also needs to develop a method of working with the government that goes beyond the current approach of simply supporting it.

The government of Georgia was elected by its people and has a commitment to democracy that, while somewhat erratic, is still stronger than that in most other nondemocratic or democratizing countries. For these reasons, the U.S. should support this government. However, programs should be developed that do more than strengthen an already strong government and do not confuse Saakashvili's state building project with democracy building. They would include, for example, creating ways to open up the policy and budget making processes to more public participation and input, working intensely with parties other than the UNM so that they can develop strategies and platforms which reflect a pro-state but anti-UNM position, and providing financial support for media outlets over which the government could exert only minimal pressure. Ironically, these are the types of programs that played such a key role in consolidating democracy in Eastern Europe in the 1990s.

Helping to recreate the vibrant civic life that characterized the late Shevardnadze years and made the Rose Revolution possible and supporting independent and critical media in Georgia are two additional ways the U.S. can help reinvigorate democratic reform in Georgia. Similar efforts to push Georgia to taking stronger steps toward democratic consolidation should include helping to build democratic institutions and willingness to publicly, but gently, criticize the government on democracy related issues. These efforts will show the Georgian government, and more important the Georgian people, that the U.S. takes democratic reform seriously.

The uncritical view of the U.S. toward Georgia's democratic development will, unfortunately, have an effect far beyond the borders of just one country. If U.S. policy towards Georgia does not continue to push for consolidation and deepening of democracy there, it will likely undermine U.S. democracy promotion efforts and lend support to those who argue that the U.S. is interested not in supporting real democracy, but simply in ensuring that friendly regimes remain in place in key regions.

Georgia should become a model for democracy in which every citizen will be equal before the law, in which every citizen will have equal opportunities to achieve success and to realize his or her abilities . . . Georgia should have a capable government responsible to the people, a government in which every citizen is represented and in which the voice of every Georgian in listened to.[8]

These are not the words of an American policy maker, Georgian NGO democracy advocate, or opponent of the new Georgian government. They come from President Saakashvili's first inaugural address. This language demonstrates that Saakashvili understands what a consolidated Georgian democracy would look like and suggests a strong commitment to that goal. It is not difficult to find this kind of rhetoric from leaders of countries that are not nearly as democratic as Georgia, so the words should not be taken simply at face value. However, these words are coming not from just any leader but from a popularly elected, Western educated president who has publicly and privately pledged his commitment to democracy. This suggests that perhaps Saakashvili should have his views taken seriously and be held to them.

The United States can only help make the Georgian president's vision a reality if we are not just supportive of his government but honest in our assessment and willing to point out shortcomings as we see them. Simply pointing to the success of Georgia's democracy and increasing our assistance without showing concerns when they arise does not help Georgian democracy and undermines U.S. legitimacy as a promoter of democracy.

Why Georgia Is Important to the United States

The Rose Revolution occurred at a critical time for the U.S. with regard to democracy assistance. Late 2003 and early 2004 marked the period when democratization began to emerge as the major rationale by the Bush administration to explain the ongoing American military presence in Iraq as well as when building democracy began to become more of an issue in post-war Afghanistan. In general, President Bush was just beginning to move to his radical pro-democracy promotion position when the Rose Revolution occurred. For the new Georgian government, this was extremely fortuitous timing.

It is likely that Bush's enthusiasm for the Rose Revolution, Saakashvili, and the new Georgian government was increased because of the timing of these events. Just as Bush was beginning to focus on democracy assistance as a major theme of his foreign policy, these policies seemed to come to fruition in Georgia. For the Bush administration the Rose Revolution served as a way to remind critics that the administration's policies and vision regarding democracy could work, making it even harder for the U.S. administration to see any blemishes on the post-Communist world's newest democracy. Had the Rose Revolution occurred a few years earlier, it would have likely drawn less attention from the White House because democratization was less of a preoccupation. Had it occurred a few years later, cynicism about Iraq would likely have cooled American enthusiasm for Georgia. Georgia quickly became the primary example toward which Bush could point to demonstrate the value and import of democracy assistance.

Nonetheless, for the U.S., Georgia is not just another country where the goal of creating democracy must compete, and is occasionally in conflict, with other foreign policy goals. While to some extent the potential for democracy is particularly important because Georgia is of strategic value to the U.S., the converse is, in fact, more true. Georgia is of strategic value to the U.S. because of the potential for democracy in that country.

Unlike neighboring Azerbaijan, Georgia does not have natural gas or other extremely valuable natural resources. As an overwhelmingly Christian country, it is not a place where there is a chance of an anti-American Islamist regime that might support terrorist activity against the U.S. coming into power, nor is it in a key location for trade or other economic issues. Georgia is strategically important in the sense that all countries are important to the U.S. as the global hegemon. One can create a narrative for why Georgia is strategically important based on its proximity to Russia, Azerbaijan, or Iran, or as a strategic energy corridor but a similar narrative can be created for dozens of countries. Moreover, it is telling that when Georgia was in a period of genuine political chaos in the early 1990s, with small wars in South Ossetia and Abkhazia and the possibility of even greater instability throughout the country, the U.S. did not really become involved or focus the level of attention it might have if Georgia's strategic value had been more significant.

Today, Georgia's strategic import to the U.S. stems, in several different ways from its democratic potential. If democracy in Georgia fails, Georgia will return to being a semidemocratic, semifailed post-Soviet state about which nobody in the U.S. or Europe will care a great deal, albeit one through which several energy pipelines pass. If, however, Saakashvili succeeds, which will mean building both democracy and the Georgian state, then Georgia will be of great strategic import because it will show that it is possible to expand democracy in the twenty-first century to countries where it had been previously thought to be extremely difficult. Georgia's ongoing strategic value to the U.S. is dependent on the growth and consolidation of Georgian democracy. A genuinely democratic Georgia will be powerful evidence to the rest of the world, including democratic activists struggling for their freedoms, that the U.S. commitment to democracy is real and that U.S. support for democracy can make a difference.

Even if the worst case is avoided and the regime remains in place but fails to bring about meaningful democratic reforms, Georgia's strategic value to the U.S. will wane. Should democracy in Georgia fail, it will be have only a moderate negative effect on the U.S., but if it should succeed, the impact and value for the U.S. will be very positive. Strategically, then, there is little reason for the U.S. to pursue a course that does not seek to move the Georgian government toward stronger and more meaningful democracy. Having Georgia become another state that is somewhat friendly to the U.S., dependent on the West for aid, and governed by a semidemocratic system of one kind or another is of little strategic value to the U.S. A state in this condition that has oil or plays a key role in the war on terror would be different, but Georgia fits neither category. However, there is reason to fear that unless additional attention is paid to democracy in Georgia, this is the direction in which it will go.

Chapter 8
Georgia and the Fading of the Color Revolutions

The United States has presented the Rose Revolution, only somewhat accurately and in very general terms, as a success story for democracy assistance policy. The transition in Georgia occurred at a time when it appeared as if the steam was running out of the third wave of democratization, and as conditions in postwar Iraq were beginning to go sour. At the time, the Rose Revolution followed by the Orange Revolution in Ukraine seemed like the beginning of another set of advances for democracy globally. Thus the Rose Revolution has occupied an important place in both American foreign policy and the ongoing narrative of democratization and democracy assistance. However, the U.S. policies of both claiming the Rose Revolution as evidence of the success of democracy assistance projects, and treating President Saakashvili's Georgia as a largely consolidated democracy reflect a lack of nuance.

Paradoxically, as shown in Chapter 6, U.S. influence on the Rose Revolution was both significant and accidental. While the myriad programs in Georgia supported by the U.S. government ended up contributing, perhaps inadvertently, to the political events and environment that formed the Rose Revolution, the event itself was in no way part of a U.S. strategy of revolution, or even of a specific vision of democratization for Georgia. On the contrary, the absence of a cohesive strategy for democratization in Georgia was striking. The policy seemed to be to implement a broad assortment of democracy assistance programs and hope for the best after Shevardnadze's term in office expired in 2005.

I have also argued that positioning Georgia as a dramatic success for democratization policy not only has meant misrepresenting the U.S. role and aims in pre-Rose Revolution Georgia, but has led to a policy toward post-Rose Revolution Georgia that may prove to be a mistake for both countries. By failing to recognize that Georgian democracy is still in its early, consolidating stage, and crafting policy and democracy assistance programs appropriate to this reality, the U.S. is sending troublingly mixed messages about the real meaning and goals of democracy assistance. These mixed messages were reinforced in November 2007 when the violent images coming out of Tbilisi were contrasted with Bush's previous rhetoric on democracy in Georgia.[1]

During the eighteen months immediately following the Rose Revolution, seemingly momentous democratic breakthroughs in Ukraine, Krygzystan, and Lebanon occurred as well, making it possible, for a time, to speak about a fourth wave of democratization, one in which U.S.-led democracy assistance seemed to have played a critical role. Georgia, it appeared, had been the beginning of an important new trend in democracy. By the middle of 2005, however, this nascent fourth wave had peaked and a period of pushback from foreign governments and domestic policy makers and pundits had begun. Democracy assistance had entered a new era, one in which resistance abroad and skepticism at home were greater, raising new challenges for U.S. democracy assistance policy.

The Rose and later Orange Revolutions convinced many remaining authoritarian leaders that democracy assistance was more than just support of pesky but largely harmless civil society organization and similar activities. These leaders began to see that democracy assistance could contribute to much more serious outcomes including, in some cases, revolution and regime change. To a significant extent, these connections were overstated, but the notion that democracy assistance could play a role in democratic breakthroughs was accurate enough. Beginning in 2004 and 2005, authoritarian leaders in the former Soviet Union who were concerned about becoming the next victim of a color revolution changed their view of democracy promotion and began to act on this new view. This development made it increasingly difficult for democracy assistance programs and organizations to function in the remaining nondemocratic countries, particularly in the former Soviet Union. Opposition to democracy assistance has become stronger in the former Soviet Union, where the color revolutions, including the Tulip Revolution in Kyrgyzstan, are viewed as products of American intervention and as American efforts to bring their preferred leaders to power.

Democracy assistance organizations in Russia, Belarus, Kazakhstan, Azerbaijan, and elsewhere in the former Soviet Union began to face increased harassment by government agencies. This harassment took the form of audits, increased surveillance, and other forms of discouragement. It has been very difficult for democracy assistance organizations to function in these countries. Laws are passed limiting how much foreign money an NGO can take; NGO activities are monitored

extremely closely; and foreigners working for democracy assistance programs increasingly are confronting problems involving visas, tax offices,
and bureaucratic hurdles. Most of these post-Soviet regimes have implemented these changes drawing on Russian support and advice. This
opposition has arisen, quite naturally, because authoritarian regimes
want to hold onto their power and while they are often willing to make
some concessions to semidemocratic processes, such as regular and
fraudulent elections, they do not want to be pushed toward genuine
democratic reform.[2]

Iraq and Democracy Assistance

The actions and words of Putin and other authoritarian leaders in the
former Soviet Union in the years following the democratic breakthroughs in Georgia and Ukraine had substantial negative impact on
democracy assistance efforts. However, the ongoing war in Iraq probably
had the greatest effect on how U.S. democracy assistance was viewed
internationally and, perhaps even more significantly, in the domestic
political context.

During 2004–2006, the Bush administration began to increasingly cite
the goal of bringing democracy to Iraq as the justification for the invasion and occupation of that country. As the war in Iraq became increasingly unpopular with the American people and violence escalated, the
administration's hopes of establishing democracy there seemed increasingly far-fetched and misguided.

The juxtaposition of daily images of suicide bombers, dead Iraqis, and
dead American soldiers with speeches by Bush and others that democracy was coming to Iraq, began to undermine the credibility of democracy assistance. Bush's statements on democracy in Iraq seemed to be
poorly thought out and unconvincing defenses of the ongoing strategy
in Iraq, rather than a genuine commitment to a broad policy of democracy assistance in different forms. In reality, these statements were probably both. Moreover, Bush's description of Iraq as a democracy, after a
few successful elections there, has raised the question, for many, of why
they would ever want to live in a democracy.

Before the war in Iraq, democracy assistance, while an important part
of American foreign policy, was not something about which most Americans, including many opinion leaders and other elites, had heard or
understood well. The war in Iraq and Bush's strong, partisan advocacy
for democracy assistance changed this. Democracy assistance became
something about which many people, including almost all opinion leaders, had heard something. Unfortunately, it remained poorly understood.

By the beginning of Bush's second term in office, democracy assistance had undergone a substantial transformation in how it was perceived. For the first fifteen years or so following the end of the Cold War, democracy assistance, to the extent Americans thought about it at all, was seen as a relatively benign, soft diplomatic, bipartisan set of policies implemented largely by NGOs. The programs were viewed as perhaps not having great impact, but at least not doing any harm either to the U.S. or to the countries in which they worked.

Linking democracy assistance to the war in Iraq changed this. U.S. democracy assistance policy in this has been unlike democracy assistance in most other countries, but because of the high visibility of Iraq many Americans assumed that democracy assistance could consist of a policy of military intervention and occupation, regime change, early and frequent elections and generally trying to export democracy wholesale to post-conflict countries. Bush's renewed rhetorical emphasis on elections as the preeminent measurement of democratization in places as diverse as Georgia and Iraq exacerbated this problematic perception. It also made it very easy for critics of democracy assistance to focus on the relatively easy issue of overemphasizing elections, a criticism that had been understood and responded to substantially in the 1990s through evolving appropriate programs and approaches. Democracy assistance in Iraq was also understood, correctly, by most Americans as a policy pursued by the U.S. without support from other countries. The partisan nature of the debate around Iraq has also made democracy assistance increasingly seen as a partisan Republican program in spite of its decades old bipartisan pedigree.

The complex and important questions regarding democracy assistance strategy raised by the experiences in Georgia before and after the Rose Revolution were overshadowed by the linkage of democracy assistance to the ongoing debacle in Iraq. Iraq quickly evolved into the 800-pound gorilla in the democracy assistance room, the massive and destructive center of debate and attention on the issue. Some who believed that the war in Iraq was a mistake see democracy promotion there as little more than American imperialism in its newest form. However, not all opponents of the war in Iraq share this view. For example, the amendment that initially called for democracy assistance in Iraq was authored by Senator Ted Kennedy (D. Mass.), one of Congress's most outspoken opponents of the war. Others believe the Bush administration should have understood that the task of building democracy in Iraq was going to be much more difficult than initially projected. Larry Diamond, a senior advisor on democratization for the Coalition Provisional Authority (CPA) in Iraq in 2003–2004, described the project as being "underresourced . . . we never had enough civilian employees, or

enough armored cars, body armor, helicopters. . . . We never had sufficient expertise on the ground. The CPA relied heavily on . . . a cadre of
eager young neophytes."[3] Still others expressed concern about the
effect U.S. support for democracy in Iraq, and Bush's calls for democracy in the Middle East more broadly, will have on U.S. relationships
with key allies in the region. Thus, Iraq has reopened many of the
debates discussed in this work, but the experience there frames these
debates in a way that is very unfavorable for democracy assistance.

Iraq may be the most visible, and controversial, current example of
democracy promotion, but in many respects it represents a completely
different situation from that in most democratizing countries. Ironically,
the increasing use of democracy promotion by the Bush administration
as the rationale for invading and continuing the occupation of Iraq has
not succeeded in winning support for U.S. actions in Iraq among either
domestic or international audiences. Instead, it has weakened support
for the policy of democracy assistance in general.

The problems in Iraq are not the only component of the new domestic backlash against democracy assistance. Hamas's resounding election
victory in the Palestinian Authority, the war between Hezbollah and
Israel, and the success of Islamist forces in elections throughout the
Arab world have led to a domestic backlash against democracy assistance
by Americans who see promoting democracy as peripheral to U.S.
national interests, particularly in the Middle East.[4]

Bombs and Ballots

Much of the domestic criticism of democracy assistance is based on an
inaccurate understanding of the policy, its impact, and its support.[5] In
some cases people writing on the subject lack detailed knowledge of the
field of democracy assistance. More troublingly, in other cases, critics
seem to have deliberately mischaracterized democracy assistance to create a straw man for their arguments.

The outsized role Iraq has played in understanding democracy assistance has allowed opposition to democracy assistance policy makers,
pundits, and scholars to focus largely on either the role of the military
or the perceived emphasis on encouraging elections—bombs and ballots. The former focus argues that democracy assistance is largely driven
by invasions and wars, linking the debate around democracy assistance
mentioned in Chapter 1 to a larger debate about the wisdom of military
interventions and invasions.

It is easy, and probably wise, to be critical of a foreign policy that seeks
to violently overthrow dictators and then try to create democracy in their
wake. However, this caricature of democracy assistance only applies to a

very small fraction of the dozens of countries throughout Africa, South America, the former communist bloc, and Asia where the U.S. and others have sought to help strengthen democracy. Opposing democracy promotion because of opposition to military intervention is making the mistake of throwing out the democracy assistance baby with the bathwater of invasions and war.

Focusing on Iraq as an example of this type of problem also raises the question of to what extent the problems in that country should be attributed to this one component of overall U.S. policy toward Iraq. Even a cursory look at Iraq's history over the last century shows its creation by the British, which put three different ethnic groups in one country; the violent Baath takeover and brutal regime of Saddam Hussein; Hussein's genocidal policies toward the Kurds and brutality toward the Shia, which exacerbated ethnic tensions; a bloody war against Iran that cost hundreds of thousands of Iraqi lives; defeat at the hands of the U.S. and its allies in the first Gulf War; the crippling sanctions following that war; and finally the toppling of Hussein's regime at the hands of the U.S. and the UK in the second Gulf War. It strains credulity and serious political analysis to claim that the current problems of instability, violence, ethnic and religious divisions, and the possibility of civil war are occurring because elections were held. Moreover, it is at least worth considering the possibility that the elections of January and December 2005 where large numbers of Iraqi people stood up to threats and intimidation to cast their ballots, was one of the few bright moments where there may have been potential for positive change in Iraq. That moment, of course, has passed now as the conflict in Iraq shows no real signs of abating.

The election-centered criticisms of democracy assistance focus on the inadequacies of balloting as a means to ensure democracy, and identify potentially explosive consequences that can occur if elections are introduced at the wrong place or time.[6] However, democracy assistance is more than just supporting and promoting elections, and election assistance continues to constitute a relatively small proportion of overall U.S. democracy assistance funding. In fiscal 2004, support for elections and political processes constituted 4.4 percent of USAID democracy and governance funding. For fiscal 2005 this number was 7.2 percent; in fiscal 2006 it was 10 percent. In each of these years, USAID democracy and governance funding for civil society and for governance exceeded elections and political processes funding.[7] As demonstrated by the case of Georgia, most democracy assistance work emphasizes building stronger democratic institutions, not simply calling for elections and putting people the U.S. likes into office, as it is frequently caricatured.[8] Georgia is, of course, not the only example of this sort of democracy assistance. Successful U.S. democracy assistance policies in recent years in countries such as Croatia, the Baltic States, and South Africa have all shared this emphasis on building democratic institutions.

Many of the warnings of the potentially negative consequences of ill-timed elections are primarily reminders of the possible perils of conducting early elections in ethnically divided countries or in countries recently emerging from civil or other conflict.[9] Maligning democracy assistance by arguing that elections alone cannot bring about, and do not constitute, democracy, is the "ballots" component of the "bombs and ballots" myth: that promoting democracy is simply pushing for more elections. Elections are, of course, a key and indispensable component of democracy, but scholars and practitioners of democracy assistance have for years been aware of the dangers of relying too heavily on elections to be the midwives of peaceful democratization.[10]

Elections are understood by most practitioners of democratic development to be only a part, albeit a critical one, of a necessary battery of democratization activities that seek to strengthen democratic institutions such as courts, legislatures, local governments, political parties, civil society, and the rule of law. Nonetheless, the promise of elections has played a key role in resolving conflicts in places as diverse as Mozambique, Sierra Leone, and El Salvador. Scholarly debates over the ideal sequencing of institution building and elections are still alive and well after several decades, but these debates are of little value to practitioners or activists in democratizing countries, who understand that in reality, strengthening institutions, supporting civil society, and conducting elections generally have to be done at the same time.[11]

We would all prefer democratizing countries to conduct elections in contexts where cohesive and accountable political parties elect people to strong legislatures in a climate where the laws are understood and enforced. However, countries that fit this description are not democratizing countries; they are democratic countries.[12] In other words, countries that are capable of conducting free and fair elections are usually already democratic and do not need very much democracy assistance. Free and fair elections, therefore, are both a symptom and a result of democracy.

Part of the "bombs and ballots" caricature of democracy assistance is that the U.S., or the West more broadly, demands elections in a post-conflict country and that balloting ends up creating more problems than it solves. The reality in many democratizing countries is different, and, as we know, most democracy assistance does not occur in post-conflict countries. Instead, elections in transitional countries generally are scheduled by the authoritarian ruler and rigged to ensure reelection of the ruling party. Clearly, the Rose Revolution was triggered by the elections in Georgia that were scheduled years in advance by Shevardnadze's government. The election served as a rallying point both logistically and substantively for democracy advocates in Georgia, as well as in Ukraine and, even as far back as the Philippines in the 1980s.

Elections like the one in Georgia in 2003 are far more common and raise a different set of challenges for democracy assistance and its critics. Democrats facing the prospect of a stolen election turn to the U.S. and Europe for help in somehow making the election fair and leveling the playing field between the government and the opposition. In these cases the West is faced with the choice of working to make the election more fair or ignoring the direct pleas of assistance from activists working hard, often at great personal risk, for democratic change in their own countries. In Georgia, the U.S. had offered moderate support of this type to the democrats for a number of years. In Serbia in 2000, the U.S. offered more significant support.

Because of the centrality of elections in democratic governance as well as the key roles elections have played in democratic breakthroughs, election work remains one of several central components of democracy assistance. A policy of supporting elections *and* helping to develop other democratic institutions is essential to the success of democracy assistance. However, it is important to distinguish this from the approach of supporting elections *but* only after other conditions have been met. By connecting support for elections to meeting pre-conditions involving the development of other democratic institutions, supporters of the latter approach generally put themselves in the de facto position of simply opposing elections.

The Future of Democracy Assistance

As Iraq continues to dominate the foreign policy debates and the color revolutions fade more into the background, looking more like aberrations than like the beginning of meaningful trends, the project of democracy assistance finds itself at a crossroads. The domestic and international political environment has become a more difficult one in which to promote democracy. Opponents of democracy assistance have used American failures in Iraq as the cornerstone of their arguments against the policy more broadly. International efforts led by Putin in Russia and various authoritarian leaders around the world have also made this environment much more difficult.

Ironically, in the context of American policy making and politics, the greatest blow to democracy assistance was delivered by the person who is perhaps democracy promotion's greatest advocate. No previous president had, ever, through his rhetoric, made democracy promotion a priority to any extent even approaching that of George W. Bush.[13] Bush made it the centerpiece of his foreign policy, funded democracy assistance in unprecedented level, and stressed the need to expand democracy as an essential battle in the war against terrorism after September 11, 2001. Before the war in Iraq, Bush's rhetorical emphasis on democracy assistance had some positive impact in places like the Middle East, as the message that the U.S. was going to take a new approach to democracy in that region began to sink in there. However, all this impact disappeared once the war in Iraq started.

During the Bush administration, democracy promotion became increasingly viewed as a partisan issue associated more with aggressive military action than with constructive NGO activity. For many, democracy promotion became inextricably linked to its leading advocate, President Bush, making it difficult to disaggregate the goal of democracy assistance with the realities of preemptive war, extraordinary rendition, excesses and mishandling of the war on terror, and other unpopular hallmarks of foreign policy during Bush's two terms in office. Opponents of the war in Iraq and of Bush's aggressive foreign policy found it easy to lump democracy assistance in with the rest of their criticisms of Bush. Bush and his supporters, on the other hand, linked democracy promotion, somewhat unrealistically, to the war on terror and presented it as the post facto reason for the invasion of Iraq. Thus both sides embraced a reductive and ideologically driven view of democracy assistance, politicizing the issue for the first time.

Nonetheless, the goals of democracy assistance remain as important, and potentially bipartisan, today as they were twenty years ago when the modern era of democracy assistance began. The debacle in Iraq and the difficulty faced by a prospective fourth wave of democratization has not diminished the value of democracy or made the need for it any less urgent. Nor has it reduced the demand for democracy and freedom among the millions of people still living under authoritarian and non-democratic governments.

When the next president's term begins in 2009, democracy promotion will play a different role in U.S. foreign policy and be viewed quite differently from the case in 2001 when George W. Bush began his presidency. Ultimately, it is likely that even if democracy promotion no longer occupies the central position in foreign policy it has in recent years, it will remain part of America's foreign policy. Democracy assistance is too cheap and too successful to succumb to the growing partisan debate around it.

For democracy promotion to remain a relevant and successful policy in the next administration, supporters and practitioners of democracy assistance will have to change somewhat. Proponents of democracy promotion must work to reposition the policy as a bipartisan issue divorced from military interventionism, preemptive war, and other hangovers from the experience in Iraq. Democracy promotion when it has been most successful has been a cooperative effort with the U.S. and Europe working together. This was certainly the case in Georgia where organizations such as the OSCE played critical roles in exposing the fraud in the 2003 elections, and European countries were important partners, albeit mostly junior partners, to the U.S. in supporting civil society during the Shevardnadze years.

The goal of democracy assistance should be to help build enduring meaningful democracies. Achieving democracy quickly or cheaply settling for unstable semidemocratic systems with pro-American leadership should not be guiding principles. The U.S. and its allies have succeeded in supporting democratic development over the last 60 years in places like Japan, Germany, Eastern Europe, and parts of Africa and South America. The democratically elected leaders of these countries do not always support the U.S., but clearly the U.S. benefits from the existence of democratic regimes in these countries.

The discussion of Georgia throughout this work suggests additional challenges for democracy promotion. American policy toward Georgia since the Rose Revolution could ultimately give credence to those who argue that democracy promotion is simply the newest American tactic for putting friendly leaders into power. The failure of the U.S. to draw attention to the shortcomings of Georgia's new leadership or to invest substantial resources in the consolidation of democracy after the Rose Revolution is a troubling indication of the priority building meaningful democracy has in American foreign policy.

Zhou Enlai, the Chinese prime minister, is said to have responded when, in the 1960s, he was asked to evaluate the impact of the French Revolution, that it is still too early to tell. This is the case for the Rose Revolution as well. The final chapter on democratic and political development in post-Soviet Georgia has not been written. Moreover, a reinvigorated democracy assistance project can have a strong effect on democratic development in Georgia. Even given all the shortcomings of post-Rose Revolution democracy, and the violent suppression of the November 2007 demonstrations, Georgia remains a place of great democratic potential. Reaching this potential will be a tremendously valuable achievement for both Georgia and the U.S.

As I have sought to show in this work, understanding the Rose Revolution requires the ability to see nuance and shades of gray. Shevardnadze was not the sainted former Soviet foreign minister who alone had the ability to change Georgia in the 1990s, nor was he an evil dictator who repressed freedom and any sign of democracy while leading Georgia. Rather, he was a complex leader with a mixed record on issues of democracy. He was also viewed in the West with a certain ambivalence as people sought to balance their respect for him with the growing reality that he had not been able to deliver for Georgia. Mikheil Saakashvili and the people around him are not creating Plato's Republic in the south Caucasus and setting the perfect example of how countries become democratic—as President Bush's comments seem to suggest— nor is Saakashvili a budding dictator with no regard for freedom, as some of his domestic and international critics suggest. Instead, Georgia's government has mixed motives and a record that contains both strengths and weaknesses. Similarly, George Soros and U.S.-supported NGOs did not plot Shevardnadze's overthrow so he could be replaced by Saakashvili, nor did the U.S. and the West have no role in the Rose Revolution. Rather the U.S. played a substantial but not overwhelming, and at times accidental, role in those events.

Georgia is, of course, not alone in this regard. Most of the world's semidemocratic or semiauthoritarian regimes today share this nuance. For every North Korea, Belarus, or Saudi Arabia, there are dozens of countries such as Armenia, Kyrgyzstan, Venezuela, or Cambodia where democratic and nondemocratic practices exist side by side, where some measures of democracy seem to be improving while others are getting worse, and where the leadership is being pulled in several different directions on questions of freedom and democracy. U.S. democracy assistance policy must reflect this understanding of the political environments in which we will be working.

Postscript—War with Russia and Georgia's Future

On August 7, 2008, Georgia found itself in the international news once again. This time it was in the spotlight not for domestic political events, but because the Georgian government had decided that it could no longer countenance the presence of and ongoing provocations by Russian forces in South Ossetia. The government decided to address this problem by launching a military effort to reassert Georgian control over South Ossetia. This was met by a swift, severe, and predictable military response by Russia. Moscow's response included not only pushing Georgian troops out of South Ossetia and expanding the Russian presence in Abkhazia, but also carrying out an air and ground assault on the rest of Georgia that included taking the major cities of Poti and Gori, displacing tens of thousands of Georgian citizens, and sending an unequivocal message that Russia was not going to tolerate a strong and truly independent Georgia.

While the conflict between Russia and Georgia would have been unimaginable if not for the Rose Revolution and the pro-Western, pro-NATO government President Saakashvili led in Georgia, it appeared on the surface to be an international event with little obvious relationship to the development of democracy in Georgia, or indeed with Georgian domestic politics more generally. A closer look at the immediate roots of the conflict, however, shows that Georgian domestic politics played an important role in the events leading up to August 7, and that the conflict between Georgia and Russia will almost certainly have an impact on democratic development in Georgia. It will also have an important effect on the U.S. role in Georgia, with the invasion sparking a broad discussion in the United States about the nature of the U.S.-Russia relationship and fear of another Cold War with Russia.

A key part of Saakashvili's state-building agenda had been reconstituting Georgia's territorial integrity and reasserting Tbilisi's sovereignty over Ajara, Abkhazia, and South Ossetia, the three regions that had been lost during the Shevardnadze years. Saakashvili was able to regain control over Ajara early in his first term through a nonviolent standoff with Abkhazian leader Aslan Abashidze that was itself something of a small-scale Rose Revolution. Not surprisingly, reasserting control over Abkhazia and South Ossetia were far greater challenges for the new Georgian government.

In the years following the Rose Revolution, expectations in Georgia were high. Saakashvili's penchant for strong rhetoric and overpromising had contributed to this. While in many respects the accomplishments of the Rose Revolution government were impressive, they were unable to meet these not entirely realistic expectations. This contributed to the unrest in Georgia in November 2007, but this unrest only led to further political gain by Saakashvili's National Movement. Thus, the demonstrations of 2007 and the presidential and parliamentary elections of 2008, rather than being an opportunity for the Georgian citizenry to express their discontent and hold their government accountable, contributed to the further consolidation of power by the National Movement. Still, the unmet political and economic expectations remained and only increased the need for the government to resolve the frozen conflicts in South Ossetia and Abkhazia and restore Georgia's territorial integrity, even as the National Movement strengthened its grip on the formal institutions of political power.

The government's rhetoric regarding Abkhazia and South Ossetia, a domestic political climate of substantially less enthusiasm for Saakashvili's administration, unwarranted overconfidence in Georgia's improved military capability, and ongoing Russian provocations formed a combination of forces that ultimately proved impossible for Saakashvili and those around him to resist. Moreover, by August 2008 the National Movement dominated the government of Georgia, which meant that policy was not being made in a way that was deliberative or included different political views. The elections of May 2008 had led to a Parliament that was even more dominated by the National Movement than the previous one. At the same time, Nino Burjanadze, who had remained a calmer, more thoughtful presence during the first years following the Rose Revolution, had left Parliament in early summer 2008 to be replaced by the less independent Davit Bakradze. Whatever voices in the Georgian government urged against a reckless military adventure were drowned out by those counseling war

Once Russia responded, the conflict became major international news, even vying with the Beijing Olympics for top coverage in the U.S. media. Saakashvili and his government launched a major media campaign to explain Georgia's position and Russia's invasion to the West. On the surface, this seemed relatively straightforward. Russia had provoked Georgia's response in South Ossetia, but had then launched an all-out war against Georgia. Russia clearly was the aggressor, and ham-fisted Russian attempts to portray Georgia and Saakashvili as genocidal for alleged war crimes in South Ossetia were largely ignored in the West.

This narrative—which U.S. media and policymakers accepted nearly unequivocally—was not so much inaccurate as appallingly simplistic. The U.S. position quickly became that small, democratic Georgia was invaded by an aggressive, hostile, or "revanchist" Russia, and that the United States needed to restore Georgia's territorial integrity (some-thing that Georgia had not really enjoyed since the Soviet era), expel Russia's troops from Georgian soil, and risk moving toward another Cold War with Russia. This view encompassed important truths, but also belied, yet again, a less than full understanding of Georgia and an almost deliberate unwillingness to comprehend Georgia in a realistic fashion. Furthermore, when this was accompanied by U.S. leaders uni-laterally appointing themselves the avatars of what was acceptable behav-ior in the twenty-first century, critics of recent U.S. policy focused not on the plight of Georgia, but on the hypocrisy of the United States and its leaders. Once again, U.S. missteps in Iraq had returned to backfire on Georgia.

A key component of this simplistic understanding of the conflict was the constant description of Georgia as democratic. The notion that Saa-kashvili's Georgia was a democracy, especially after the events in Novem-ber 2007 and the two elections since then, was one that reflected a consensus in Washington but virtually nowhere else. Of course, U.S. sup-port for Georgia against what was clearly an aggressive and unwarranted Russia attack should not depend on the state of Georgian democracy. The United States should have supported Georgian independence and sovereignty even though its democracy is imperfect. Issues of national sovereignty apply to all countries, whether or not they are democracies. Overemphasizing Georgia's democratic claims, however, did not strengthen support for Georgia so much as weaken American credibility on the issue.

Similarly, conflating Georgia's territorial integrity with its future as a sovereign state, and the right of the Georgian people to choose their own future with regard to both domestic and international questions, was deceptive and intellectually lazy. It ultimately condemns Georgia to a long uphill struggle that, if successful, will result in increasing the country's size but will guarantee problems of governance and national harmony for decades. This is not to say that Georgia's claims on Ab-khazia and South Ossetia are not legitimate, but simply that U.S. policy-makers should think long and hard before determining that these issues are not up for debate and are as important as the future of Georgia itself. Jeopardizing the U.S. relationship with Russia over the future of

Georgia, and the implications that has for other American allies in Eastern Europe, is very different from taking this risk for the cause of Georgia's territorial integrity. The former is perhaps an unfortunate necessity; the latter would be an enormous mistake.

The unwillingness on the part of the United States to criticize post-Rose Revolution Georgia remained in place during and immediately after the conflict in Georgia. Thus, the American position on the war between Georgia and Russia was again completely without any nuance. This approach has not been good for democratic development in Georgia and ultimately was not and will not be good for Georgia's efforts to coexist with Russia. One of the central lessons Georgia learned from this conflict was that. no matter how close it is to the United States, and no matter how much the United States may want to help Georgia, Russia is still able to run roughshod over Georgia, sending troops deep into Georgian territory, so Georgia has no option but to find a way to coexist with Russia.

Georgia's actions on August 7, while far from unprovoked or in some abstract way unjust, not only led directly to a Russian attach that was very damaging to Georgia, but also catalyzed rapid deterioration of relations between Russia and the United States. Additionally, it forced the United States into a difficult position with some of its European allies, who prefer a less confrontational approach with Russia.

It is not clear that this conflict was avoidable. Russian frustration with Georgia under Saakashvili and with Saakashvili's efforts to turn Georgia toward the West and eventually become part of NATO were always going to exacerbate tensions with Russia. Nonetheless, it is certainly possible that a less bellicose Georgian approach to Russia, and a less encouraging attitude toward Georgia from the United States, might have led to a less hostile approach from Russia.

The 2008 elections and the war with Russia marked the end of the post-Rose Revolution era in Georgia. The promise the Rose Revolution once held has given way to the consolidation of a semi-democratic regime through two less than free and fair elections. At the same time, doubts have now been raised about Georgia's sovereignty not only by the Russian invasion but by the failure of Russian troops to completely evacuate Georgia.

The post-Rose Revolution era will remain challenging for Georgia and will pivot on two key questions. The first, and most important, is whether Russia will permit Georgia enough space to once again become a sovereign state and direct its own destiny. Clearly, the United States and other European—especially Eastern European—countries are committed to supporting this effort, but if Russia digs in its heels and refuses to leave

Georgia, it is not clear what the level of commitment or range of options available to the West will be.

The future of Georgia's domestic political institutions is the second question. As the war with Russia winds down, several competing urges in Georgian domestic politics will emerge. It is likely that Saakashvili will continue to stress nationalist rhetoric and the unrealistic goals of restoring territorial integrity in order to deflect attention from what will likely be a grim economic situation as well as from the inevitable questions about why he decided to try to retake South Ossetia, knowing full well what the Russian response was likely to be. There will almost certainly be a corresponding effort from opposition parties in Georgia to hold the government accountable for this mistake. This will create tensions that will very likely stretch Georgia's already weak democratic institutions and tradition of political tolerance.

Notes

Chapter 1. Georgia and the Democracy Promotion Project

1. See, e.g., MacKinnon (2007). He argues that the Rose Revolution and similar breakthroughs in Ukraine, Serbia, and elsewhere were engineered largely by the U.S. and are part of a "new Cold War" on its part.

2. Quoted from McLaughlin (2004).

3. See Kandelaki (2006).

4. Kandelaki was active in Kmara—an NGO funded by American billionaire George Soros's Open Society Institute that I discuss in depth later—during the months leading up to the Rose Revolution.

5. This remark was made in English, so the colorful language is a direct quote.

6. House International Relations Subcommittee on International Terrorism, Nonproliferation and Human Rights Holds Hearing on Supporting Human Rights and Democracy, July 7, 2004.

7. Tarnoff (2002). This support included a broad gamut of programs from nonproliferation and war on terrorism to money for agriculture and health as well as, of course, democracy assistance.

8. The Open Society Institute is the foundation of George Soros. Based in New York, it works on both domestic and international issues to promote free and open societies.

9. The resource curse is the notion that countries with abundant natural resources will rely on these as engines for economic growth, thus stunting other forms of economic and political development. See Auty (1993).

10. Georgia has generated more than its fair share of scholarly attention for a country of its size and relative importance to the United States and Europe, but not a great deal of this has focused on domestic politics. There have been only a few significant books in English about the politics of post-Soviet Georgia. These include Karumidze and Wertsch (2005), Wheatley (2005), Suny (1993, 1994), and Nodia and Hanf (2000). The first two are largely about the Rose Revolution and the events leading up to it; Karumidze and Wertsch includes valuable interviews with numerous Georgian and foreign participants in the events of 2003. Wheatley is more analytical but focuses largely on Georgia and does not place the Rose Revolution in the broader context of democratization or democracy promotion. Suny's and Nodia's books were written in the 1990s and seek to explain the Georgian political environment of that period. Suny takes a historical perspective, looking at politics and society in pre-Soviet Georgia as well as the Soviet period to try to explain the politics of newly independent Georgia.

Nodia looks closely at the sociology of post-Soviet Georgia. These works are helpful for understanding the early years of independent Georgia, as well as some of the foundation of the country's current political situation, but they were written years before the Rose Revolution.

11. For example, Legvold and Coppiters's (2005) edited volume addresses a number of the critical issues involving Georgia and Russia.

12. Monten (2005) discusses the influence of Christianity on American perceptions of its role in the world since the country's founding. He specifically note the influence on seventeenth-century Calvinism on democracy promotion throughout the centuries.

13. Jeanne Kirkpatrick's *Dictatorships and Double Standards* (1982) is the most well known and influential of these works.

14. Carothers (1999)

15. See McFaul (2004) and Sen (2001).

16. Vienna Declaration and Programme of Action, adopted by the World Conference on Human Rights June 25, 1993.

17. See Sen (1991) and McFaul (2004, 2005) for more on this.

18. The 2006 NED budget was $80 million, an increase from $60 million in 2005. The 2006 IRI budget was $74.1 million and that of NDI exceeded $100 million, both substantial increases from 2005. The USAID global budget for democracy in governance increased from $781 million in 2005 to $2.69 billion in 2007. Of course, NDI and IRI get some of their money from sources other than USAID. http://www.usaid.gov/policy/budget/cbj2007/summtabs/st_2abc .pdf.

19. According to Huntington (1991), the first wave of democracy occurred in Europe in the mid-nineteenth century and the second wave during the years immediately following World War II.

20. There is some literature emerging on this issue. See, e.g., Melia (2006).

21. Ivie (2001) offers a good analysis of this debate in a review article that examines works by Gowa (1999), Kozhemiakin (1998), Gilbert (1999), Weart (1998), Elman (1997), and Rummel (1997). Other recent work on this question includes Ray (1997), Gat (2005), Mansfield and Snyder (2002, 2005), and Cox, Ikenberry and Inogushi (2000).

22. Quoted in Weisman (2006). Zakaria (2003) makes this point with somewhat more nuance.

23. Cavell (2002) and Encarnación (2003) are good scholarly examples of this view of American democracy assistance. Other examples can be seen on thousands of websites and blogs. A very limited list of these blogs includes www.redpepper.blogs.com, the British Helsinki Human Rights Group www .bhhrg.org, www.internetactivist.org, www.petitiononline.com/closened, www .antiwarr.com, www.wsws.org, www.internationalist.org.

24. See, e.g., Weart (1998), Rummel (1975–1981, 1997), Maoz and Russett (1996), Ray (1997).

25. NED (2002), 4.

26. See Talbott, (1994) for an explanation of this view which came to be very influential during the Clinton administration. The Clinton administration's 1995 National Security Strategy Document "A National Security Strategy of Engagement and Enlargment" also relies on this approach and explanation.

27. Sen (1999) argued another economic angle, that famines do not occur in democracies.

28. Cox, Ikenberry, Inoguchi (2000) offer a collection of essays addressing these and other related questions.

29. See Mansfield and Snyder (2005).

30. For more on this view see, for example, Schweller (2000), Mousseau (1998), or Reiter and Huth (1996).

31. The debate over the wisdom of making democracy promotion an increasingly central part of foreign policy has led to further discussions within the academy and policy communities about sequencing, the relative import of elections, the central role of civil society and the efficacy of American democracy promotion practices in general. See, for example, Mansfield and Snyder (2006), Fukuyama (2006), or Zakaria (2003).

32. See http://www.freedomhouse.org/template.cfm?page=15 for a description of this index and how it is determined.

33. See, for example, Goble (1997), Collier and Levitsky (1997), Ottaway (2002), Schedler (2006). Chapter 2 of the present volume includes a discussion of this literature with regards to pre-Rose Revolution Georgia.

Chapter 2. Illusions of Democracy

1. Other works that provide significant depth on Georgian nationalism and its pre-Soviet history include Tuminez (2003), Kolsto (1996), and Nodia (1995).

2. Nodia (1995).

3. In a discussion with the author in July 2004, Shevardnadze made this point very clearly. He named his return to Georgia and his work at the end of the Cold War as the two accomplishments of which he was most proud.

4. Transparency International (1995–).

5. Freedom House is a U.S.-based NGO. According to its mission, statement, "Freedom House is an independent nongovernmental organization that supports the expansion of freedom in the world. Freedom is possible only in democratic political systems in which the governments are accountable to their own people; the rule of law prevails; and freedoms of expression, association, and belief, as well as respect for the rights of minorities and women, are guaranteed."

6. OSCE/ODIHR (2000), 1, 15.

7. Human Rights Watch (2001).

8. OSCE/ODIHR (1999).

9. The term "majoritarian" refers to what are generally known as single mandate districts, where one person represents one specific area of a country. However, majoritarian is the word usually used to describe these districts in Georgia, so I use it in this work.

10. "Rayon" is a Soviet administrative term comparable to "county" in the United States.

11. The Georgian parliament, like many parliaments in the former Soviet Union, is organized into factions that are officially recognized and, as will be discussed later, are given perks and power in parliament.

12. OSCE/ODIHR (1999), 26.

13. The New Rights credentials as an opposition party were further weakened because Gamkrelidze had earned much of his fortune through a monopoly on the insurance industry from Shevardnadze's government, making it difficult to believe that he was actually in opposition to the man who had made him very rich through questionably legal and ethical policies.

14. Vazha Lortkipanidze, a former State Minister of Georgia under Shevardnadze, referred to these types of small parties in Georgian as being like *djonjoli* (a pickled herb often served as a side dish at traditional Georgian supras). His point was that this dish, like most at these parties, is pleasant enough to have around but you don't really notice if it is not there.

15. The mayor of Tbilisi is still not directly elected. This remains a contentious issue in Georgia.

16. Carothers (2002).

17. Schedler (2006), 3.

18. Ottaway (2002), 3.

19. Levitsky and Way (2002), 51.

Chapter 3. The Accidental Revolution

1. This chapter draws heavily on notes taken while in Georgia during almost all of 2003, closely monitoring the English and Georgian language media as well as conversations with hundreds of Georgian politicians, government officials, civic activists, and ordinary voters.

2. Election monitoring was one of many rule-of-law-related projects GYLA did with this funding.

3. One of the stranger rumors concerning inking was that it would cause impotence. When asked what she was going to do about this rumor, CEC chair Nana Devadiriani responded in a frustrated tone, "it is not my fault if some people do not understand what part of the body will be inked."

4. After the New Rights, NM, and UD led a march to protest CUG unwillingness to support a strong new election law in June 2003, Natalashvili remarked that "the new CUG is protesting the old CUG on the streets of Tbilisi."

5. In mid-2003, Ghia Nodia, one of Georgia's leading political observers, and currently the Minister of Education explained the relationship between these three to me in a private conversation by saying "don't forget, they all went to high school together." While not literally true, this captured the depth, length, and personal nature of the rivalries.

6. See Devdariani (2003).

7. See Anteleva (2003).

8. A similar program brought election monitors from Azerbaijan to monitor the elections in the heavily Azeri region of Kvemo Kartli, also notorious for particularly bad elections.

9. Abashidze, of course, had more than just some organized crime connections and was something of a criminal kingpin himself.

10. Minutes after the exit poll numbers were released, I spoke with one of Saakashvili's top aides and said, "So, I guess the campaign for president starts tonight." He laughed warmly and said "Absolutely."

11. Although I have no concrete proof of this, leaders of both the BD and the NM, during these days, told me these deals had been proposed by the government and rejected by their parties.

12. Saakashvili (2004a).

13. During that first week of demonstrations I asked a senior NM leader whether they were "going by the seat of their pants"; he chuckled and said "yes."

14. Shortly after Shevardnadze resigned, a senior NM leader told me that the

party had been ready to call an end to the demonstrations if Shevardnadze would accept the PVT results. The centrality of the PVT rather than the exit poll in this negotiation speaks to the relative value placed on each by the Georgian people and politicians.

15. Lortkipanidze was a moderate and decent politician, albeit one who was rumored to have stolen millions of dollars during his tenure as state minister under Shevardnadze. He brought his Christian Democratic Union of Georgia (CDUG) into the FNG in exchange for the number one spot on the FNG list. He was one of the most palatable politicians in the top FNG positions.

Chapter 4. How Democratic Was the Rose Revolution?

1. The dacha to which Shevardnadze retired to write his memoirs had previously been the presidential mansion, but Shevardnadze privatized it and bought if for a very low price late in his presidency. This made Shevardnadze's remarks upon resigning—"I am going home"—somewhat disingenuous because he didn't actually go anywhere but turned around and walked back into the house that he had all but stolen from the people of Georgia.

2. The parliamentary elections in March 2004 were only for the 150 party list members of the parliament. The 75 single mandate representatives who were elected in the fraudulent elections of November, 2003 were allowed to keep their seats.

3. From Georgia Extraordinary Presidential Election 4 January 2004 OSCE/ODIHR. (2004).

4. See Bunce and Wolchick (2006) for a discussion of these breakthroughs.

5. *Khachapuri*, a kind of cheesebread, is Georgia's national dish.

6. See, for example, Bunce (2006), Fairbanks (2004), or Mitchell (2004).

7. Tarnoff (2003) estimates that Georgia received more U.S. foreign assistance in both 2002 and 2003 than any other post-Soviet state other than Ukraine, Russia, and Armenia. However, not all this assistance was for democracy work.

8. Carothers (1999), 85.

Chapter Five. Governance by Adrenaline

1. In a speech at the Council on Foreign Relations in New York on February 26, 2004 (Saakashvili 2004b), Saakashvili's words made it clear that there was reason for great hope and expectations in Georgia. "A new era nonetheless exists. For anyone who ever thought or hoped that Georgia was a failed state, our revolution and our people proved that forever wrong. Emerging from a glorious revolution, Georgia is stronger than ever, more united than ever, and more resolute in its commitments to build a stable and prosperous state than ever."

2. The Venice Commission Report "Opinions on the Draft Amendments to the Constitution of Georgia" (2004) provides a balanced assessment of the proposed changes, but its central finding that more time was needed to discuss these changes was mute when the report was issued on March 15. This was less than two months after the amendments had been proposed, but by this time they had already been passed into law.

3. Burjanadze had also been plagued by rumors that both her husband and

her father had enriched themselves by corruption during the Shevardnadze regime. This was not lost on Saakashvili.

4. This was also ironic because nobody had been more responsible for building parliament into a relevant political institution during the Shevardnadze years than Zhvania.

5. For example, Alexander Shalaberidze, a Georgian MP, has referred to "certain Russian forces" behind Zhvania's death. Irina Sarashvili Chanturia is a fringe politician in post-Shevardnadze Georgia but her remarks at a press conference following Zhvania's death—"I can't understand why Zurab Zhvania's death was initially declared an accident, or why the Georgian government refuses to have independent experts. join the investigation"—capture some of the concern around the government's declaration that the death was an accident. See Blagov (2005). Shevardnadze himself stated in a March 2006 interview with the *Washington Post* that "He was murdered," but did not speculate who might have been behind the murder; see Quinn-Judge (2006). In September 2007, former Defense Minister Irakle Okruashvili, upon announcing that he was moving into the opposition, made a number of serious charges against Saakashvili's government, including implying that Saakashvili was behind the death of Zhvania.

6. A piece by John Laughland in *The Guardian* on April 1, 2004 (2004a) was clearly planted by Abashidze and the Ajaran authorities and is makes Abashidze's views on the Rose Revolution clear. The piece refers to Zhvania as a "thug" compares Saakashvili to fellow Georgians Stalin and Beria and asserts that "November's 'revolution of roses' was stage-managed by the Americans."

7. As evidence that George Soros, whom I have never met, and I were in cahoots, Natalashvili pointed out that we were both Democrats. I responded that we also both lived in New York City but that didn't mean we spoke to each other every day. I resisted the temptation to point out that Soros and I are also both Jewish and to ask Natalashvili what kind of post-Soviet demagogue he was if he couldn't even find a way to blame the Jews at a time like this.

8. One way to see the difference in elections before and after the Rose Revolution is to compare the OSCE/ODIHR report on the flawed 2003 parliamentary elections conducted which brought about the transition in Georgia (http://www.osce.org/documents/odihr/ 2004/01/1992_en.pdf) and the same organization's report on the repeat of these parliamentary elections in 2004 during the early months of Saakashvili's presidency (http://www.osce.org/documents/odihr/2004/03/2488_en.pdf).

9. http://www.freedomhouse.org/template.cfm?page = 22&year = 2005&country = 6 7 41.

10. http://www.freedomhouse.org/template.cfm?page = 22&country = 7181&year = 2 007.

11. The full English language text of the letter, dated 10/18/04, can be found on http://www.civil.ge/eng/article.php?id = 8100. Signatories on the letter included Ghia Nodia and Davit Usupashvili, two of Georgia's best known intellectuals among both foreign and domestic audiences. Both were active opponents of Shevardnadze's and supporters of the Rose Revolution.

12. Pepys (2006), Devdariani, Kandelaki, and Lomsadze (2004), Kupcham (2006).

13. Mikheil Saakashvili, "Remarks H.E. The President of Georgia Mikheil Saakashvili, European Parliament Strasbourg," November 14, 2006, www.president.gov.ge

14. Condorcet, Dodgson, and Arrow are among the best-known scholars to explore this point.

15. For example, Levan Ramishvili of the Liberty Institute, a prominent pro-government NGO with very close ties to the administration, commented in October 2006. "Today Russia has more allies in the political parties in Georgia that are cooperating with Russia openly or covertly, and their number is higher than it seems with just one glance." Khutsidze and Sepashvili (2006).

16. This allusion was undoubtedly broadly understood in Georgia, where *The Godfather* remains a very popular movie.

17. David the Builder ruled Georgia from 1089 until 1125. He is remembered by Georgians for creating a strong Georgian army, unifying the Georgian Orthodox Church, issuing Georgian currency and defeating several amassed Muslim armies at the battle of Didgori in 1121.

18. See Ostrovsky (2004). Saakashvili's comparison with Ben Gurion is notable as not too many world leaders would publicly identify an Israeli political figure as a role model, but Israel is very well liked in Georgia and the two countries have close relations. This connection is based on both the good relations between Jewish and Christian Georgians during the last two and a half millennium as well as Georgian respect for Israel's military and economic strength.

19. *Supporting Human Rights and Democracy: The U.S. Record 2003–2004 Report* (U.S. Department of State 2004a). Note Armitage's use of the past tense indicating that democracy had already been achieved in Georgia.

20. In fact, the government has been pushed in this direction by the opposition as well, most notably the New Rights Party. Party leader David Gamkrelidze challenged President Saakashvili at an October 16, 2006 press conference. "Why is President Saakashvili not fulfilling the provisions set by the Georgian Parliament's July 18 resolution. Why is President Saakashvili ignoring our proposals to unilaterally cease Russian peacekeeping and to quit the Commonwealth of Independent States (CIS) . . . ? What are President Saakashvili's plans in respect to the independence referendum planned for November 12 in breakaway South Ossetia, and what will Georgia's response be to Russia's potential decision to recognize Abkhazia and South Ossetia?" "Opposition Leader Questions Saakashvili on Ties with Russia" (2006).

21. See, for example, Coppieters and Legvold (2005), Hunter (2006), and Lynch (2004) for more on this important issue.

22. Tedo Japardize, former Georgian Foreign Minister and Ambassador to the U.S., phrased this distinction this way.

23. Sedov (2006).

24. Finn (2006).

25. Chachua and Kurashvili (2006).

26. Levitsky and Way (2006); see also Levitsky and Way (2002).

27. Diamond and Plattner (2002), Ottaway (2002), Mandaville and Mandaville (2007) offer criticisms of the transition paradigm. The work cited by Carothers also offers a description and critique of the paradigm.

28. Goble (1997) introduced the term "hyphenated democracy."

Chapter Six. The U.S. Role in the Rose Revolution

1. Sussman (2006). Sussman's statements are not accurate, but similar views can be seen in countless blogs and other anti-war websites and articles.

2. Laughland (2004b). This article appears on the BHHRG website. The BHHRG's previous contribution to Georgian politics had been putting their stamp of approval on Abashidze's stolen elections in Ajara.

3. Cited in Champion (2006).

4. Statement of John Tefft, ambassador-designate to Georgia, before the Senate Foreign Relations Committee May 24, 2005 (U.S. Senate 2005).

5. The September 2005 edition of *Democracy Rising* (USAID 2005) comes close to making this claim, particularly in a chart on page 7 indicating how $91 million in U.S. foreign assistance for democracy has been used in Georgia since 1994.

6. This estimate comes from King (2004). Additionally, the U.S. State Department estimated in January 2007 that the U.S. had provided "approximately $1.7 billion in assistance" to Georgia since 1991. See U.S. Department of State (2007).

7. Two exceptions to this were longtime Shevardnadze aides Gela Charkviani and Tedo Japardize, who stayed with Shevardnadze to the end while trying to push him more toward democracy and fair elections. Unfortunately, by 2003 these two were a minority among Shevardnadze's aides and advisors.

8. NDI went so far as to honor Shevardnadze with its W. Averell Harriman Democracy Award in 1999.

9. USAID/Caucasus (2003), 7.

10. As shown in Chapter 3, not all these programs, notably support for the voter list, were successful or effective.

11. General Shalikashvili was very well known in Georgia and enjoyed great prestige there not only because of the high ranking positions he had held in the American military, but also because he perhaps the highest profile Georgian American. Shalikashvili's father had been born in Georgia and, of course, his last name is unmistakably Georgian.

12. The role of opposition coalitions in electoral breakthroughs is quite significant. Howard and Roessler's (2006) description of why coalitions can play a central role applies to Georgia reasonably well. Van de Walle (2006) also provides insight into how coalitions can help combat likely election fraud.

13. For example, in 2004, the last year of Akaev's presidency in Kyrgyzstan, the country received $50 million in U.S. assistance of which only $12.2 million went toward democracy assistance. U.S. Department of State (2004a).

Chapter 7. Georgia and the United States After the Revolution

1. Numerous civil society activists who played key roles in 2003 are now in government. Giga Bokeria, a leading figure in the Liberty Institute, is now an MP. Zurab Tchiarabashvili, who directed ISFED during the 2003 election cycle, became chair of the CEC and mayor of Tbilisi before being sent abroad as a diplomat. Kaha Lomaia, director of the Open Society Institute Georgia office, became minister of education and national science advisor. These are only some examples.

2. Bush (2005).

3. This information is taken from the democracy and governance section of the USAID Georgia website, http://georgia.usaid.gov/programs/democracy_and_governance.html. Note that the parliamenaary strengthening project is meant to respond to the priorities of the government, meaning the executive branch. This somewhat defeats the purpose of a strong parliament which, virtually by definition, should be setting its own priorities.

4. Asatiani (2005).

5. Interview with author, March 5, 2007. Evans served as Chief of Party for IREX in 2002–2005.

6. Interview with author, March 18, 2007.

7. Officials from the U.S. government have made concerns about the pace and character of democratization known to the Georgian government privately, but this does not have the same impact as public statements, particularly because of the high regard in which official American opinion is held in Georgia.

8. Saakashvili (2005).

Chapter 8. Georgia and the Fading of the Color Revolutions

1. Applebaum (2007), Almond (2007), *New York Times* (2007).

2. For a description of how views of democracy assistance have changed among authoritarian governments in the former Soviet Union, and Russia's role in this, see Carothers (2006) and Gershman and Allen (2007).

3. Diamond (2005), 289.

4. See, for example, Cordesman (2004), Ikenberry (2004).

5. This section draws on some material from Mitchell (2007).

6. Richard Haass (2005), for example, introduces his critique of the role of elections in democracy assistance by writing "many observers equate democracy and elections. One does not guarantee the other." The second sentence is clearly true, but there are few serious observers, or practitioners, of democracy assistance who equate elections and democracy.

7. Data from USAID Office of Democracy and Governance website, www .usaid.gov/policy/budget.

8. The often insightful criticisms of moving too quickly toward elections made by Snyder and Mansfield (2005) are weakened somewhat because they extrapolate criticisms of democracy assistance more broadly from this insight.

9. See, for example, Snyder and Mansfield (2005), Zakaria (1997), Chua (2003).

10. Carothers (2002), O'Donnell (2002), and many others have addressed this question.

11. Carothers (2007) and Berman (2007) address this point, arguing that sequencing is not even an accurate reading of democratic development in most countries.

12. See O'Donnell (2002) for a more in depth discussion of this point.

13. As discussed in Chapter 1, President Clinton made democracy promotion one of the central pillars of his 1995 National Security Strategy, but even Clinton's public statements on the issue were not as frequent or impassioned as those of President Bush.

Bibliography

Almond, Mark. 2007. "The West Should Stop Picking Losers." *International Herald Tribune*, November 13.

Anteleva, Natalia. 2003. "Radical Opposition Party Tops Opposition Poll in Georgia as Parliament Election Looms." *Eurasia Insight*, October 28.

Applebaum, Anne. 2007. "Georgia's Leap Backward." *Washington Post*, November 13.

ARD, Inc. 2001. "USAID Caucasus/Georgia Civil Society Assessment (Including NGO Development, Media and Political Processes)." Burlington, Vt.: ARD, June.

———. 2002. "USAID/Georgia Democracy and Government Assessment of Georgia." Burlington, Vt.: ARD, December.

Arrow, Kenneth. 1951. *Social Choice and Individual Values*. New York: Wiley.

Asatiani, Giorgi. 2005. "USAID Final Project Report: Support to the New Government of Georgia" Bethesda, Md.: Development Associates International.

Associated Press. 1999. "Sea of Blood Predicted in Georgia Battle." December 31.

Associated Press-Reuters. 1992. "Rebels Consider Role for Shevardnadze." January 7.

Auty, Richard. 1993. *Sustaining Development in Mineral Economies: The Resource Curse Thesis*. London: Routledge

Baaklini, Abdo, and Helen Desfosses, eds. 1997. *Designs for Democratic Stability: Studies in Viable Constitutionalism* Armonk, N.Y.: M.E. Sharpe.

Baker, Peter. 2001. "A Hero to the West, a Villain at Home: Shevardnadze Leads Georgians to Hardship." *Washington Post*, April 14.

Berg-Schlosser, Dirk, and Raivo Vetik, eds. 2001. *Perspectives on Democratic Consolidation in Central and Eastern Europe* New York: Columbia University Press.

Berman, Shari, 2007. "How Democracies Emerge: Lessons from Europe." *Journal of Democracy* 18, 1: 28–41.

Bjorlund, Eric, 2004. *Beyond Free and Fair: Monitoring Elections and Building Democracy*. Baltimore: Johns Hopkins University Press.

Blagov, Sergei. 2005. "Post-Zhvania, Georgia-Russia Ties Face New Challenges." *Eurasia Insight*, February 8.

Bunce, Valerie, and Sharon Wolchick, 2006. "International Diffusion and Postcommunist Electoral Revolutions" *Communist and Postcommunist Studies* 39, 3: 283–304.

Bush, George W. 2005. "President Addresses and Thanks Citizens in Tbilisi, Georgia." May 10.

Carothers, Thomas. 1999. *Aiding Democracy Abroad: The Learning Curve* Washington, D.C.: Carnegie Endowment for International Peace.

————. 2002. "The End of the Transition Paradigm." *Journal of Democracy* 13, 1: 5–21.

————. 2004 *Critical Mission: Essays on Democracy Promotion.* Washington, D.C.: Carnegie Endowment for International Peace;

————. 2006a. "The Backlash Against Democracy Promotion." *Foreign Affairs* (March/April).

————. 2006b. *Confronting the Weakest Link: Aiding Political Parties in New Democracies* Washington, D.C.: Carnegie Endowment for International Peace.

————. 2007. "How Democracies Emerge: The Sequencing Fallacy." *Journal of Democracy* 18, 1: 12–27.

Cavell, Colin. 2002. *Exporting "Made-in-America" Democracy: The National Endowment for Democracy and U.S. Foreign Policy.* Lanham, Md.: University Press of America.

Chachua, Diana, and Nana Kurashvili. 2006. "Georgia: Opposition's Poor Election Showing Rings Alarm Bells." *Institute for War and Peace Reporting,* October 12.

Champion, Marc. 2006. "In Bloom: As Georgia's 'Rose Revolution' Blossoms, Thorny Issues Emerge: President Cultivates Economy, Energy, Industry, but Rankles Critics, Russia." *Wall Street Journal Europe,* July 6.

Civil Georgia. 2006a. "Authorities See Tycoon as Political Foe." March 29. www.civil.ge.

————. 2006b. "Opposition Leader Questions Saakashvili on Ties with Russia." October 16. www.civil.ge.

Collier, David, and Steven Levitsky. 1997. "Research Note: Democracy with Adjectives: Conceptual Innovation in Comparative Research." *World Politics* 49, 3: 30–51.

Connell, Christopher, 1992. "U.S. Opens Full Diplomatic Ties with Shevardnadze's Georgia." Associated Press, March 24.

Cordesman, Anthony. 2004. "U.S. Policy in Iraq: A 'Realist' Approach to Its Challenges and Opportunities." Working Paper, Center for Strategic and International Studies, Washington, D.C., August 6.

Cox, Michael, G. John Ikenberry, and Takashi Inogushi, eds. 2000. *American Democracy Promotion: Impulses, Strategies, and Impacts.* Oxford: Oxford University Press.

Crabtree, John, ed. 2006. *Making Institutions Work in Peru: Democracy, Development and Inequality Since 1980.* London: Institute for the Study of the Americas.

Crossette, Barbara. 1992. "Baker Visits Georgia to Help a Friend." *New York Times,* May 26.

Dahl, Robert. 1989. *Democracy and Its Critics.* New Haven, Conn.: Yale University Press.

Devdariani, Jaba. 2003. "The Popularity of an Opposition Moderate Coalition Surges in Georgia." *Eurasia Insight,* September 25.

Devdariani, Jaba, Giorgi Kandelaki, and Giorgi Lomsadze. 2004. "Saakashvili Opponents in Georgia Say President Is Using Anti-Democratic Methods to Advance." EurasiaNet.org, March 1.

Diamond, Larry. 2002. "Thinking About Hybrid Regimes." *Journal of Democracy* 13, 2: 21–35.

————. 2005. *Squandered Victory: The American Occupation and the Bungled Effort to Bring Democracy to Iraq.* New York: Holt

Diamond, Larry, and Richard Gunther. 2001. *Political Parties and Democracy.* Baltimore: Johns Hopkins University Press.

Diamond, Larry, and Marc Plattner, eds. 2001. *The Global Divergence of Democracies*. A Journal of Democracy Book. Baltimore: Johns Hopkins University Press.

Dodgson, Charles Lutwidge. 1994. *The Mathematical Pamphlets of Charles Lutwidge Dodgson and Related Pieces*. Ed. Francis Abeles. New York: Lewis Carroll Society of North America; Charlottesville: Distributed by the University Press of Virginia.

Dreze, Jean, and Amartya Sen. 1999. *The Amartya Sen and Jean Dreze Omnibus: Poverty and Famines; Hunger and Public Action; India Economic Development and Social Opportunity*. New York: Oxford University Press.

Domingo, Pilar. 1999. "Judicial Independence and Judicial Reform in Latin America." In *The Self-Restraining State: Power and Accountability in New Democracies*, ed. Andreas Schedler, Larry Diamond, and Marc Plattner. Boulder, Colo.: Lynne Rienner.

Elman, Miriam Fendius, ed. 1997. *Paths to Peace: Is Democracy the Answer?* Cambridge, Mass.: MIT Press.

Encarnación, Omar. 2003. *The Myth of Civil Society: Social Capital and Democratic Consolidation in Spain and Brazil*. New York: Palgrave Macmillan.

Fairbanks, Charles. 2004. "Georgia's Rose Revolution." *Journal of Democracy* 15, 2: 110–24.

Finn, Peter. 2006. "Putin and Georgia Officials Intensify Rhetoric in Dispute: President Calls Russians' Arrests 'State Terrorism'." *Washington Post*, October 2.

Freedom House. 2006. *Freedom in the World Country Ratings 1972–2006*. New York: Freedom House. http://www.freedomhouse.org.

Fukuyama, Francis. 2006. *America at the Crossroads: Democracy, Power, and the Neoconservative Legacy*. New Haven, Conn.: Yale University Press

Gat, Azar. 2005. "The Democratic Peace Theory Reframed: The Impact of Modernity." *World Politics* 58, 1: 73–100.

Gershman, Carl, and Michael Allen. 2007. "The Assault on Democracy Assistance." *Journal of Democracy* 17, 2: 36–51.

Gilbert, Alan. 1999. *Must Global Politics Constrain Democracy? Great-Power Realism, Democratic Peace, and Democratic Internationalism*. Princeton, N.J.: Princeton University Press.

Gunther, Richard P. Nikiforos Diamandouros, and Hans-Jürgen Puhle, eds. 1995. *The Politics of Democratic Consolidation: Southern Europe in Comparative Perspective*. Baltimore: Johns Hopkins University Press.

Gray, John. 1992. "Analysis: Eduard Shevardnadze, Known Internationally as a Reformer, Is Remembered in His Native Georgia as a Hard-Line Communist: Old Memories Taint Homecoming." *Globe and Mail*, March 9.

Grey, Robert, ed. 1997. *Democratic Theory and Post-Communist Change*. Upper Saddle River, N.J.: Prentice-Hall.

Goble, Paul. 1997. "Hyphenated Democracy." *Central Asia Monitor* 3.

Gowa, Joanne. 1999. *Ballots and Bullets: The Elusive Democratic Peace*. Princeton, N.J.: Princeton University Press

Gunther, Richard, José Montero, and Juan Linz. 2002. *Political Parties: Old Concepts and New Challenges*. Oxford: Oxford University Press

Haass, Richard. 2005. *The Opportunity: America's Moment to Alter History's Course*. New York: Public Affairs.

Hahn, Jeffrey. 1996. *Democratization in Russia: The Development of Legislative Institutions*. Armonk, N.Y.: M.E. Sharpe.

Henderson, Sarah. 2003. *Building Democracy in Contemporary Russia*. Ithaca, N.Y.: Cornell University Press.

Howard, Marc and Philip Roessler. 2006. "Liberalizing Electoral Outcomes in Competitive Authoritarian Regimes." *American Political Science Review* 50, 2.

Human Rights Watch. 2001. *World Report 2001: Georgia.* www.hrw.org/wr2k1/europe/georgia

Hunter, Shireen. 2006. "Borders, Conflict, and Security in the Caucasus: The Legacy of the Past." *SAIS Review* 26, 1: 111–25.

Huntington, Samuel. 1991. *The Third Wave: Democratization in the Late Twentieth Century.* Norman: University of Oklahoma Press.

Ignatiev, Noel. 1995. *How the Irish Became White.* New York: Routledge.

Ikenberry, G. John. 2004. "The End of the Neoconservative Moment." *Survival* 46, 1.

Ivie, Robert. 2001. "Democratizing for Peace." *Rhetoric and Public Affairs* 4, 2: 309–22.

Jones, Stephen. 2000. "Georgian Nationalism: A Reassessment." *Analysis of Current Events* 12, 5–6: 3–5.

Jones, Stephen, and Robert Parsons. 1996. "Georgia and the Georgians." In *The Nationalities Question in the Post-Soviet States,* ed. Graham Smith. Harlow: Longman. 291–313.

Kandelaki, Giorgi. 2006. "Georgia's Rose Revolution: A Participant's Perspective." U.S. Institute of Peace Special Report. Washington D.C.: USIP.

Karumidze, Zurab, and James Wertsch, eds. 2005. *Enough! The Rose Revolution in the Republic of Georgia 2003.* New York: Nova Science.

Khutsidze, Nino, and Giorgi Sepashvili. 2006. "Some See Foreign Factors Behind Saakashvili's Surprise Proposal." *Civil Georgia,* October 20. www.civil.ge.

King, Charles. 2004. "A Rose Among Thorns: Georgia Makes Good." *Foreign Affairs* (March/April).

Kirkpatrick, Jeanne. 1982. *Dictatorships and Double Standards: Rationalism and Reason in Politics.* New York: Simon and Schuster.

Kolsto, Pal. 1996. "Nation-Building in the Former USSR." *Journal of Democracy* 7, 1: 118–32.

Kozhemiakin, Alexander. 1998. *Expanding the Zone of Peace? Democratization and International Security.* New York: St. Martin's Press.

Kupcham, Charles. 2006. "Wilted Rose: Is Georgia Reverting to Tyranny?" *New Republic,* January 30.

Laughland, John. 2004a. "Georgia on Their Mind: Laughland in Batumi." *The Guardian,* April 1.

———. 2004b. "The Technique of a Coup d'État." British Helsinki Human Rights Group, Sanders Research Associates, January 12.

Legvold, Robert, and Bruno Coppieters. 2005. *Statehood and Security: Georgia After the Rose Revolution.* Cambridge, Mass.: American Academy of Arts and Sciences, MIT Press.

Levitsky, Steven, and Lucan Way. 2002. "The Rise of Competitive Authoritarianism." *Journal of Democracy* 13, 2: 51–65.

———. 2006. "Auhoritarian Failure: How Does State Weakness Strengthen Electoral Competition." In *Electoral Authoritarianism: The Dynamics of Unfree Competition,* ed. Andreas Schedler. London: Lynne Rienner.

Linz, Juan, and Alfred Stepan, eds. 1978. *The Breakdown of Democratic Regimes: Latin America.* Baltimore: John Hopkins University Press.

———. 1996. *Problems of Democratic Transition and Consolidation: Southern Europe, South America, and Post-Communist Europe* Baltimore: Johns Hopkins University Press.

Linz, Juan, and ArturoValenzuela, eds. 1994. *The Failure of Presidential Democracy.* Baltimore: Johns Hopkins University Press.

Lynch, Dov. 2004. *Engaging Eurasia's Separatist States: Unresolved Conflicts and De Facto States.* Washington D.C.: U.S. Institute of Peace Press.

MacKinnon, Mark. 2007. *The New Cold War: Revolutions, Rigged Elections, and Pipeline Politics in the Former Soviet Union.* New York: Carroll and Graf.

Mandaville, Alicia Phillips, and Peter P. Mandaville. 2007. "Rethinking Democratization and Democracy Assistance" *Development* 50, 1.

Mansfield, Edward, and Jack Snyder. 2002. "Democratic Transitions, Institutional Strength, and War." *International Organization* 56, 2: 297–337.

———. 2005. *Electing to Fight: Why Emerging Democracies Go to War.* Cambridge, Mass.: MIT Press.

Maoz, Zeev, John O'Neal, Frances O'Neal, and Bruce Russett. 1996. "The Liberal Peace: Interdependence, Democracy, and International Conflict, 1950–85." *Journal of Peace Research* 33, 1: 11–28.

McFaul, Michael. 1993. *Post-Communist Politics: Democratic Prospects in Russia and Eastern Europe.* Washington, D.C.: Center for Strategic International Studies.

———. 2004–5. "Democracy Promotion as a World Value." *Washington Quarterly* 28, 1: 147–63.

McFaul, Michael, and Kathryn Stoner-Weiss, eds. 2004 *After the Collapse of Communism: Comparative Lessons of Transition.* Cambridge: Cambridge University Press.

McLaughlin, Daniel. 2004. "Putin Accuses West of Backing Revolutions." *Irish Times*, December 24.

McLean, Iain, and Fiona Hewitt, eds. 1994. *Condorcet: Foundations of Social Choice and Political Theory.* Aldershot: Elgar.

Melia, Thomas O. 2006. "The Democracy Bureaucracy." *American Interest* 1, 4.

Mitchell, Lincoln. 2004. "Georgia's Rose Revolution." *Current History* 103, 675: 342–48.

———. 2006. "Democracy in Georgia Since the Rose Revolution." *Orbis* 50, 4: 669–76.

———. 2007 "Beyond Bombs and Ballots: Dispelling Myths about Democracy Assistance." *National Interest* 88: 32–36.

Monten, Jonathan. 2005. "The Roots of the Bush Doctrine: Power, Nationalism, and Democracy Promotion in U.S. Strategy." *International Security* 29, 4: 112–56.

Moore, Barrington. 1965. *Social Origins of Dictatorship and Democracy: Lord and Peasant in the Making of the Modern World.* Boston: Beacon Press.

Moses, Joel, ed. 2003. *Dilemmas of Transition in Post-Soviet Countries.* Chicago: Burnham.

Mousseau, Michael. 1998. "Democracy and Compromise in Militarized Interstate Conflicts, 1816–1992." *Journal of Conflict Resolution* 42, 2: 210–23.

National Endowment for Democracy. 2002. *Strategy Document.* Washington, D.C.: NED, January.

"A National Security Strategy of Engagement and Enlargement." 1995. Washington, D.C.: Office of the President.

New York Times. 2007. "Roses and Reality in Georgia." November 10.

Nichol, Jim. 2006. "Armenia, Azerbaijan and Georgia: Political Developments and Implications for U.S. Interests" Congressional Research Service, July 24.

Nodia, Ghia. 1995. "Georgia's Identity Crisis." *Journal of Democracy* 6, 1: 104–16.

Nodia, Ghia, and Theodor Hanf. 2000. *Georgia, Lurching to Democracy: From Agnos-*

tic Tolerance to Pious Jacobinism: Societal Change and People's Reactions. Baden-Baden: Nomos.

O'Donnell, Guillermo. 2002 "In Partial Defense of an Evanescent 'Paradigm'." *Journal of Democracy* 13, 3: 6–12.

O'Donnell, Guillermo, Philippe Schmitter, and Laurence Whitehead, eds. 1986a. *Transitions from Authoritarian Rule: Prospects for Democracy.* Baltimore: Johns Hopkins University Press.

———, eds. 1986b. *Transitions from Authoritarian Rule: Latin America.* Baltimore: Johns Hopkins University Press.

OSCE/ODIHR. 1999. "Georgia Parliamentary Elections Final Report 31 October and 14." Warsaw: OSCE/ODIHR.

———. 2000. "Republic of Georgia: Presidential Elections Final Report." Warsaw: OSCE/ODIHR.

———. 2003. "Georgia Parliamentary Elections Report 2 November 2003." Warsaw: OSCE/ODIHR.

———. 2004a. "Georgia Extraordinary Presidential Election 4 January 2004: OSCE/ODIHR Election Observation Mission Final Report." Warsaw: OSCE/ODIHR.

———. 2004b. Georgia Partial Repeat Parliamentary Elections 28 March 2004." Warsaw: OSCE/ODIHR.

——— 2008. "Georgia Extraoridnary Presidential Election January 2008 OSCE/ODIHR Election Observation Mission Final Report." Warsaw: OSCE/ODIHR.

Ostrovsky, Arkady. "How to Be a Founding Father." *Financial Times,* July 10.

Ottaway, Marina. 2002. *Democracy Challenged: The Rise of Semi-Authoritarianism.* Washington, D.C.: Carnegie Endowment for International Peace.

Ottaway, Marina, and Theresa Chung. 1999. "Toward a New Paradigm." *Journal of Democracy* 10, 4: 99–113.

Pepys, Mary Noel. 2006. "Combating Judicial Corruption in the Republic of Georgia." *International Judicial Monitor* 1, 5.

Quinn-Judge, Paul. 2006. "Shevardnadze the Survivor. *Washington Post,* March 19.

Ray, James. 1997. "The Democratic Path to Peace." *Journal of Democracy* 8, 2: 49–64.

Reuters. 1992a. "Georgians Welcome Shevardnadze Home." March 8.

Reuters. 1992b. "Well-Wishers Celebrate Shevardnadze's Return." March 9.

Rostow, Dankwart. 1970. "Transitions to Democracy: Toward a Dynamic Model." *Comparative Politics* 2 (April): 337–63.

Rousseau, David L., Christopher Gelpi, Dan Reiter, and Paul Huth. 1996. "Assessing the Dyadic Nature of the Democratic Peace" *American Political Science Review* 90, 3: 512–33.

Rummel, R. J. 1975–81. *Understanding Conflict and War.* 5 vols. Beverly Hills, Calif.: Sage.

———. 1997. *Power Kills: Democracy as a Method of Nonviolence.* New Brunswick, N.J.: Transaction Publishers.

Saakashvili, Mikheil. 2004a. "Georgia's Progress: Fulfilling the Promise of the Rose Revolution." *International Herald Tribune,* November 30.

———. 2004b. "The Russell C. Leffingwell Lecture with Mikhail Saakashvili." Council on Foreign Relations, February 26.

———. 2004c. "Speech Delivered by President Mikheil Saakashvili at the Parade Dedicated to the Independence Day of Georgia." Tbilisi, May 26. President .gov.ge.

———. 2005. "Inaugural Address." Tbilisi, January 10. President.gov.ge.

———. 2006. "Remarks H.E. The President of Georgia Mikheil Saakashvili, European Parliament Strasbourg," Strasbourg, November.

Saxton, Alexander. 1990. *The Rise and Fall of the White Republic: Class Politics and Mass Culture in Nineteenth-Century America*. London: Verso.

Schedler, Andreas, ed. 2006. *Electoral Authoritarianism: The Dynamics of Unfree Competition*. London: Lynne Rienner.

Schedler, Andreas, Larry Diamond, and Marc Plattner, eds. 1999. *The Self-Rrestraining State: Power and Accountability in New Democracies*. Boulder, Colo.: Lynne Rienner.

Schodolski, Vincent. 1992. "Georgia Victors Want Shevardnadze to Return: Invited to Seek Presidency After Gamsakhurdia Toppled." *Chicago Tribune*, January 7.

Schwartz, Herman, 1999. "Surprising Success: The New Eastern European Constitutional Courts." In *The Self-Restraining State: Power and Accountability in New Democracies*, ed. Andreas Schedler, Larry Diamond, and Marc Plattner. Boulder, Colo.: Lynne Rienner.

Schweller, Randall, 2000. "From War to Peace: Altered Strategic Landscapes in the Twentieth Century," *Journal of Cold War Studies* 4, 4: 133–35.

Sedov, Dmitry. 2006. "Georgia if War Breaks Out Tomorrow." *Strategic Culture Magazine*, July 17.

Sen, Amartya. 2001. "Democracy as a Universal Value." In Diamond, Larry and Plattner, Marc *The Global Divergence of Democracies*, ed. Larry Diamond and Marc Plattner. A Journal of Democracy Book. Baltimore: Johns Hopkins University Press. 3–17.

Serafin, Joan, ed. 1994. *East-Central Europe in the 1990s*. Boulder, Colo.: Westview Press.

Smith, Graham, ed. 1996. *The Nationalities Question in the Post-Soviet States*. Harlow: Longman.

Spectator Wire Services. 1992. "Georgia Welcomes Its Famous Native Son." March 9.

Sundstrom, Lisa. 2006. *Funding Civil Society: Foreign Assistance and NGO Development in Russia* Stanford, Calif.: Stanford University Press.

Suny, Ronald Grigor. 1993. *The Revenge of the Past: Nationalism, Revolution, and the Collapse of the Soviet Union*. Stanford, Calif.: Stanford University Press.

———. 1994. *The Making of the Georgian Nation*. Bloomington: University of Indiana Press.

Sussman, Gerald. 2006. "The Myths of 'Democracy Assistance': U.S. Political Intervention in Post-Soviet Eastern Europe." *Monthly Review* 58, 7.

Talbott, Strobe. 1994. "The New Geopolitics: Defending Democracy in the Post-Cold War Era." Speech delivered at Oxford University, October 20.

Tarnoff Curt. 2002. "The Former Soviet Union and U.S. Foreign Assistance." Issue Brief for Congress, May 20.

———. 2003. *The Former Soviet Union and U.S. Foreign Assistance*. Washington, D.C.: Congressional Research Service, Library of Congress.

Transparency International. 1995–. Corruption Perceptions Index. http://www .transparency.org/policy_research/surveys_indices/global/cpi

Tuminez, Astrid. 2003. "Nationalism, Ethnic Pressures, and the Breakup of the Soviet Union." *Journal of Cold War Studies* 5, 4: 81–136.

USAID. 2005. "Georgia's Rose Revolution." *Democracy Rising* (September).

USAID/Caucasus. 1996. Georgia Program Strategic Plan FY 1996–2000.

————. 2003. Georgia Country Strategy FY 2004–2008. August 7.

U.S. Department of State. 2004a. *Supporting Human Rights and Democracy: The U.S. Record 2003–2004.* Washington, D.C.: GPO.

————. 2004b. "U.S. Assistance to Georgia—Fiscal Year 2004." *Fact Sheet, Bureau of European and Eurasian Affairs.* Washington, D.C.: Bureau of European and Affairs, August 17.

————. 2007. *Background Note: Georgia.* Washington, D.C.: Bureau of European and Affairs, January.

U.S. House of Representatives. 2004. House Subcommittee on International Terrorism, Nonproliferation and Human Rights, July 7.

U.S. Senate. 2005. Foreign Relations Committee Statement by John Tefft, Ambassador-Designate to Georgia, May 24.

Van de Walle, Nicolas. 2006. "Tipping Games: When Do Opposition Parties Coalesce?" In *Electoral Authoritarianism: The Dynamics of Unfree Competition*, ed. Andreas Schedler. London, Lynne Rienner.

Venice Commission. 2004. "Opinion on the Draft Amendments to the Constitution of Georgia adopted by the Venice Commission at its 58th Plenary Session, Venice, 12–13 March. CDL-AD(2004)008. Strasbourg, March 29.

Vignasky, Mikheil. 2005. "Premier's Death Heralds Challenging Days for Georgia." *Kvali Online Magazine*, February 10.

Washington Post. 2003. Editorial, "Potemkin Democracy." May 30.

Weart, Spencer. 1998. *Never at War: Why Democracies Will Not Fight One Another.* New Haven, Conn.: Yale University Press.

Weisman, Steven. 2006. "Diplomatic Memo; Democracy Push by Bush Attracts Doubters in Party." *New York Times*, March 17.

Wheatley, Jonathan. 2005. *Georgia from National Awakening to Rose Revolution: Delayed Transition in the Former Soviet Union.* Aldershot: Ashgate.

Whitehead, Laurence, ed. 1996. *The International Dimensions of Democratization: Europe and the Americas.* Oxford: Oxford University Press

Whitehead, Laurence, and John Crabree. 2001. *Toward Democratic Viability: The Bolivian Experience.* New York: Palgrave in association with St. Antony's College, Oxford.

Widner, Jennifer. 1999. "Building Judicial Independence in Common Law Africa." In *The Self-Restraining State: Power and Accountability in New Democracies*, ed. Andreas Schedler, Larry Diamond, and Marc Plattner. Boulder, Colo.: Lynne Rienner.

World Bank 2000. "Corruption in Georgia: Survey Evidence." Poverty Reduction and Economic Management Department Europe and Central Asia Region Report 19276. Washington, D.C.: World Bank, June.

World Conference on Human Rights. 1993. "Vienna Declaration and Programme of Action." June 25.

Zakaria, Fareed. 2003. *The Future of Freedom: Illiberal Democracy at Home and Abroad.* New York: Norton.

Index

Acknowledgments

I am thankful to several people for helping me make this book a reality. Dean Lisa Anderson and the Arnold A. Saltzman Institute of War and Peace Studies at Columbia University's School of International and Public Affairs provided me with office space and the time needed to write most of this book. Columbia University's Harriman Institute also provided support to me during the writing of this book. Craig Charney encouraged me constantly to write about the Rose Revolution. Tom Carothers and Michael McFaul provided valuable feedback on early drafts. Bill Finan at the University of Pennsylvania Press played an essential role in helping make this book a reality. I am also grateful for NDI for the opportunity to become involved in democracy in the former Soviet Union.

A number of people in Georgia, including Khatuna Khvichia and Natia Jikia, read early drafts, offered comments, and helped track down documents, people and information when I needed it. Mark Mullen, my former colleague in Georgia who remains involved in civil society and politics in Georgia, provided very helpful advice and opinions regarding the book.

During my years working in Georgia and writing this book, I spoke frequently with many Georgians discussing politics, the Rose Revolution, Shevardnadze's regime, post-Rose Revolution Georgia, and countless other questions. It is not possible to list them all, but they include President Mikheil Saakashvili, President Eduard Shevardnadze, late Prime Minister Zurab Zhvania, Speaker of Parliament Nino Burjanadze, David Gamkrelidze, Shalva Natalashvili, Ghia Nodia, David Usupashvili, Giorgi Arveladze, Giorgi Margvelashvili, and many others who provided key information and background for this book.

I am particularly grateful to Tinatin (Tiko) Ninua for reading numerous drafts of the book, pointing out my mistakes and answering many of my questions about Georgian history and details about Georgian politics. I am certain that a few mistakes remain, but they are mine alone. Before I started writing this book, Tiko worked with me for two years in

Georgia serving as my translator and political advisor. Her insights into Georgian politics, language skills and regular briefings during this time were extremely helpful.

My wife, Marta Sanders, uprooted her life to move to Georgia for two years and then had to listen to me talk about Georgian politics for several years after our return to New York. I am thankful to her for putting up with all this. Lastly, this book is dedicated to our two sons, Asher and Reuben, who remember Georgia not for the politics and revolution but for the dances, khachapuri, and our pink house in the hills of Tbilisi.